AF732157

digits™

PEARSON

Boston, Massachusetts • Chandler, Arizona • Glenview, Illinois • Upper Saddle River, New Jersey

Acknowledgments: Illustrations by Ralph Voltz and Laserwords

PEARSON

ISBN-13: 978-0-13-326694-8
ISBN-10: 0-13-326694-X
2 3 4 5 V016 17 16 15 14 13

digits™ System Requirements

Supported System Configurations

	Operating System (32-bit only)	Web Browser* (32-bit only)	Java® Version**
PC	Windows® XP (SP3) Windows Vista (SP1) Windows 7	Internet Explorer® 7 Internet Explorer 8 Internet Explorer 9 Mozilla Firefox® 11 Google Chrome™	1.4.2 1.5 [5.0 Update 11 or higher] 1.6 [6.0 through Update 18]
Mac	Macintosh® OS 10.6.x, 10.7.x	Safari® 5.0 Safari 5.1 Google Chrome™	1.5 [5.0 Update 16 or higher]

* Pop-up blockers must be disabled in the browser.
** Java (JRE) plug-in must be installed and JavaScript® must be enabled in the browser.

Additional Requirements

Software	Version
Adobe® Flash®	Version 10.4 or higher
Adobe Reader® (required for PC*)	Version 8 or higher
Word processing software	Microsoft® Word®, Open Office, or similar application to open ".doc" files

* Macintosh® OS 10.6 has a built-in PDF reader, Preview.

Screen Resolution

PC
Minimum: 1024 x 768*
Maximum: 1280 x 1024
Mac
Minimum: 1024 x 768*
Maximum: 1280 x 960
*recommended for interactive whiteboards

Internet Connection

Broadband (cable/DSL) or greater is recommended.

AOL® and AT&T™ Yahoo!® Users

You cannot use the AOL or AT&T Yahoo! browsers. However, you can use AOL or AT&T as your Internet Service Provider to access the Internet, and then open a supported browser.

For *digits*™ Support

go to **http://support.pearsonschool.com/index.cfm/digits**

digits™ Learning Team

My Name: ____________________

My Teacher's Name: ____________________

My School: ____________________

Francis (Skip) Fennell
***digits* Author**
Approaches to mathematics content and curriculum, educational policy, and support for intervention

Art Johnson
***digits* Author**
Approaches to mathematical content and support for English language learners

Helene Sherman
***digits* Author**
Teacher education and support for struggling students

Stuart J. Murphy
***digits* Author**
Visual learning and student engagement

Janie Schielack
***digits* Author**
Approaches to mathematical content, building problem solvers, and support for intervention

Eric Milou
***digits* Author**
Approaches to mathematical content and the use of technology in middle grades classrooms

William F. Tate
***digits* Author**
Approaches to intervention, and use of efficacy and research

Grant Wiggins
***digits* Consulting Author**
Understanding by Design

Randall I. Charles
***digits* Advisor**

Jim Cummins
***digits* Advisor**
Supporting English Language Learners

Jacquie Moen
***digits* Advisor**
Digital Technology

Log into **MyMathUniverse**

Be sure to save all of your your log-in information by writing it here.

Class URL: ______________________________

My Username: ______________________________

My Password: ______________________________

1 First, go to MyMathUniverse.com.

2 After you've logged in, choose your class from the **home page.**

3 When you have chosen your class, this is your **Overview page.**

Click **To Do** to view your due items.

Click **Practice** to explore ***digits*** lessons on your own.

Click **Done** to view your past due and completed items.

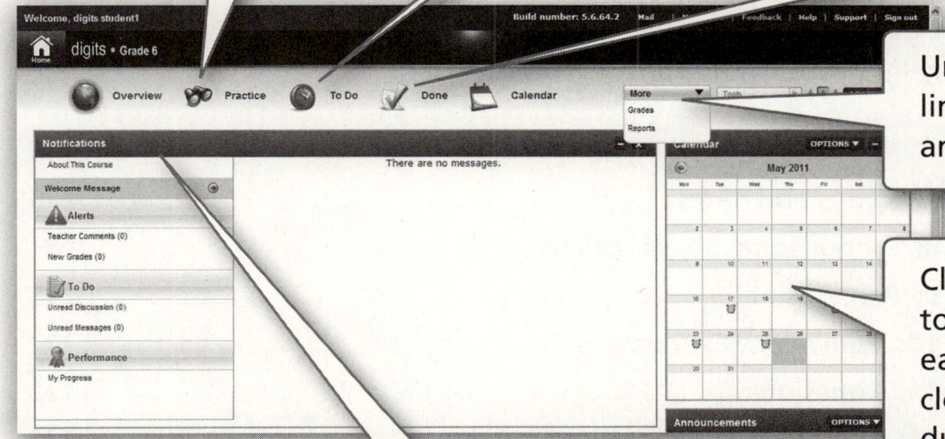

Under **More** you can link to your **Grades** and **Reports**.

Click the **Calendar** to view items due each day. Red alarm clocks are for past due assignments!

Check your **Notifications**, including:

- Teacher Comments
- Grades posted
- Messages from your teacher
- Your progress in ***digits***

As you work online, make sure to hit "Save" so you don't lose your work!

Save

Contents

Welcome to digits

Using the Student Companion

digits is designed to help you master mathematics skills and concepts in a way that's relevant to you. As the title ***digits*** suggests, this program takes a digital approach. The Student Companion supports your work on ***digits*** by providing a place to demonstrate your understanding of lesson skills and concepts in writing.

Your companion supports your work on ***digits*** in so many ways!

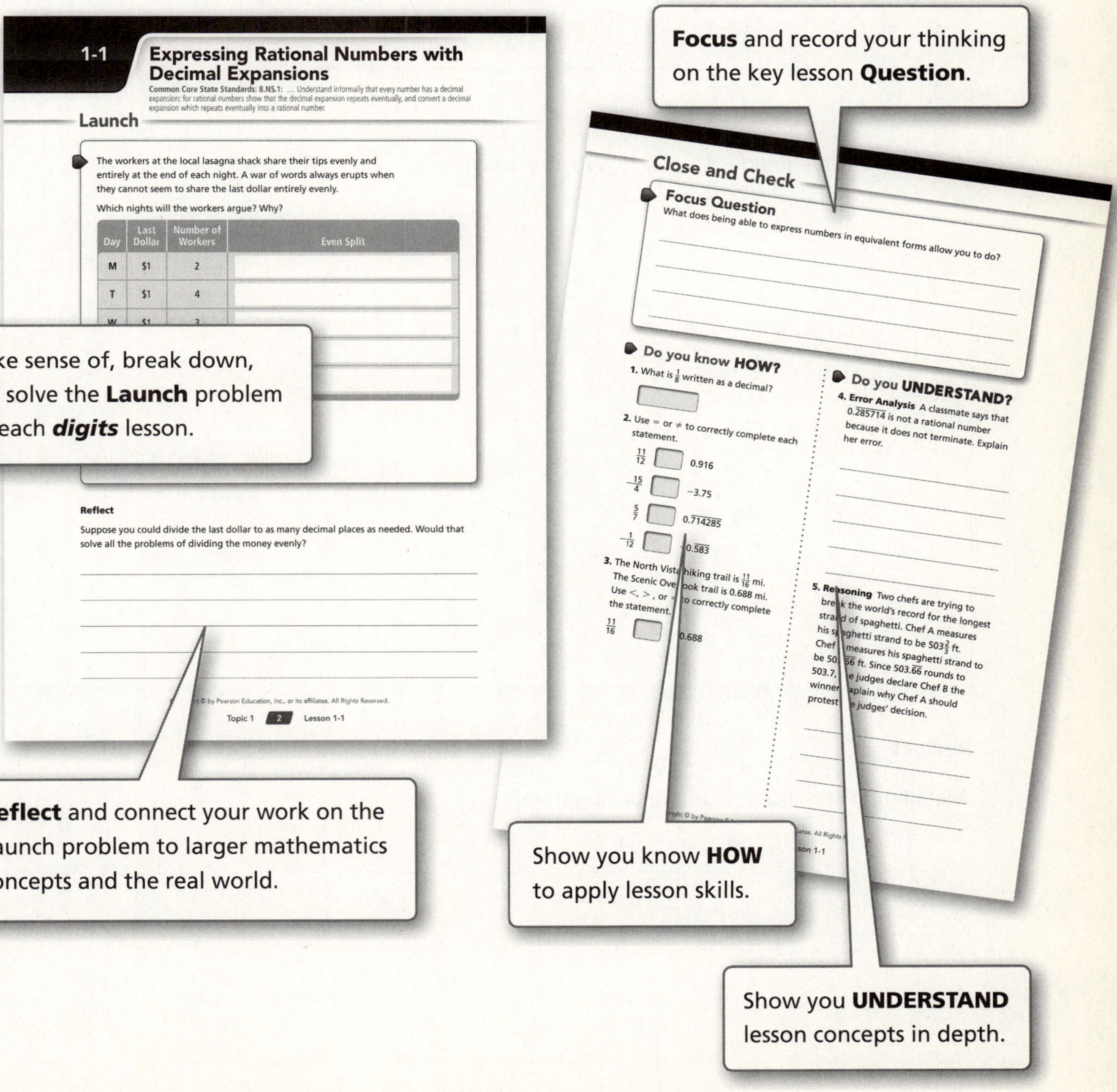

Focus and record your thinking on the key lesson **Question**.

Make sense of, break down, and solve the **Launch** problem for each ***digits*** lesson.

Reflect and connect your work on the Launch problem to larger mathematics concepts and the real world.

Show you know **HOW** to apply lesson skills.

Show you **UNDERSTAND** lesson concepts in depth.

1-1 Rational Numbers, Opposites, and Absolute Value

Common Core State Standards: 7.NS.1: Apply and extend previous understandings of addition and subtraction . . . . **7.NS.1.a:** Describe situations in which opposite quantities combine to make 0.

Launch

Why do we need −1? Couldn't we just count forward from 0 by ones and use those numbers?

On this number line, write −1 and two other missing numbers you think we need. For each number you place provide an example of why it's needed.

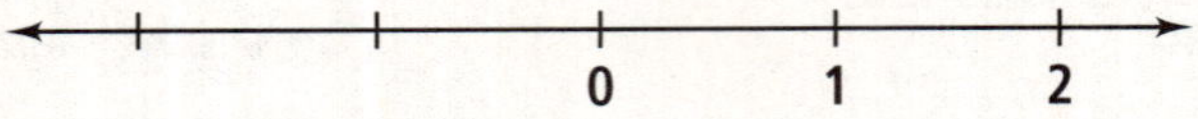

Why we need −1	Why we need	Why we need

Reflect

Are all numbers either positive or negative?

Close and Check

Focus Question

When is it helpful to use a number's opposite?

Do you know HOW?

1. Circle the set(s) of numbers to which $4\frac{2}{7}$ belongs.

A. Whole numbers

B. Integers

C. Rational numbers

2. List the values in order from least to greatest.

$$\left|-\frac{4}{5}\right|, |0.5|, |-2|, |1|$$

3. Write a positive or negative number to represent the change described in the situation. Describe the opposite change in words and with a number.

	Words	Number
Situation	You spend $37 at the mall.	
Opposite		

Do you UNDERSTAND?

4. Vocabulary Is zero a rational number? Explain.

5. Reasoning How many rational numbers are there between −10 and 10? Explain.

1-2 Adding Integers

Common Core State Standards: 7.NS.1.b: Understand $p + q$ as the number located a distance $|q|$ from p, in the positive or negative direction … . Show that a number and its opposite have a sum of 0 … . Interpret sums of rational numbers by describing real-world contexts. Also, **7.NS.1.**

Launch

Two rounds remain in a friendly video game of Zombie Pretzel Attack 2! Each zombie pretzel cheesed scores 100 points. Each player cheeses three zombie pretzels.

Write each player's new score. Tell how you found each score.

Player	Current Score	New Score
1	200 points	
2	−400 points	
3	−200 points	

Reflect

Did any player's score change from negative to positive? Explain why.

Close and Check

Focus Question

What does it mean to add less than nothing to something?

Do you know **HOW?**

1. Complete the statement. Then find the sum.

$-8 + 5$ is ☐ units from -8 in the ☐ direction.

$-8 + 5 =$ ☐

2. Is the value of the expression $75 + (-75)$ *less than zero*, *equal to zero*, or *greater than zero*?

3. Write and simplify an addition expression for the model.

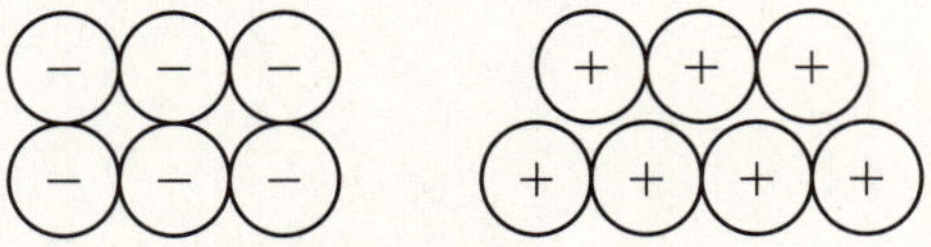

Do you **UNDERSTAND?**

4. Reasoning Does every rational number have an additive inverse? Explain.

5. Error Analysis A classmate says that the additive inverse of any rational number is negative. Is he correct? Explain.

1-3 Adding Rational Numbers

Common Core State Standards: 7.NS.1.b: Understand $p + q$ as the number located a distance $|q|$ from p, in the positive or negative direction . . . . Interpret sums of rational numbers by describing real-world contexts. **7.NS.1.d:** Apply properties of operations . . . to add . . . rational numbers.

Launch

Without adding, tell whether $A + B$, $B + C$, and $A + C$ would result in a negative or positive sum.

Tell how you know.

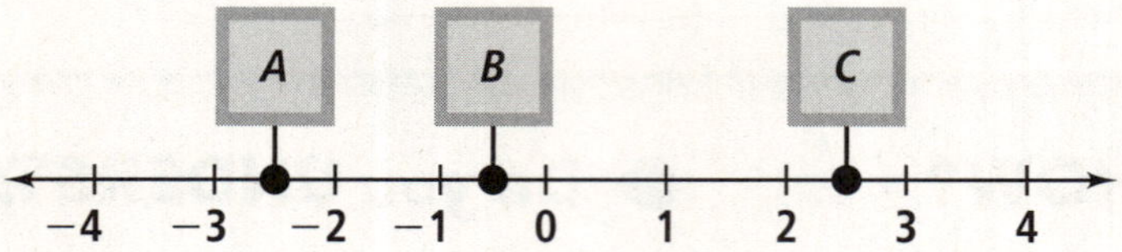

Reflect

Would you solve the problem differently if *A*, *B*, and *C* were integers? Explain.

Close and Check

Focus Question

How is adding rational numbers different than adding whole numbers?

Do you know HOW?

1. Identify the property of addition used to complete the 2nd step of the equation: *Commutative*, *Associative*, *Inverse*, *Identity*, or *Zero*.

$$-\frac{7}{9} + \frac{2}{3} = \left(-\frac{1}{9}\right) + \left(-\frac{2}{3} + \frac{2}{3}\right)$$

$$-\frac{7}{9} + \frac{2}{3} = \left(-\frac{1}{9}\right) + 0$$

2. What is the sum of $-\frac{7}{10} + \frac{1}{4}$?

3. What is the sum of $-4\frac{5}{6} + \left(-2\frac{5}{9}\right)$?

4. A homeowner owes the electric company \$72.45. She pays \$57.50. Write and simplify an expression to model this situation.

Do you UNDERSTAND?

5. Writing Describe a strategy you can use to find the sum of a positive and a negative integer.

6. Reasoning How can you tell without solving whether the sum or difference of a positive number and a negative number will be less than zero, equal to zero, or greater than zero?

1-4 Subtracting Integers

Common Core State Standards: 7.NS.1: Apply and extend previous understandings of … subtraction to … subtract rational numbers; represent … subtraction on a … number line diagram. **7.NS.1.c:** Understand subtraction of rational numbers as adding the additive inverse, $p - q = p + (-q)$ … .

Launch

Player 3 goes last in the final round of Zombie Pretzel Attack 2! She loses 500 points when caught by two zombie pretzels.

What's her new score? How many points does she need to catch Player 1? Tell how you found out.

Player	Current Score	New Score
1	500 points	300 points
2	−100 points	−200 points
3	100 points	

Reflect

How could the Zombie Pretzel Attack 2! game work without negative numbers? Would the game be as good? Explain.

Close and Check

Focus Question

What does it mean to subtract less than nothing from something?

Do you know HOW?

1. Write equivalent subtraction and addition expressions for the number line model.

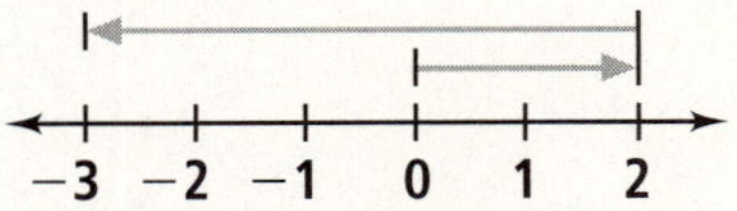

☐ − ☐ = ☐ + ☐

2. The highest point in California is Mt. Whitney at 14,494 ft above sea level. The lowest point in the state is Death Valley, which is 14,776 ft lower than Mt. Whitney. Write and simplify a subtraction expression to represent the lowest point in California.

3. Write and simplify an equivalent expression.

$$-12 - (-8)$$

Do you UNDERSTAND?

4. Compare and Contrast How is adding two negative integers the same as and different from subtracting two positive integers?

5. Writing Explain why subtracting a positive number and adding a negative number result in the same solution.

1-5 Subtracting Rational Numbers

Common Core State Standards: 7.NS.1: Apply … previous understandings of addition and subtraction to … subtract rational numbers; represent … subtraction on a … number line diagram. **7.NS.1.b:** … Interpret sums of rational numbers by describing real-world contexts.

Launch

Without subtracting, tell whether $A - C$, $A - B$, and $B - A$ would result in a negative or positive difference.

Tell how you know.

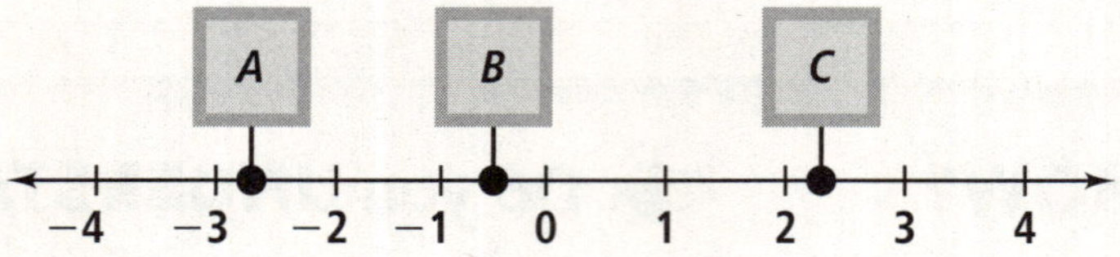

Reflect

Would you solve the problem differently if *A*, *B*, and *C* were integers? Explain.

Close and Check

Focus Question

How is subtracting rational numbers different than subtracting whole numbers?

Do you know HOW?

1. Is $-\frac{5}{9} - \left(-\frac{7}{9}\right)$ *less than zero, equal to zero,* or *greater than zero*?

2. Write and simplify a subtraction expression for the number line model.

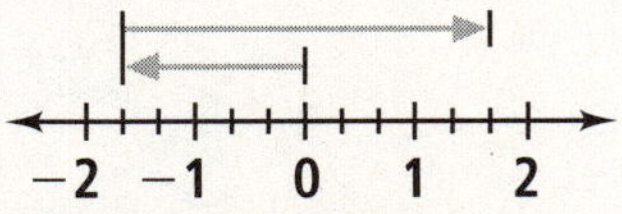

3. The lowest point in the United States is Death Valley with an elevation of −282 ft in relation to sea level. The lowest point on land in the world is the shore of the Dead Sea at −1,385 ft. What is the difference between the two elevations?

Do you UNDERSTAND?

4. Writing How would you explain the meaning of subtracting negative numbers to someone who had never heard of it?

5. Error Analysis The record high temperature in the United States is 134°F and the record low temperature is −80°F. A classmate writes an equation to find the difference between the two temperatures. Explain her error and give the correct answer.

$$134 - 80 = 54$$

1-6 Distance on a Number Line

Common Core State Standards: 7.NS.1.c: Understand subtraction of rational numbers as adding the additive inverse … . Show that the distance between two rational numbers on the number line is the absolute value of their difference, and apply this principle in real-world contexts.

Launch

A family of runners position themselves near the starting line of a race to make the race fair.

Which runner has the greatest head start over another runner? Which runner has the least head start over another runner?

Reflect

What number did you always use to make all the comparisons of head starts? Why?

Close and Check

Focus Question

Subtraction is not commutative. In what situations does the order in which you subtract two numbers *not* matter?

Do you know HOW?

1. A space shuttle can orbit the earth at 330 mi above sea level. The average commercial airplane can fly at 5.7 mi above sea level. What is the distance between the two aircraft?

2. The lowest point on Earth is in the Mariana Trench in the Pacific Ocean. It is $-10{,}924$ m from sea level. The highest point on Earth is Mount Everest in the Himalaya Mountains at 8,850 m from sea level. What is the distance between the highest and lowest points on Earth?

3. Write an expression using absolute value to represent the distance between -12 and 12 on the number line.

Do you UNDERSTAND?

4. Writing Explain when to use absolute value in solving integer equations and when not to use it.

5. Error Analysis The Roman Empire lasted from 27 BC to 476 AD. Using 0 as the division between BC and AD, a classmate says he can find the total length of the Roman Empire using the equation $-27 + 476 = x$. Is he correct? Explain.

1-7 Problem Solving

Common Core State Standards: 7.EE.3: Solve multi-step real-life and mathematical problems posed with positive and negative rational numbers in any form (whole numbers, fraction, and decimals), using tools strategically. Also, **7.NS.1.b** and **7.NS.1.c.**

Launch

In the game of golf, players try to get negative scores, not positive scores, on each hole. Draw lines to order the players from 1st to 4th place. Then write how many shots each player was behind the winner. Explain your work.

Reflect

Can a player in any game be −5 points behind the lead player? Explain why or why not.

Close and Check

Focus Question

What kinds of problems can you solve by adding the different types of rational numbers? What kinds of problems can you solve by subtracting the different types of rational numbers?

Do you know **HOW?**

1. One cat weighs $5\frac{1}{4}$ lbs. Another cat's weight differs by $1\frac{5}{8}$ lbs. Place points on the number line to represent the possible weights of the second cat. Write the weights.

or

2. Find the value of x.

$$x + 17.3 = -5.2$$

$x =$

Use the data set for Exercises 3 and 4.

−2, 6, −15, 0, 11, −9, 17, 9

3. Find the range of the data.

4. Find the interquartile range of the data.

Do you **UNDERSTAND?**

5. Reasoning The elevation of the basement floor of an office building is −18 ft. The height of the building above ground is 216 ft. To find the total distance between the basement floor and the top of the building, would you add or subtract the integers? Explain.

6. Writing Write another integer word problem about the office building that uses subtraction. Write the expression and solve the problem.

2-1 Multiplying Integers

Common Core State Standards: 7.NS.2.a: Understand that multiplication is extended … to rational numbers by requiring that operations … satisfy … the distributive property, leading to … rules for multiplying signed numbers. Interpret products of rational numbers … . Also, **7.NS.2, 7.NS.2.c.**

Launch

Complete the multiplication table. Describe at least one rule for multiplying integers based on what you see in the table.

x	−3	−2	−1	0	1	2	3
3							9
2							6
1							3
0							0
−1							−3
−2	6	4	2	0	−2	−4	−6
−3							−9

Reflect

What do you notice about the signs of the products in the four shaded sections of the grid?

Close and Check

Focus Question

How does knowing how to add positive and negative integers help you multiply positive and negative integers? How do properties of addition and multiplication help you multiply positive and negative integers?

Do you know HOW?

1. Find the product of $-5(8)$.

2. Find the product of $-9(-9)$.

3. Circle the products that are equivalent to -100.

A. $-5 \cdot 2(-10)$

B. $-1(25 \cdot 4)$

C. $-4 \cdot 5^2$

D. $(-2)(25)(-2)$

4. Suppose a and b are nonzero integers with the same signs. Is the product of a and b positive or negative?

Do you UNDERSTAND?

5. Writing Draw a model to show the product of a and b, where $a < 0 < b$. Explain your model.

6. Compare and Contrast How does the sign of the product of a positive and a negative number compare with the sign of the sum of a positive and a negative number?

2-2 Multiplying Rational Numbers

Common Core State Standards: 7.NS.2: Apply and extend previous understandings of multiplication and division of fractions to multiply and divide rational numbers. **7.NS.2.a:** Understand … the rules for multiplying signed numbers. Interpret products … by describing real-world contexts.

Launch

Sort the tiles into two groups. Describe each group.

$1.5 \cdot 3$	$1.5 \cdot (-3)$	$3 \cdot 1.5$	$-3 \cdot 1.5$
$-1.5 \cdot 3$	$-1.5 \cdot (-3)$	$3 \cdot (-1.5)$	$-3 \cdot (-1.5)$

Group 1	Group 2

Reflect

How would solving this problem be different if both factors of each expression were integers? Explain.

Close and Check

Focus Question

How is multiplying rational numbers like multiplying fractions and multiplying decimals? How is it different?

Do you know HOW?

1. Write **P** next to the positive products and **N** next to the negative products.

$\frac{5}{9} \cdot \left(-\frac{3}{7}\right)$

$(-4.8)(-0.2)$

$\left(-3\frac{2}{5}\right)\left(6\frac{1}{3}\right)\left(-1\frac{1}{9}\right)$

$14.2 \cdot (-2)\left(-5\frac{2}{7}\right)(-0.25)$

2. Find the product of $-5.8(3)(-2.2)$.

3. In 1911, the temperature in Rapid City, South Dakota, dropped at an amazing rate of about 3.1°F per minute. This remarkable temperature change took place in a span of 15 minutes. Write the change in temperature.

Do you UNDERSTAND?

4. Reasoning Will the product of -3^{17} be positive or negative? Explain.

5. Error Analysis A classmate says that you can tell the sign of a product by comparing the number of positive and negative factors. If there are more negative factors, then the product will be negative. If there are more positive factors, then the product will be positive. Do you agree? Explain.

2-3

Dividing Integers

Common Core State Standards: 7.NS.2.b: Understand that integers can be divided, provided that the divisor is not zero, and every quotient of integers (with non-zero divisor) is a rational number. If p and q are integers, then $-\left(\frac{p}{q}\right) = \frac{(-p)}{q} = \frac{p}{(-q)}$ . . . . Also, **7.NS.2.**

Launch

Draw arrows to show how to redistribute the integer chips equally among the bags. Then write two equations, one using multiplication and one using division, to describe your distribution.

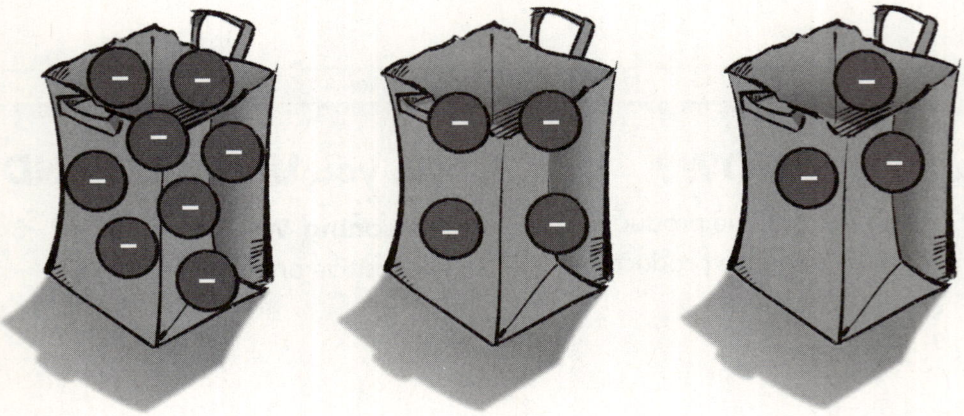

Reflect

How is dividing integers similar to and different from dividing whole numbers?

Close and Check

Focus Question

How does the relationship between multiplication and division help you divide integers? When does division of integers not have meaning and why?

Do you know HOW?

1. Write **P** next to the positive quotients, **N** next to the negative quotients, and **U** next to the quotients that are undefined.

   $-3 \div (-7)$

   $-4 \div 0$

   $-12 \div 2$

   $14 \div 7$

2. Solve $\frac{-75}{a} = -25$.

3. The stock market lost 7,695 points in a 17-month period. Express the change in the stock market as a unit rate. Round your answer to the nearest integer.

Do you UNDERSTAND?

4. **Reasoning** Show that the quotient of two negative numbers is a positive number. Use multiplication to support your reasoning.

5. **Writing** Explain why division by 0 is undefined. Use an example.

2-4 Dividing Rational Numbers

Common Core State Standards: 7.NS.2: Apply and extend previous understandings of multiplication and division of fractions to multiply and divide rational numbers. **7.NS.2.b:** … Interpret quotients of rational numbers by describing real-world contexts.

Launch

Sort the tiles into two groups. Describe your groups.

$7\frac{1}{2} \div 3$ | $-7\frac{1}{2} \div 3$ | $7\frac{1}{2} \div (-3)$ | $-7\frac{1}{2} \div (-3)$

Group 1	Group 2

Reflect

How would solving this problem be different if the dividend and divisors were always integers? Explain.

Close and Check

Focus Question

How does the relationship between multiplication and division help you divide rational numbers?

Do you know HOW?

1. Write the reciprocal of each number.

-30

$\frac{1}{12}$

6

$-\frac{6}{11}$

2. Write $-\frac{7}{8} \div \frac{3}{5}$ as a multiplication expression.

3. The equation $d = -\frac{3}{5}t$ describes the change in degrees Fahrenheit d after t hours. The temperature falls a total of $7\frac{1}{2}$ degrees. How long does it take the temperature to fall?

Do you UNDERSTAND?

4. **Reasoning** Can the product of reciprocals ever be equal to -1? Explain.

5. **Writing** Explain why multiplying by the reciprocal of a number is the same as dividing by that number. Use the equation in your explanation.

$$-\frac{7}{9} \div \frac{3}{8} = -\frac{7}{9} \cdot \frac{8}{3}$$

2-5 Operations with Rational Numbers

Common Core State Standards: 7.NS.2.c: Apply properties of operations as strategies to multiply and divide rational numbers. **7.NS.3:** Solve real-world and mathematical problems involving the four operations with rational numbers. Also, **7.NS.2.**

Launch

Is the value of this expression *positive* or *negative*? Show how to change the expression so that its value switches to the other sign. Do not change or move any numbers or operation symbols.

$$2 + \frac{1}{2} \cdot 1\frac{3}{4} - 3$$

Positive	Negative

Reflect

How are the expression as shown and the expression after your change alike? How are they different?

Close and Check

Focus Question

Many problems involve more than one operation with rational numbers. How do you decide the order in which to carry out the operations?

Do you know HOW?

1. Write and simplify an equivalent expression by using the Distributive Property.

$$-7\left(\frac{5}{7} - \frac{12}{21}\right)$$

2. Antarctica holds the record for the lowest recorded temperature of −129°F. Use the formula to find the equivalent temperature in °C.

$$C = \frac{5}{9}(F - 32)$$

3. Simplify the complex fraction.

$$\frac{-\frac{3}{8}}{\frac{5}{7} - 2}$$

Do you UNDERSTAND?

4. Writing Describe another method for solving the expression in Exercise 1. Does this method always work? Explain.

5. Error Analysis Explain the error and find the correct answer.

$$\frac{\frac{7}{15}}{\frac{1}{6} - 1} = \frac{\frac{7}{15}}{-\frac{5}{6}} = \frac{7}{15} \cdot -\frac{5}{6} = -\frac{7}{18}$$

2-6 Problem Solving

Common Core State Standards: 7.NS.3: Solve real-world and mathematical problems involving the four operations with rational numbers. **7.EE.3:** Solve multi-step real-life and mathematical problems posed with positive and negative rational numbers in any form ... .

Launch

A not-so-jazzed New Orleans dog forgets where she buries her favorite bone. She picks a spot and digs at a rate of 0.4 ft every 10 minutes for an hour to find it.

Write and evaluate an expression to represent the dog's elevation in relation to sea level after digging for one hour.

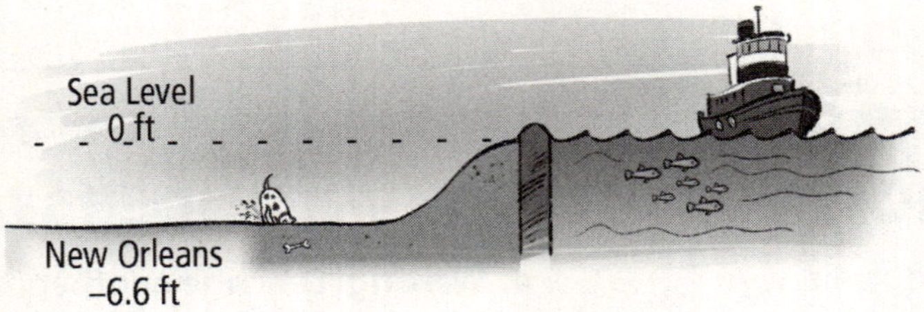

Reflect

Is there one right expression to represent the dog's situation? Explain.

Close and Check

Focus Question

What types of problems can you solve using operations with rational numbers?

Do you know HOW?

1. Many places on land are located below sea level. The table shows the altitude of various locations. Find the mean altitude in relation to sea level. Round your answer to the nearest tenth.

Position Relative to Sea Level					
Altitude (ft)	−11	−13	−16	−20	−23
Frequency	2	4	6	2	4

2. Insert a pair of parentheses to make the expression true.

$$6 - 5 + 4 + 9 = 6$$

3. Complete the table to show the change in the water table levels during a severe drought. Assume the relationship is proportional.

Months of drought	3	5	8
Change in water level (cm)		−130	

Do you UNDERSTAND?

4. Writing An airplane descends from 35,000 ft at a rate of 33 feet per second. Explain how to use this information to find the altitude of the airplane after 12 minutes.

5. Error Analysis A classmate says that simplifying the expression is the same with or without parentheses. Do you agree? Explain.

$$-9 \times (6 + 3) + 8$$

3-1 Repeating Decimals

Common Core State Standards: 7.NS.2.b: Understand that integers can be divided, provided that the divisor is not zero . . . . **7.NS.2.d:** Convert a rational number to a decimal using long division; know that the decimal form of a rational number terminates in 0s or eventually repeats.

Launch

Use a picture, words, and a number to represent the quantity 2 out of 3 in three other ways. Tell which of these ways may be best for problem solving and why.

A Picture	Words	A Number

Reflect

When have you represented quantities in different ways in your past mathematics work? How was that helpful?

Close and Check

Focus Question

When is it helpful to be able to write fractions as decimals? Why is it helpful to show that a decimal repeats?

____

____

____

____

Do you know HOW?

1. Circle the repeating decimal(s).

12.34345 $\qquad$ $9.\overline{012}$

5.25... $\qquad$ $23.4380\overline{2}$

2. Write $\frac{1}{13}$ as a decimal.

3. Write $6\frac{5}{12}$ as a decimal.

4. An electrician cuts away a 7.2-inch long section of drywall to make repairs to the electrical system. He has several scraps of drywall he can use to repair the hole. Circle the length(s) of drywall that is large enough to repair the hole.

$7\frac{2}{13}$ $\qquad$ $7\frac{3}{14}$ $\qquad$ $7\frac{5}{21}$

Do you UNDERSTAND?

5. Writing Your friend compares the values in Exercise 4. She writes the mixed number as an improper fraction. Next she divides the numerator by the denominator to find the decimal value of each number. Describe a shorter method.

____

____

____

____

6. Reasoning When converting a fraction to a decimal by using long division, how can you know when the decimal is beginning to repeat?

____

____

____

____

____

3-2 Terminating Decimals

Common Core State Standards: 7.NS.2.d: Convert a rational number to a decimal using long division; know that the decimal form of a rational number terminates in 0s or eventually repeats. Also, **7.NS.2.b.**

Launch

A certain surly friend of yours likes 1 ÷ 2 far better than 1 ÷ 3. He says, "At least you can clearly see the answer to 1 ÷ 2."

Show and explain with decimals what might make your certain friend surly about 1 ÷ 3, but happy about 1 ÷ 2.

Reflect

How could writing 1 ÷ 2 and 1 ÷ 3 each as fractions make your friend less surly?

Close and Check

Focus Question

When is it helpful to be able to write fractions as decimals? How is a fraction written as a terminating decimal different from a fraction written as a repeating decimal?

Do you know HOW?

1. Circle the terminating decimal(s).

10.243444 2.010110111...

5.25... 43.98769876

2. Circle the fraction(s) that can be written as a terminating decimal.

$8\frac{7}{12}$ $19\frac{12}{25}$

$4\frac{3}{11}$ $26\frac{2}{15}$

3. The pediatrician weighs a newborn baby on a digital scale. He tells the parents that their baby weighs $6\frac{5}{8}$ pounds. What decimal number did the pediatrician read on the scale?

4. A customer purchases $7\frac{13}{16}$ gallons of gas. What is the decimal equivalent of this mixed number?

Do you UNDERSTAND?

5. Reasoning To compare the values of a decimal and a fraction, should you convert the decimal to a fraction or the fraction to a decimal? Explain.

6. Error Analysis Your friend says every decimal is a repeating decimal because there are an infinite number of 0s at the end of every decimal number. Explain the error in her reasoning.

3-3 Percents Greater Than 100

Common Core State Standards: 7.NS.3: Solve real-world and mathematical problems involving the four operations with rational numbers.

Launch

During a heated origami-making argument, you tell your surly friend that you always give 150% effort in folding paper animals. Your surly friend says that he doesn't even know what 150% looks like.

Show a way to represent 150% with pictures or numbers. Explain why your representation works.

Reflect

Can you really give more than 100% effort? Provide a possible way in words.

Close and Check

Focus Question

What does it mean to have more than 100% of something?

Do you know HOW?

1. Circle the best estimate for 450% of 15.
   A. greater than 0 but less than 30
   B. greater than 30 but less than 60
   C. greater than 60 but less than 100
   D. greater than 100

2. Suppose a small business employs 45 people. Five years later, the same small business employs 380% of the original number of employees. How many employees are there now?

   ☐ employees

3. Bacterial colonies multiply very quickly. Assume there is a small colony of 560 bacteria that increases 675%. Circle the true statement(s).
   A. The change in the number of bacteria is between 3,000 and 4,000.
   B. The total number of bacteria is 675 times greater than 560.
   C. The total number of bacteria grows to 3,780.

Do you UNDERSTAND?

4. **Compare and Contrast** Compare finding 150% of a number and finding 15% of a number.

5. **Reasoning** The selling price of a sweater is a 175% increase of the purchase price. The markup is $36.75. Explain how to find the purchase price and the selling price.

3-4 Percents Less Than 1

Common Core State Standards: 7.NS.3: Solve real-world and mathematical problems involving the four operations with rational numbers.

Launch

Explain how these three shaded squares could be used in a representation of 300% or 30%. Use pictures, words, and numbers to model the mathematics.

How the Squares Could Model 300%:

How the Squares Could Model 30%:

Reflect

What fractions and decimals would your models model?

Close and Check

Focus Question

What does it mean to have a fractional percent of something?

Do you know HOW?

1. Circle the number(s) that is equivalent to $\frac{1}{5}$%.

20%	$\frac{2}{100}$
0.002	0.20

2. Find the solutions.

What is $\frac{1}{8}$% of 800?

3 is what percent of 1,200?

19.5 is 0.75% of what?

3. The unemployment rate falls 0.4%. Out of 3,500 unemployed workers, how many people find jobs?

people

4. Washington, D.C., comprises about 0.0016% of the total area of the U. S. The U. S. covers about 3,790,000 square miles. About how many square miles is Washington, D.C.? Round your answer to the nearest whole number.

square miles

Do you UNDERSTAND?

5. Writing Write a real-world problem that includes a percent less than 1%. Show how to solve your problem.

6. Compare and Contrast What is the same and different about a percent less than 100 and a fractional percent?

3-5 Fractions, Decimals, and Percents

Common Core State Standards: 7.NS.2.d: Convert a rational number to a decimal using long division . . . . **7.NS.3:** Solve real-world and mathematical problems involving the four operations with rational numbers. Also, **7.NS.2.b.**

Launch

The results of an international origami competition show how many animals top folders perfectly folded in fifty minutes.

How could the origami competition organizers use fractions, decimals, or percents to better represent the results? Explain.

Origami Animal Folding Results

Contestant	Perfectly Folded	Folded
Happy Friend	8	12
Surly Friend	6	10
New Friend	4	8
Not a Friend	10	15

Reflect

Would you rule out using any form of these representations—fractions, decimals, or percents—to improve the results for any reason? If so, why?

Close and Check

Focus Question

Why are there different representations of rational numbers?

Do you know HOW?

1. There are 87 varieties of cetaceans (whales, dolphins, and porpoises). 11 cetacean species are baleen whales. What percent of cetaceans are baleen whales? Round your answer to the nearest tenth.

2. Cows eat 2.5% of their body weight in dry food each day. The average cow weighs 1,660 lbs. How many pounds of dry food will the average cow eat each day?

pounds

3. Complete the table below by filling in equivalent values in different forms.

Fraction	$\frac{1}{4}$			
Decimal		0.04		0.005
Percent			112.5%	

Do you UNDERSTAND?

4. Writing Is it easier to change a fraction to a decimal and then to a percent, or is it easier to change a fraction directly to a percent? Explain.

5. Error Analysis A score of at least 85% of 220 points is needed to advance to the semi-finals. Can the equation be used to find the number of points needed to advance? Explain.

$$220x = 0.85$$

3-6 Percent Error

Common Core State Standards: 7.RP.3: Use proportional relationships to solve multistep ratio and percent problems. *Examples: … percent error.*

Launch

The surly friend and his remaining friends set out to set up an origami shop with a goal of selling 200 animals the first week. After the first week, the surly friend says, "Our sales total is 3 percent from the goal."

Tell how many animals the group sold. Explain whether they made their goal.

Reflect

Was the surly friend clear about the sales results? If not, how could he have been clearer?

Close and Check

Focus Question

How are percents helpful to describe and understand variability in data?

Do you know HOW?

1. Find the percent error of the estimated value to the nearest whole percent.
Estimated value: 547
Actual value: 562

2. An event planner predicts 215 people will attend the party. The number actually attending is 241. To the nearest tenth, find percent the event planner's prediction is off.

3. The actual diameter of a redwood tree is 12.4 feet. To the nearest tenth, find the greatest percent error in the data.

Diameter of a Redwood

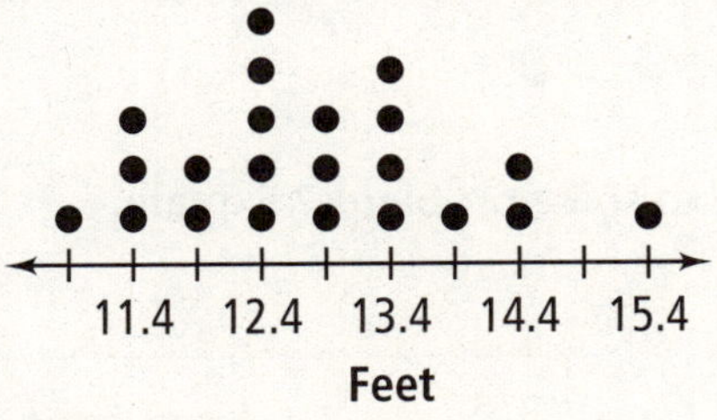

Do you UNDERSTAND?

4. Reasoning How does understanding percent error impact making decisions based on a set of data?

5. Error Analysis A classmate finds the percent error in Monday's predicted high temperature of 71°F and the actual high temperature of 78°F. Explain her error.

$$\frac{(71 - 78)}{78} = -\frac{7}{78} = -9\%$$

3-7 Problem Solving

Common Core State Standards: 7.NS.3: Solve real-world and mathematical problems involving the four operations with rational numbers.

Launch

Your surly friend plans a 400-ft^2 garden to improve his mood. 40% of the garden will be fruit, $\frac{1}{4}$ will be vegetables, 0.1 will be herbs, and the rest flowers.

Choose only one representation—fractions, decimals, or percents—to find the area of each part of the garden. Explain your choice after completing the area calculations.

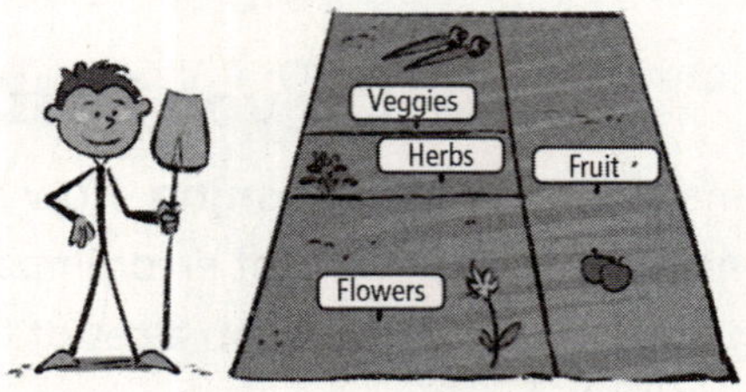

Reflect

Do you use fractions, decimals, or percents more often to solve problems? Explain.

Close and Check

Focus Question

How does understanding the relationships among fractions, decimals, and percents help you solve problems?

Do you know HOW?

1. The minimum wage in 2007 was $5.85. The minimum wage rose 24% by 2009. To the nearest cent, find the minimum wage in 2009.

2. On Saturday, a store sells $2,700 in merchandise. The store makes a profit of 15.25% on all sales. The remaining income pays for the store's expenses. How much money goes toward expenses on Saturday?

3. Three roommates split their rent based on the sizes of their bedrooms. Roommate 1's bedroom takes up $\frac{3}{7}$ (43%) of total space. Roommate 2's and Roommate 3's each take up $\frac{2}{7}$ (29%). Find the estimated amount they will pay if total rent is $1900. Then find the percent error on the rent paid.

Estimated amount:

Percent error:

Do you UNDERSTAND?

4. **Writing** Explain how to use estimation to check the reasonableness of your solution to Exercise 2.

5. **Reasoning** If you were one of the roommates from Exercise 3, could you avoid overpaying your rent while still splitting costs according to your room sizes? Explain.

4-1 Expressing Rational Numbers with Decimal Expansions

Common Core State Standards: 8.NS.1: … Understand informally that every number has a decimal expansion; for rational numbers show that the decimal expansion repeats eventually, and convert a decimal expansion which repeats eventually into a rational number.

Launch

The workers at the local lasagna shack share their tips evenly and entirely at the end of each night. A war of words always erupts when they cannot seem to share the last dollar entirely evenly.

Which nights will the workers argue? Why?

Day	Last Dollar	Number of Workers	Even Split
M	$1	2	
T	$1	4	
W	$1	3	
TH	$1	5	
F	$1	6	

Reflect

Suppose you could divide the last dollar to as many decimal places as needed. Would that solve all the problems of dividing the money evenly?

Close and Check

Focus Question

What does being able to express numbers in equivalent forms allow you to do?

Do you know HOW?

1. What is $\frac{1}{8}$ written as a decimal?

2. Use $=$ or $\neq$ to correctly complete each statement.

$\frac{11}{12}$ ☐ 0.916

$-\frac{15}{4}$ ☐ -3.75

$\frac{5}{7}$ ☐ $0.\overline{714285}$

$-\frac{1}{12}$ ☐ $-0.\overline{583}$

3. The North Vista hiking trail is $\frac{11}{16}$ mi. The Scenic Overlook trail is 0.688 mi. Use $<$, $>$, or $=$ to correctly complete the statement.

$\frac{11}{16}$ ☐ 0.688

Do you UNDERSTAND?

4. Error Analysis A classmate says that $0.\overline{285714}$ is not a rational number because it does not terminate. Explain her error.

5. Reasoning Two chefs are trying to break the world's record for the longest strand of spaghetti. Chef A measures his spaghetti strand to be $503\frac{2}{3}$ ft. Chef B measures his spaghetti strand to be $503.\overline{66}$ ft. Since $503.\overline{66}$ rounds to 503.7, the judges declare Chef B the winner. Explain why Chef A should protest the judges' decision.

4-2 Exploring Irrational Numbers

Common Core State Standards: 8.NS.1: Know that numbers that are not rational are called irrational. Understand informally that every number has a decimal expansion; for rational numbers show that the decimal expansion repeats eventually … .

Launch

Complete the table and then draw each square. Provide exact lengths. Describe any problems you have.

	Side Length	Area
Square 1		1 unit^2
Square 2		2 units^2
Square 3		4 units^2

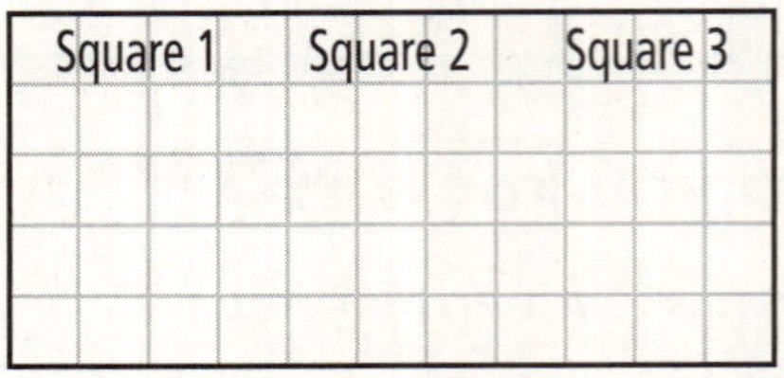

Reflect

Do you think you could find an exact side length for all of the squares if you kept trying? Explain.

Close and Check

Focus Question

What is the difference between an irrational number and a rational number? Can a number be both irrational and rational?

Do you know HOW?

1. Circle the irrational numbers.

$\sqrt{111}$ $\sqrt{400}$ $\sqrt{160}$

$\sqrt{144}$ $\sqrt{220}$ $\sqrt{200}$

2. Circle the rational numbers. Assume each pattern continues.

4.014014 6.232342345

0.717717 1.594593592

12.12211222 9.96939693

3. Indicate all the possible names for each number.

	$\sqrt{36}$	$-\frac{1}{6}$	$\sqrt{11}$
Natural Number			
Whole Number			
Integer			
Rational Number			
Irrational Number			
Real Number			

Do you UNDERSTAND?

4. Reasoning Can an irrational number ever be a natural number? A whole number? Explain.

5. Compare and Contrast What is the difference between locating $\frac{3}{5}$ on a number line and locating $\sqrt{5}$ on a number line?

4-3 Approximating Irrational Numbers

Common Core State Standards: 8.NS.2: Use rational approximations of irrational numbers to compare the size of irrational numbers, locate them approximately on a number line diagram, and estimate the value of expressions.

Launch

Due to the sauciness of their sauce, the local lasagna shack decides to expand its old square napkin to a new square napkin.

Find the approximate side length of the new square napkin. Explain what you did.

Old Napkin
100 in.^{2}

New Napkin
150 in.^{2}

Reflect

Why would it be useful to write the side length of the new square napkin as an approximate length instead of an exact length?

Close and Check

Focus Question

How do you estimate an irrational number? Why might you need to be able to estimate an irrational number?

Do you know HOW?

1. On a number line, between which two whole numbers would $\sqrt{136}$ be located?

   and

2. The square root of an integer n is between 6 and 7. Write an inequality that expresses all the possible values for n.

3. Which value is farther to the right on a number line?

   2.5^2 $\sqrt{81}$

4. A square sandbox has an area of 42 ft^2. What is the approximate perimeter of the sandbox to the nearest hundredth?

Do you UNDERSTAND?

5. **Reasoning** Two classmates estimate the location of $\sqrt{60}$ on a number line. One student locates the point at 7.7. The other student says the point is located at 7.75. Can both students be correct? Explain.

6. **Writing** Pi (π) is an irrational number used to find the circumference and area of circles. Are the circumference and area of a circle actual or estimated measures? Explain.

4-4 Comparing and Ordering Rational and Irrational Numbers

Common Core State Standards: 8.NS.2: Use rational approximations of irrational numbers to compare the size of irrational numbers, locate them approximately on a number line diagram, and estimate the value of expressions.

Launch

For people who prefer pizza, the local lasagna shack also offers thin crust pizzas in three different shapes. Each costs $20.

Which deal is the best and which deal is the worst? Explain.

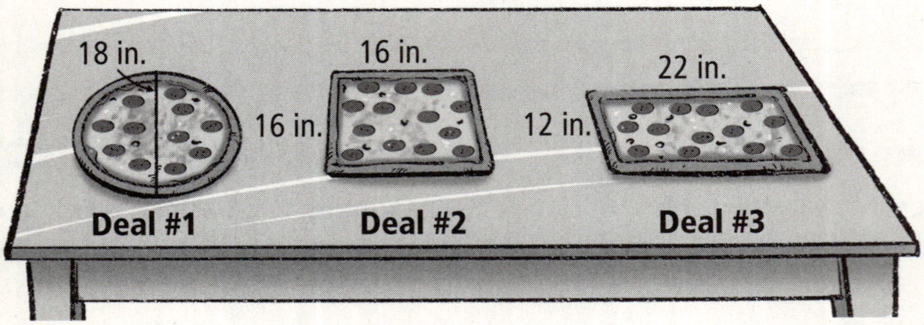

Reflect

Do you think all the pizza areas are rational? Explain.

Close and Check

Focus Question

How can you compare rational and irrational numbers? Why might you want to?

Do you know HOW?

1. Use $<$, $>$, or $=$ to complete each statement.

$7 \ \square \ \sqrt{7}$

$\sqrt{121} \ \square \ 11$

$-16 \ \square \ -\sqrt{225}$

$\sqrt{8} \ \square \ \frac{21}{8}$

2. Order the values from least to greatest

$\frac{25}{7}$ $\quad \sqrt{3}$ $\quad 5.85$ $\quad 4^2$ $\quad \pi$

$\square \ \square \ \square \ \square \ \square$

3. Match each point on the number line to the nearest value.

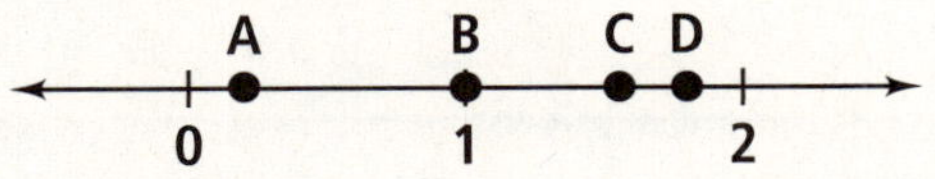

$\sqrt{1} \ \square$ $\qquad \frac{19}{12} \ \square$

$\sqrt{3} \ \square$ $\qquad \frac{2}{11} \ \square$

Do you UNDERSTAND?

4. Reasoning The owners want to remake the pizza in Deal #3 of the Launch. Can they make a square pizza with exactly the same area? Explain.

5. Writing What strategies can you use to order the numbers in Exercise 2 without changing them all to decimals?

4-5 Problem Solving

Common Core State Standards: 8.NS.1: Know that numbers that are not rational are called irrational … and convert a decimal expansion which repeats eventually into a rational number. **8.NS.2:** Use rational approximations of irrational numbers to … estimate the value of expressions.

Launch

Your friend said the square root of 14 is somewhere in between 3 and 4 as shown.

Explain whether you agree. Then show where would be a more precise spot to place the square root of 14 and tell why your estimate is better.

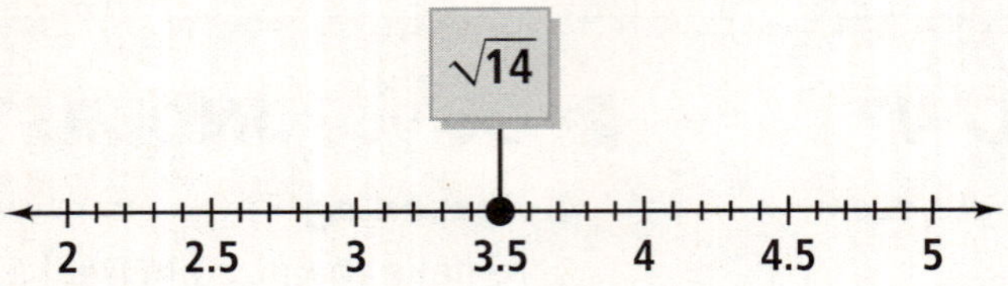

Reflect

When is precision important and when is it not so important? Provide an example for each.

Close and Check

Focus Question

How is solving a problem that includes rational numbers similar to solving a problem that includes irrational numbers? How is it different?

Do you know HOW?

1. If $x = 6$, what is the smallest natural number y that makes $\sqrt{x^2 + y^2}$ rational?

   $y =$

2. A carnival ride must be enclosed within a fence. The ride requires 676 ft^2 of space to operate. What is the minimum number of feet of fencing required to enclose the ride?

   ft

3. A square billboard is shown below. What is the approximate length and width of the billboard to the nearest hundredth?

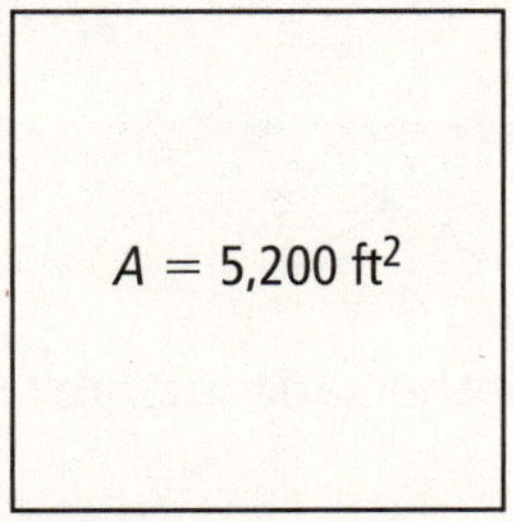

Do you UNDERSTAND?

4. **Reasoning** A square pool with side lengths of 16 ft sells for $\frac{2}{3}$ the price of a circular pool with a diameter of 18 ft. If the shape does not matter, which is the better deal? Explain.

5. **Error Analysis** Your friend says that 0.2 and $0.\overline{2}$ can both be written as the fraction $\frac{1}{5}$. Explain his mistake.

5-1 Perfect Squares, Square Roots, and Equations of the Form $x^2 = p$

Common Core State Standards: 8.EE.2: Use square root and cube root symbols to represent solutions to equations of the form $x^2 = p$ and $x^3 = p$, where p is a positive rational number. Evaluate square roots of small perfect squares and cube roots of small perfect cubes.

Launch

Your friend claims that x^2 is the same as $2x$. Tell how he could have come to that conclusion. Explain whether you agree.

Reflect

When have you used expressions with exponents like x^2 in mathematics before? Explain.

Close and Check

Focus Question

How can you apply what you know about squares and square roots to write and solve equations of the form $x^2 = p$? How can you use equations in that form?

Do you know HOW?

1. Solve each equation.

A. $x^2 = 36$

B. $x^2 = 64$

C. $x^2 = 400$

D. $x^2 = 121$

2. Solve $y^2 = \frac{144}{169}$.

3. A square flower garden has an area of 136 ft^2. Find the length of one side of the garden to the nearest tenth of a foot.

ft

4. A square playground has an area of 1,500 ft^2. Find the length of one side of the playground to the nearest tenth of a foot.

ft

Do you UNDERSTAND?

5. Vocabulary What is the relationship between perfect squares and square roots? Give an example.

6. Error Analysis The square-shaped downtown region of a town has an area of 144 km^2. Your friend says the length of one side can be represented by $\sqrt{144} = \pm 12$. Explain the error she made in her solution.

5-2 Perfect Cubes, Cube Roots, and Equations of the Form $x^3 = p$

Common Core State Standards: 8.EE.2: Use square root and cube root symbols to represent solutions to equations of the form $x^2 = p$ and $x^3 = p$, where p is a positive rational number. Evaluate square roots of small perfect squares and cube roots of small perfect cubes.

Launch

Draw a line from each measurement to the figure it could represent. Explain how you know you are correct.

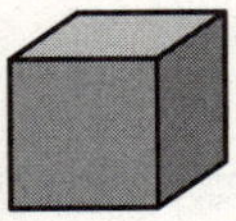

64 in.^{2}

64 in.^{3}

Reflect

Could one of the measurements somehow represent something about both figures? Could the other?

Close and Check

Focus Question

How is solving an equation that includes cubes similar to solving an equation that includes squares? How is it different?

Do you know HOW?

1. Solve each equation.

A. $x^3 = 343$

B. $x^3 = -1{,}000$

C. $x^3 = -729$

D. $x^3 = 216$

2. Solve $y^3 = \frac{27}{512}$.

3. A storage unit in the shape of a cube has a volume of 3,000 cubic feet. Find the length of one side of the storage unit to the nearest tenth of a foot.

ft

4. An abstract sculpture in the shape of a cube has a volume of 925 ft^3. Find the approximate length of one side of the sculpture to the nearest tenth of a foot.

ft

Do you UNDERSTAND?

5. Error Analysis A salesperson says the volume of a cube-shaped birdcage is 64 ft^3. What error does the salesperson make when solving the equation? Write the correct solution and explain what it means.

$$x^3 = 64$$
$$\sqrt[3]{x^3} = \sqrt[3]{64}$$
$$x = \pm 4$$

6. Reasoning Can the cube root of a positive number ever be negative? Explain.

5-3 Exponents and Multiplication

Common Core State Standards: 8.EE.1: Know and apply the properties of integer exponents to generate equivalent numerical expressions. *For example,* $3^2 \times 3^{-5} = 3^{-3} = \frac{1}{3^3} = \frac{1}{27}$.

Launch

The city's second-best scientist's first rocket fails to reach orbit. He promises his second rocket will fly twice as fast as his first and his third rocket will fly twice as fast as the second.

How fast will Rockets 2 and 3 fly? Show how you know.

Rocket 1	Rocket 2	Rocket 3
2^{14} mph		

Reflect

What do you know about the factors in the expression 2^{14}? Explain.

Close and Check

Focus Question

How can you apply what you know about multiplying numerical expressions to multiplying algebraic expressions containing exponents?

Do you know HOW?

1. Simplify the expression.
$4x^6 \cdot 12x^9$

2. Simplify the expression.
$(f^8)^3$

3. Simplify the expression.
$(4st)^4$

4. Simplify the expression.
$(7q^7r^3)^3$

5. Circle the expression(s) that is equivalent to $216a^9b^{15}c^{27}$.

A. $(72a^6b^{12}c^{24})^3$

B. $(72a^3b^5c^9)^3$

C. $(6a^6b^{12}c^{24})^3$

D. $(6a^3b^5c^9)^3$

Do you UNDERSTAND?

6. Writing Use arithmetic to prove it is incorrect to add the exponents of unlike bases. Use the equation $a^2b^2 \neq (ab)^4$.

7. Error Analysis A classmate says $3s^4 \cdot 5s^2 = (15s)^6$. Explain why your classmate is incorrect. Rewrite the equation to make a true statement.

5-4 Exponents and Division

Common Core State Standards: 8.EE.1: Know and apply the properties of integer exponents to generate equivalent numerical expressions. *For example,* $3^2 \times 3^{-5} = 3^{-3} = \frac{1}{3^3} = \frac{1}{27}$.

Launch

The city's second-best scientist likes to look overly complex. That's why he's second best. He presents the cost of a rocket bolt on Rocket 1 as shown.

How much does a bolt really cost? Show how you know.

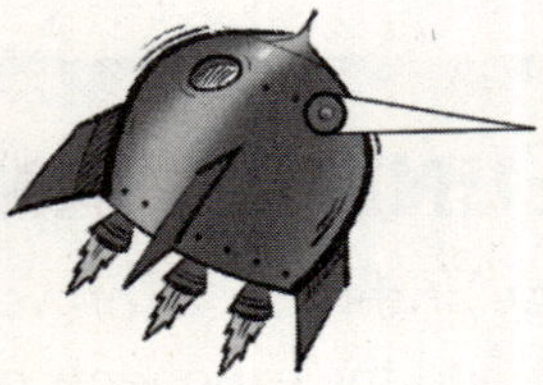

$$\frac{5 \cdot 6 \cdot 2 \cdot 17 \cdot 31 \cdot 4 \cdot 4}{31 \cdot 4 \cdot 2 \cdot 17 \cdot 6 \cdot 5}$$ **dollars each**

Reflect

What was the key to solving this problem? Explain.

Close and Check

Focus Question

How can you apply what you know about dividing numerical expressions to dividing algebraic expressions containing exponents?

Do you know HOW?

1. Simplify the expression.

$\frac{x^{27}}{x^{13}}$

2. Simplify the expression.

$\frac{r^{55}}{r^{32}}$

3. Simplify the expression.

$\left(\frac{2r^9}{3m}\right)^3$

4. Simplify the expression.

$\left(\frac{2d^3g^{12}}{4s^{12}w^6}\right)^5$

Do you UNDERSTAND?

5. **Writing** Can the exponent in the denominator be subtracted from the exponent in the numerator when the bases are different? Explain.

6. **Error Analysis** When asked to simplify the expression, your classmate writes the following:

$$\left(\frac{c^3}{3d^5}\right)^2 = \frac{2c^5}{6d^7}$$

What errors did your classmate make? What should she have written?

5-5 Zero and Negative Exponents

Common Core State Standards: 8.EE.1: Know and apply the properties of integer exponents to generate equivalent numerical expressions. *For example,* $3^2 \times 3^{-5} = 3^{-3} = \frac{1}{3^3} = \frac{1}{27}$.

Launch

Complete the table. Describe three patterns you see in the table.

2^x	10^x
$2^5 = 32$	$10^5 = 100{,}000$
$2^4 = 16$	$10^4 = 10{,}000$
$2^3 = 8$	$10^3 = 1{,}000$
$2^2 = 4$	$10^2 = 100$
$2^1 =$	$10^1 =$
$2^0 =$	$10^0 =$
$2^{-1} =$	$10^{-1} =$

Reflect

Did you figure out the pattern in the left or right column first? Explain.

Close and Check

Focus Question

When do you need an exponent that is equal to zero? When do you need an exponent that is negative? What makes these exponents useful?

Do you know HOW?

1. Simplify the expression.

$\frac{n^{15}}{n^{15}}$

2. Simplify the expression.

$\frac{12k^{15}}{3k^{18}}$

3. Tell whether each expression is > 1, < 1, or $= 1$.

5^{-3}

100^{0}

25^{-2}

7^{2}

Do you UNDERSTAND?

4. Reasoning In the expression $\frac{a^3}{a^3}$, why can the variable *not* be equal to 0? Use substitution to justify your argument arithmetically.

5. Error Analysis Your classmate simplified the expression below. Explain his error and write the correct simplified expression.

$$\frac{6w^{12}}{3w^{12}} = 2w^0 = 2 \cdot 0 = 0$$

5-6 Comparing Expressions with Exponents

Common Core State Standards: 8.EE.1: Know and apply the properties of integer exponents to generate equivalent numerical expressions. *For example,* $3^2 \times 3^{-5} = 3^{-3} = \frac{1}{3^3} = \frac{1}{27}$.

Launch

Use the tiles to create an expression with the least value and an expression with the greatest value. For each expression, you must use each number tile and the negative sign tile in only one location.

Tell how you decided the tile locations.

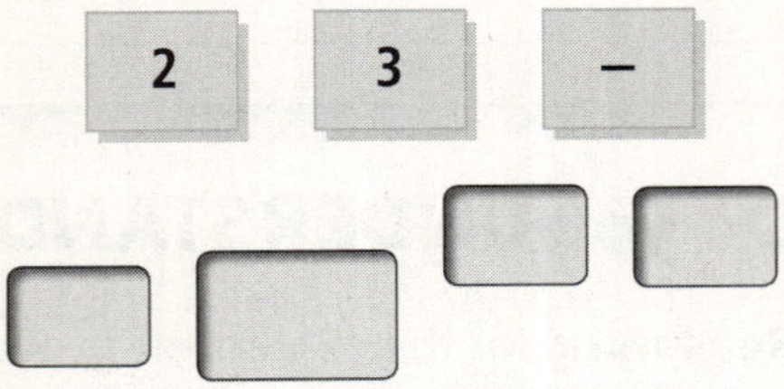

Least Value

Greatest Value

Reflect

What did you decide first in solving the problem? Explain.

Close and Check

Focus Question

What does being able to write expressions with exponents in equivalent forms allow you to do?

Do you know HOW?

1. Which expression(s) is equivalent to 6^{12}?

I. $2^{10} \cdot 3^2$

II. $6^0 \cdot 6^{12}$

III. $(6^{10})^2$

IV. $(6^2)^6$

2. Use >, <, or = to complete each statement.

8^0 ☐ $\frac{8^3}{1^3}$

12^6 ☐ $(12^2)^3$

25^8 ☐ 125^5

27^{12} ☐ $(9^6)^3$

$(8^6)^6$ ☐ $(4^4 \cdot 2^2)^6$

Do you UNDERSTAND?

3. Compare and Contrast What is the difference between comparing exponential numbers with like bases and comparing those with unlike bases?

4. Error Analysis A classmate writes equivalent expressions. Her work is shown below. Is she correct? Explain.

$$(4^2 \cdot 3^2)^6 = (12^4)^6 = 12^{24}$$

5-7 Problem Solving

Common Core State Standards: 8.EE.1: Know and apply the properties of integer exponents to generate equivalent numerical expressions. *For example,* $3^2 \times 3^{-5} = 3^{-3} = \frac{1}{3^3} = \frac{1}{27}$.

Launch

Look for a pattern in the table.

Based on the pattern, what value of x makes the statement $4^{15} = 2^x$ true?

Powers of 4	Powers of 2
$4^2 = 16$	$2^4 = 16$
$4^3 = 64$	$2^6 = 64$
$4^4 = 256$	$2^8 = 256$
$4^5 = 1024$	$2^{10} = 1024$

Reflect

What property of exponents did you apply to help you solve this problem?

Did you use an equation to find the value of x? If so, what equation did you use?

Close and Check

Focus Question

What kind of problems can you solve using expressions and equations containing exponents?

____

____

____

____

Do you know HOW?

1. Circle the value(s) of s for which the expression $-9s^3$ is reasonable for representing the volume of a cube.

A. $s = 0$

B. s can be any negative number.

C. s can be any positive number.

2. Circle the value(s) of y for which the expression $35y^2$ is reasonable for representing the number of square yards your friend mows.

A. $y = 0$

B. y can be any negative number.

C. y can be any positive number.

3. For what values of d, if any, will $2d^4 = 1{,}250$?

Do you UNDERSTAND?

4. Reasoning How would the solution to Exercise 3 change if the equation was $2d^4 = -1{,}250$? How do you know?

____

____

____

____

____

5. Error Analysis Your friend writes an expression to represent the score of a game. Is his expression useful? Explain.

$$\frac{5p^6}{(p^2)^3}$$

____

____

____

____

6-1 Exploring Scientific Notation

Common Core State Standards: 8.EE.3: Use numbers expressed in the form of a single digit times an integer power of 10 to estimate very large or very small quantities .... **8.EE.4:** Perform operations with numbers expressed in scientific notation .... .

Launch

Order the tiles from least to greatest numeric value.
Explain how you know your order is correct.

30,000	$3 \cdot 10^3$	30	$3 \cdot 10^2$
300	$3 \cdot 10^1$	3,000	$3 \cdot 10^4$

Reflect

Is there a pattern between the numbers and the expressions? If so, describe it.

Close and Check

Focus Question

Why might you use powers of 10 to write numbers?

Do you know HOW?

1. Order the numbers from least to greatest.

Least

7.29×10^0

7.29×10^{-5}

7.29×10^3

7.29×10^{-3}

Greatest

2. Circle the numbers that are expressed in scientific notation.

34.5×10^7 5.02×10^3

2×10^9 0.4×10^1

3. Suppose your calculator display shows 6.5E+21. Express this result in scientific notation.

4. Write 745,000 in scientific notation.

Do you UNDERSTAND?

5. Reasoning Explain the strategy you used to order the numbers in Exercise 1.

6. Vocabulary How is scientific notation useful in mathematics?

6-2 Using Scientific Notation to Describe Very Large Quantities

Common Core State Standards: 8.EE.3: Use numbers expressed in the form of a single digit times an integer power of 10 to estimate very large or very small quantities, and to express how many times as much one is than the other . . . .

Launch

Your friend writes 5×2^6 as a shortcut for writing 1×10^6. Explain your friend's shortcut thinking. Is your friend's thinking more science or fiction?

Reflect

Why is it helpful to write numbers in scientific notation using powers of 10? Why is this better than using powers of 2? Explain.

Close and Check

Focus Question

How can positive powers of 10 make large numbers easier to write and compare?

Do you know HOW?

1. The X-15 aircraft holds the world speed record at 23,865,600 ft/hr. Express the world record speed in scientific notation.

2. The population on Earth increased by about 7.62×10^8 people during the first decade of the 21st century. Express the population growth in standard form.

   people

3. One giant ant colony is reported to have about 3.06×10^8 worker ants and 1.02×10^6 queen ants. The number of worker ants is how many times the number of queen ants?

Do you UNDERSTAND?

4. **Writing** Your best friend has never learned about scientific notation. Explain how to use scientific notation to rewrite very large numbers.

5. **Error Analysis** A friend says the average distance to the moon is 382,500 km. Is the number he wrote accurate? Explain.

   3.825×10^6

6-3 Using Scientific Notation to Describe Very Small Quantities

Common Core State Standards: 8.EE.3: Use numbers expressed in the form of a single digit times an integer power of 10 to estimate very large or very small quantities, and to express how many times as much one is than the other … .

Launch

Your friend says a zeptometer is 1×10^{-21} based on its standard form. Explain your friend's zepto-reasoning. Is your friend's thinking more science or fiction?

Unit	Scientific Notation (m)	Standard Form (m)
Meter	1×10^{0}	1
Decimeter	1×10^{-1}	0.1
Centimeter	1×10^{-2}	0.01
Millimeter	1×10^{-3}	0.001
Zeptometer		0.00000000000000000001

Reflect

Does it make more sense to use scientific notation or standard form to represent 1 zeptometer?

Close and Check

Focus Question

How can negative powers of 10 make small numbers easier to write and compare?

Do you know HOW?

1. The diameter of an average snowflake is about 10 micrometers. That is approximately 0.0003937 in. Express the diameter of a snowflake in scientific notation.

2. The diameters of atoms can vary. One particular atom has a diameter of 5.0×10^{-8} cm. Express the diameter of the atom in standard form.

3. The measurement 8.16 micrometers equals 8.16×10^{-6} meter. The measurement 2.04 centimeters equals 2.04×10^{-2} meter. How many times greater is the centimeter measurement than the micrometer measurement?

Do you UNDERSTAND?

4. Writing Do you agree or disagree with the statement below? Explain.

> Scientific notation is a method used to rewrite very large or very small numbers as a number *n* greater than 0 times an integer power of 10.

5. Error Analysis An earthworm travels 0.0000425 miles per second. A friend writes the rate as 4.25×10^{5} mps. Explain her error. Write the correct rate in scientific notation.

6-4 Operating with Numbers Expressed in Scientific Notation

Common Core State Standards: 8.EE.3: Use numbers expressed in the form of a single digit times an integer power of 10 . . . . **8.EE.4:** Perform operations with numbers expressed in scientific notation, including problems where both decimal and scientific notation are used.

Launch

The scientific notation cards shown represent place values. Arrange at least six of the cards in place-value order to represent a three-digit number.

Then write your number in standard form and explain why the cards you chose represent your number.

1×10^2 1×10^2 1×10^0 1×10^1 1×10^1

1×10^1 1×10^0 1×10^2 1×10^2 1×10^2

Reflect

How is using the cards the same as using place value blocks? How is it different?

Close and Check

Focus Question

You previously learned how to multiply and divide expressions with exponents. How can you apply what you know to operations with numbers in scientific notation?

Do you know **HOW?**

1. Simplify.
$(6.9 \times 10^{12}) - (2.6 \times 10^{12}) + (3.4 \times 10^{12})$

2. One gram of dust can contain 2.5×10^5 dust mite droppings. The average six-room home collects about 1.5×10^3 grams of dust each month. In scientific notation, how many dust mite droppings can be found in an average home each month?

droppings

3. The smallest ant is about 4.9×10^{-4} m in length. The distance around the earth at the equator is about 4×10^7 m. In scientific notation to the nearest tenth, how many of these small ants would it take to circle the earth at the equator?

ants

Do you **UNDERSTAND?**

4. Compare and Contrast How are the processes for multiplying and dividing numbers written in scientific notation alike and different?

5. Error Analysis Your friend says this problem has no solution because 8.3 cannot be subtracted from 2.5. Do you argee? Explain.

> Statistically, 2.5×10^7 plastic beverage bottles are used each day. If 8.3×10^6 bottles are recycled, how many end up in landfills?

6-5 Problem Solving

Common Core State Standards: 8.EE.4: Perform operations with numbers expressed in scientific notation . . . . Use scientific notation and choose units of appropriate size for measurements of very large or very small quantities . . . . Also, **8.EE.1**, **8.EE.3.**

Launch

Approximate population data for adults and children in the most and least populous U.S. states in one year, according to the U.S. Census Bureau, are shown.

What is the total population for each state in scientific notation? Justify your answers.

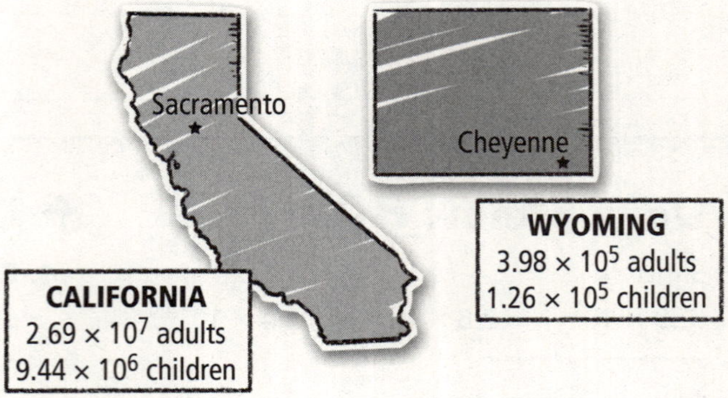

Reflect

How can you tell that California has more people than Wyoming just by comparing the adult and children populations?

Close and Check

Focus Question

How can you use scientific notation to help you solve problems?

Do you know HOW?

1. It takes light 8.5 minutes to travel from the sun to the earth. Light travels at 9.82×10^8 feet per second. How far does light travel from the sun to the earth? Express this distance in scientific notation using the most appropriate unit from the given list.

$$5280 \text{ ft} = 1760 \text{ yd}$$
$$1760 \text{ yd} = 1 \text{ mi}$$

2. The area of the world's largest country is about 6.6×10^6 mi^2. The area of the world's smallest country is about 1.7×10^{-1} mi^2. About how many times larger is the area of the largest country than the area of the smallest country? Express your answer in scientific notation.

3. Find the value of n.
$1.887 \times 10^{12} = (5.1 \times 10^8)(3.7 \times 10^n)$

4. Find the value of n.
$(4.5 \times 10^9) \div (9 \times 10^n) = 5 \times 10^2$

Do you UNDERSTAND?

5. **Reasoning** Explain why you chose the unit of measure that you did in Exercise 1. Explain why you did not choose the others.

6. **Compare and Contrast** How can understanding operations on exponential numbers help you solve problems involving scientific notation?

7-1 Equivalent Ratios

Common Core State Standards: 7.RP.1: Compute unit rates associated with ratios of fractions, including ratios of lengths, areas and other quantities measured in like or different units.

Launch

Your friend can't help but compare. During a game of stickball in the street, you notice him making all sorts of number comparisons. He asks for help making number comparisons on one building.

Name at least five number comparisons you can make by looking at the building.

Reflect

Do you make number comparisons? Provide an example of a number comparison you've made and why you made it.

Close and Check

Focus Question

What does it mean if two different ratios describe the same situation? How can being able to describe the situation in multiple ways help you to solve problems?

Do you know HOW?

1. Write the ratio of the number of bees to the number of flowers in three different ways.

2. Find a ratio equivalent to $\frac{63}{77}$ with lower terms.

3. A baby boy weighs 7 lb 8 oz. A five-year-old boy weighs 48 lb. Write the ratio of the baby's weight to the boy's weight as a fraction in simplest form.

Do you UNDERSTAND?

4. Vocabulary How can the terms of a ratio be used to write an equivalent ratio?

5. Reasoning Two students each write a ratio comparing the two shapes in the group. Can both students be correct? Explain.

$\frac{6}{4}$ $\frac{2}{3}$

7-2 Unit Rates

Common Core State Standards: 7.RP.1: Compute unit rates associated with ratios of fractions, including ratios of lengths, areas and other quantities measured in like or different units.

Launch

Three teams train turtles for the Third Annual Turtle Trot, a 30-foot race. If the turtles trot at their training pace, which turtle will win the race? By how many minutes? Explain your reasoning.

Team 1 Turtle	**Team 2 Turtle**	**Team 3 Turtle**
18 feet in 6 minutes	12 feet in 4 minutes	10 feet in 2 minutes

Reflect

Could you have solved the problem without unit rates? Explain.

Close and Check

Focus Question

How can you identify a rate? How can unit rates help you to solve problems?

Do you know HOW?

1. The Earth rotates 1.25 degrees in 5 minutes. How many degrees does it rotate in 1 minute?

[ ] degrees

2. A driver fills his tank with 15 gallons of gas for $45.60 at a gas station. The next time he stops he fills up with 12 gallons for $39.00. Find the unit price for gas at each station and circle which has the better deal.

1st Station: [ ]

2nd Station: [ ]

3. There are approximately 195 babies born each hour in the United States. Find the approximate number of babies born in the United States every 20 minutes.

[ ] babies

Do you UNDERSTAND?

4. Writing A company earns a profit of $50 for every 10 items sold. Explain how the company can find the amount of profit for 50 items sold.

5. Error Analysis A classmate writes a rate for Exercise 1 to express the degrees rotated in 2 minutes. Explain her error and give the correct rate.

$$\frac{1.25 \div 2}{5 \div 2} = \frac{0.625}{2.5}$$

7-3 Ratios With Fractions

Common Core State Standards: 7.RP.1: Compute unit rates associated with ratios of fractions, including ratios of lengths, areas and other quantities measured in like or different units.

Launch

How many pears must you place on Plate 3 so that the ratios of apples to pears are equivalent for all three plates?

Write the ratio of apples to pears for each plate. Explain your reasoning.

Plate 1

☐ : ☐
apples to pears

Plate 2

☐ : ☐
apples to pears

Plate 3

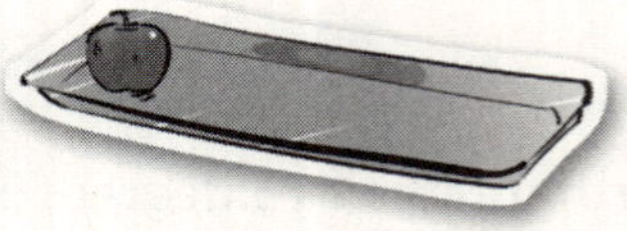

☐ : ☐
apples to pears

Reflect

Can you compare quantities that aren't in whole number units? Explain.

Close and Check

Focus Question

Previously you have written ratios as fractions. How can you write a ratio if at least one term is a fraction? How is this different from writing a ratio where both the terms are whole numbers?

Do you know HOW?

1. A bakery has $\frac{3}{4}$ dozen whole-grain muffins and 6 dozen mixed-berry muffins. Write the ratio of whole-grain muffins to mixed-berry muffins as a fraction in simplest form.

2. Write the ratio $\frac{\frac{6}{7}}{\frac{8}{9}}$ in simplest form.

3. A scale model of a van is $4\frac{1}{5}$ feet long. The actual van is $22\frac{2}{5}$ feet long. What is the ratio of the length of the model to the actual length of the van in simplest form?

Do you UNDERSTAND?

4. **Reasoning** Can any ratio be written as a unit rate? Explain.

5. **Error Analysis** A store sells 8 unscented candles for \$2 or 9 scented candles for \$3. A classmate writes the unit rates $\frac{4}{1}$ and $\frac{3}{1}$. She says one scented candle costs \$3, and one unscented candle costs \$4. Do you agree? Explain.

7-4 Unit Rates With Fractions

Common Core State Standards: 7.RP.1: Compute unit rates associated with ratios of fractions, including ratios of lengths, areas and other quantities measured in like or different units.

Launch

Two clowns get a call as they race to the circus. Clown 2 pleads, "We're going 10 miles per half-hour. We can't go any faster." The caller replies, "You'd better double your speed or you'll never make it."

Show two different ways to write a speed that is twice as fast. Explain your reasoning.

Reflect

Is reporting speed in miles per half hour useful? Is there a better way? Explain.

Close and Check

Focus Question

How can you write a unit rate if at least one term is a fraction? How is this different from writing a unit rate where both terms are whole numbers?

Do you know HOW?

1. A craft project requires $\frac{5}{6}$ yard of ribbon to make 4 refrigerator magnets. How many inches of ribbon are needed for each magnet?

   ☐ inches

2. If it takes $\frac{5}{6}$ yard of ribbon to make 4 magnets, how many complete magnets can be made with $\frac{2}{3}$ yard of ribbon?

   ☐ magnets

3. Machine A packs $4\frac{1}{4}$ cartons in $\frac{1}{5}$ hour. Machine B packs $4\frac{3}{5}$ cartons in $\frac{1}{4}$ hour. Which machine packs faster? How many cartons per hour can the faster machine pack?

   Machine: ☐

   Unit Rate: ☐

Do you UNDERSTAND?

4. **Writing** How do you convert a rate to a unit rate?

5. **Error Analysis** An elevator has a floor area of 38 ft^2 and holds a load of 3,500 lb. The engineer writes this equation to find the number of pounds per square foot.

$$\frac{\frac{3500}{1}}{\frac{38}{1}} = \frac{\frac{3500}{1} \cdot \frac{38}{1}}{1} = \frac{133{,}000}{1}\ \text{lb/ft}^2$$

   Explain his error and write the correct pounds per square foot.

7-5 Problem Solving

Common Core State Standards: 7.RP.1: Compute unit rates associated with ratios of fractions, including ratios of lengths, areas and other quantities measured in like or different units.

Launch

Two nosy neighbors constantly try to outdo each other. Neighbor 1 mows her lawn in $1\frac{3}{4}$ hours. Neighbor 2 insists she's faster and she took $2\frac{1}{4}$ hours.

Who's correct? Show how you know.

Reflect

How were unit rates useful in this problem? Explain.

Close and Check

Focus Question

In this topic you have learned how to compare quantities other than whole numbers. Are some comparisons more helpful for solving problems than others?

Do you know HOW?

1. Your neighbor is replacing her old TV. The old TV screen is $14\frac{2}{5}$ in. tall by $21\frac{1}{2}$ in. wide. The new TV screen is $28\frac{4}{5}$ in. tall and 43 in. wide. What is the ratio of the area of the old TV screen to the area of the new TV screen?

2. A mountain bike race is two laps around a $25\frac{1}{2}$ mi course. Rider A completes the first lap in $1\frac{1}{4}$ hours and the second lap in $1\frac{1}{2}$ hours. Rider B completes both laps at a constant speed of 20 miles per hour. Which rider had the faster combined time for both laps?

3. A recipe for lemonade calls for a ratio of 1 part fresh lemon juice to 8 parts cold water. You have $\frac{2}{3}$ cup of lemon juice. How much water should you add?

Do you UNDERSTAND?

4. **Writing** In one weekend, you earn \$27 and your friend earns \$35. Would a ratio or a unit rate be more helpful to compare the two amounts? Explain.

5. **Reasoning** An entertainment center for the new TV in Exercise 1 has an area of 1,548 ft^2. Explain how to find the ratio of the area of the entertainment center to the area of the TV. What is the unit ratio?

8-1 Proportional Relationships and Tables

Common Core State Standards: 7.RP.2: Recognize and represent proportional relationships .... **7.RP.2.a:** Decide whether two quantities are in a proportional relationship, e.g., by testing for equivalent ratios in a table or graphing on a coordinate plane and observing whether the graph is a straight line through the origin.

Launch

A company manufactures custom car paints. A manager receives orders for 25, 35, and 105 gallons of their Powerful Purple paint shade. The paint manager panics and says, "None of the orders match our mixing chart. How can we make these orders?"

Provide a solution for the panicked paint man.

Powerful Purple Mixing Guide

Gallons of Red Paint	Gallons of Blue Paint
2	3
4	6
20	30
40	60

Reflect

How do you know if two ratios are equivalent?

Close and Check

Focus Question

What does it mean for two quantities to have a proportional relationship? How can you tell if a table shows a proportional relationship between two quantities?

Do you know HOW?

1. The table shows a proportional relationship between the number of teachers and the number of students. Complete the table.

Teachers	3	5		10
Students		75	120	
Ratio students/ teachers				

2. Tell whether the relationship between x and y shown in the table is *proportional* or *not proportional*.

x	1	2	3	4
y	0	6	12	18

3. Circle the ratios that are proportional to $\frac{27}{9}$.

$\frac{9}{3}$ $\frac{36}{4}$ $\frac{3}{1}$

$\frac{6}{2}$ $\frac{54}{18}$ $\frac{1}{9}$

Do you UNDERSTAND?

4. Writing Explain how you determined the proportional ratios in Exercise 3.

5. Writing Give a real-world example of when you might use proportional relationships. Explain why it is proportional.

8-2 Proportional Relationships and Graphs

Common Core State Standards: 7.RP.2.a: Decide whether two quantities are in a proportional relationship, e.g., … graphing on a coordinate plane and observing whether the graph is a straight line through the origin. Also, **7.RP.2.d.**

Launch

The manager of the car paint company prepares orders for its Granny Apple Green paint.

Tell how the graph can help you find the amounts of blue and yellow paint needed to make 8 gallons, 24 gallons, and 56 gallons of Granny Apple Green paint.

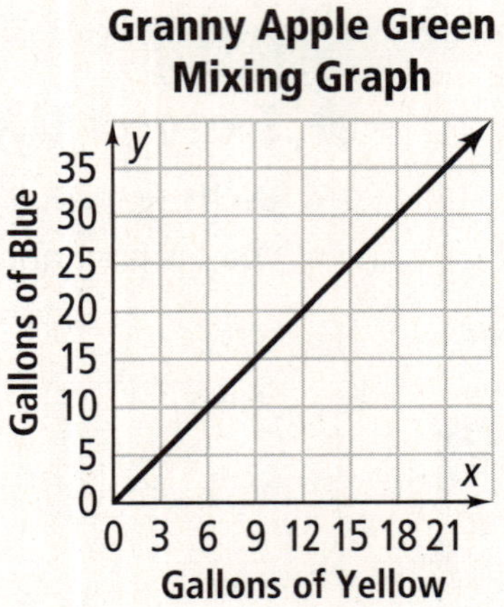

Reflect

Do you think a graph or a table makes it easier for the company to find the correct mix of blue and yellow paint to make Granny Apple Green?

Close and Check

Focus Question

How can you tell if a graph shows a proportional relationship between two quantities?

Do you know HOW?

1. The relationship between time x and distance y can be represented by the equation $y = 2x$. Complete the table and graph.

$y = 2x$

x	y
0	
1	
2	
3	
4	
5	

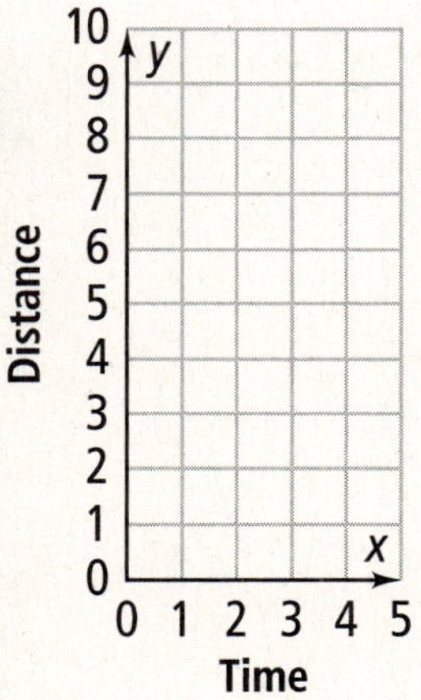

2. What is the distance when time is equal to 15?

units

3. What is the unit rate of the graph?

Do you UNDERSTAND?

4. Writing Does the graph in Exercise 1 represent a proportional relationship? Explain how you know.

5. Reasoning Do all linear graphs represent proportional relationships? Explain.

6. Error Analysis A classmate says that not all proportional relationships are linear. Do you agree? Explain.

8-3 Constant of Proportionality

Common Core State Standards: 7.RP.2: Recognize and represent proportional relationships between quantities. **7.RP.2.b:** Identify the constant of proportionality (unit rate) in tables, graphs, equations, diagrams, and verbal descriptions of proportional relationships. Also, **7.NS.2.d.**

Launch

The car paint company provides a perplexing pay graph for new managers.

What does the graph show? Which point—*A*, *B*, or *C*—might be the most useful? Explain.

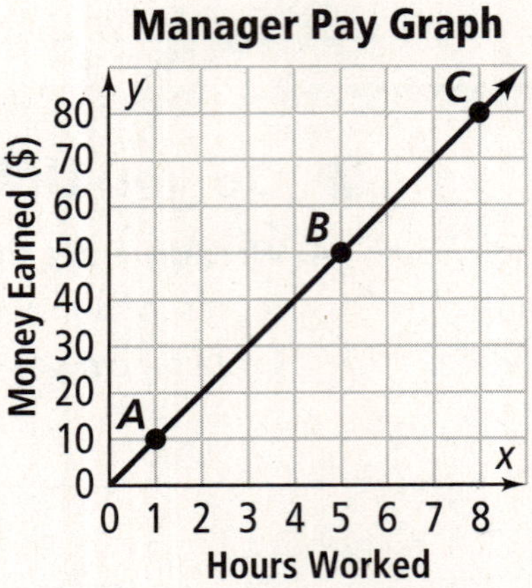

What the Graph Shows:

Which Point Might Be Most Useful:

Reflect

Which point may be the least useful? Explain.

Close and Check

Focus Question

What is a constant of proportionality? What does the constant of proportionality tell you?

Do you know HOW?

1. Each bus carries 24 passengers. The number of buses needed for a field trip depends on the number of students going on the trip. What is the constant of proportionality for this situation?

   ______ per ______

2. Your class collects cans for a local food bank. On Monday, 7 students collect 63 cans. Using the constant of proportionality, find the number of students who collect 90 cans on Tuesday.

   ______ students

3. The table shows the number of concert tickets sold based on the number hours the tickets are available. What is the constant of proportionality for this situation?

Ticket Sales

Time (hr)	Tickets
3	240
5	400
9	720
15	1200

______

Do you UNDERSTAND?

4. **Writing** Which variable in Exercise 3 represents the independent variable and which represents the dependent variable? Explain.

5. **Reasoning** How can you use the relationship between the independent and dependent variables to write a unit rate?

8-4 Proportional Relationships and Equations

Common Core State Standards: 7.RP.2: Recognize and represent proportional relationships between quantities. **7.RP.2.b:** Identify the constant of proportionality (unit rate) in … equations … of proportional relationships. **7.RP.2.c:** Represent proportional relationships by equations … .

Launch

The paint company manager grows tired of answering a particular pay question from employees. He mulls over two equations to help the employees.

What question could employees keep asking? Which equation would help them? Explain.

Reflect

If you could have had one more piece of information before starting to answer the problem, what would it be and why?

Close and Check

Focus Question

How can you tell if an equation shows a proportional relationship between two quantities? How can you identify the constant of proportionality in an equation that represents a proportional relationship?

Do you know **HOW?**

1. The equation $q = 12c$ represents the quantity q of t-shirts in any number of cartons c.

a. What is the constant of proportionality?

b. How many shirts are in 8 cartons?

shirts

2. A car manufacturer completes 81 cars every 180 seconds. Write an equation to represent the total number of cars y for x seconds of production.

3. Use the table to write an equation to find how much money y is received for x ounces of silver on the open market.

Silver Exchange Rate

Silver (oz)	5	9	12
Price ($)	151.35	272.43	363.24

Do you **UNDERSTAND?**

4. Writing Can setting up a proportion help you find the constant of proportionality in a relationship? Explain.

5. Error Analysis Assume 130 out of 150 students buy lunch each day. There are 180 school days in a year. A classmate writes an equation to find how many lunches will be sold in one school year. Is he correct? Explain.

$$\frac{130}{150} = \frac{x}{180}$$

8-5 Maps and Scale Drawings

Common Core State Standards: 7.G.1: Solve problems involving scale drawings of geometric figures, including computing actual lengths and areas from a scale drawing and reproducing a scale drawing at a different scale.

Launch

A peculiar professor wants a perfectly proportioned poster of a photo of her pet paper cup. She brings the 4-inch by 6-inch photo to your store and says the poster must be at least three feet tall.

Identify the side lengths of two possible posters.

4 in.

6 in.

Reflect

What will the pet paper cup look like if the poster is not proportional to the photo? Explain.

Close and Check

Focus Question

How can you use proportional relationships to solve problems that involve maps and scale drawings?

Do you know HOW?

1. A replica of a popular car is built to a scale of 1 in. : 24 in. The length of the replica car is 5.6 inches. What is the length, in inches, of the actual car?

2. The official ratio of length to width of the U. S. flag is 1.9 : 1. If the width of a flag is 3 ft, what is the area of the flag?

3. A company designs a billboard to advertise their grand opening. They used a scale of 1 in. : 10 ft. What would be the dimensions of the billboard in the drawing if they use a scale of 2 in. : 25 ft instead?

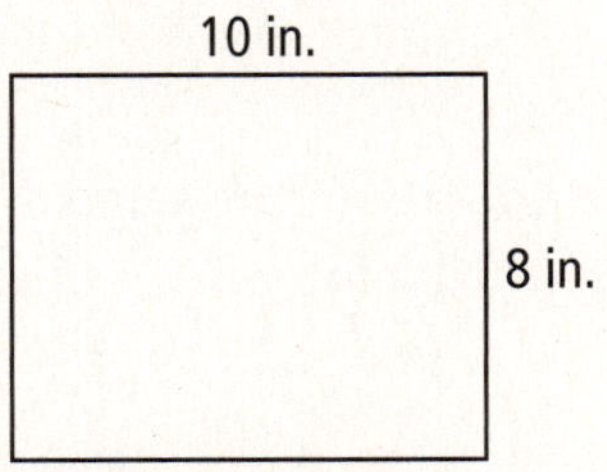

Do you UNDERSTAND?

4. Writing Can understanding scale drawings help you make decisions? Explain.

5. Compare and Contrast How are scale and ratio related?

8-6 Problem Solving

Common Core State Standards: 7.G.1: Solve problems involving scale drawings of geometric figures, including computing actual lengths and areas from a scale drawing and reproducing a scale drawing at a different scale. Also, **7.RP.2, 7.RP.2.a, 7.RP.2.b, 7.RP.2.c,** and **7.RP.2.d.**

Launch

The peculiar professor plans a room addition for her pet paper cup and poster. The scale of the model is 1 in. = 3 ft.

Draw a net for the walls and ceiling of the room on the inch grid. Label the dimensions.

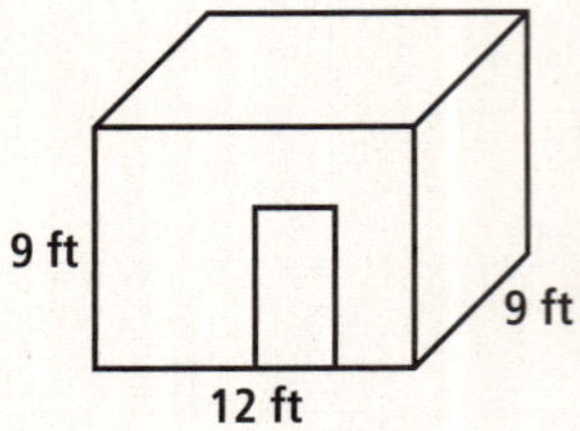

Reflect

Is the ratio of the length to the width of the ceiling in the actual room the same as the ratio of the length to the width of the ceiling in the scale drawing? Explain.

Close and Check

Focus Question

In this topic you have studied different ways to represent proportional relationships. In what ways can you represent proportional relationships? How can knowing how to represent proportional relationship in different ways be useful in solving problems?

Do you know **HOW?**

1. Circle the situation(s) that describes proportional relationships.

A. The number of roller coaster riders is 12 more than the number of seats.

B. There are 2 pieces of pizza for every friend.

C. There are 3 times as many books as there are children.

2. An office is drawn to a scale of 3 in. : 10 ft. The drawing measures 4.5 in. by 7.5 in. How many square feet of carpet are needed to carpet the office?

3. The Statue of Liberty is 151 ft tall from the base to the top of the torch. You make a scale drawing of the monument using a scale of 1 in. : 20 ft. Your friend uses a scale of 1 in. : 25 ft.

a. Whose drawing is larger?

b. How much larger?

Do you **UNDERSTAND?**

4. Writing Explain how you decided which relationships were proportional in Exercise 1 and which ones were not.

5. Reasoning The scale drawing in Exercise 2 is redrawn to a scale of 4 in. : 9 ft. Is this second drawing larger or smaller than the first? Explain.

9-1 The Percent Equation

Common Core State Standards: 7.RP.2.b: Identify the constant of proportionality (unit rate) in tables, graphs, equations, diagrams, and verbal descriptions of proportional relationships. **7.RP.2.c:** Represent proportional relationships by equations . . . . Also, **7.RP.2.**

Launch

A down-in-the-dumps drummer scours the internet for a new kit to improve his mood and swing. Based on buyers' reviews, which kit should he get? Show how you decided.

Kit 1: 9 of 13 buyers love this kit!

Kit 2: 15 of 21 buyers love this kit!

Reflect

Do you like the method of showing buyers' reviews (e.g., 9 of 13)? Explain.

Close and Check

Focus Question

How do percents and the percent equation help describe things in the real world?

Do you know HOW?

1. Is the question "What percent of 8 is 5?" looking for the *part*, the *percent*, or the *whole*?

2. Read each statement. Write **T** if it is true or **F** if it is false.

   9 is 15% of 60.

   12% of 120 is 10.

   32 is 40% of 80.

   90% of 180 is 162.

3. A shoe store is having a closeout sale. All the prices are 80% of the original price. The shoes you want originally cost $40. Find the sale price of the shoes.

Do you UNDERSTAND?

4. **Writing** The total bill at a restaurant equals $65.38. The waiter typically receives a tip equal to 15% of the total bill. He is given a $13 tip. Should he be happy with the amount of the tip? Explain.

5. **Vocabulary** Explain how to solve "72 is 18% of what number?" by using the terms *part*, *percent*, and *whole*.

9-2 Using the Percent Equation

Common Core State Standards: 7.RP.2: Recognize and represent proportional relationships between quantities. **7.RP.3:** Use proportional relationships to solve … percent problems. *Examples: … tax, gratuities and commissions … .*

Launch

A movie studio sets two offers in front of a movie star to act in a blockbuster upcoming action flick. The star can choose only one offer.

Make a case for accepting each offer. Then explain which offer you would choose.

Reflect

Which offer has a constant of proportionality? Explain.

Close and Check

Focus Question

In what situations are fixed numbers better than percents of an amount? In what situations are percents better than fixed numbers?

Do you know HOW?

1. You pay \$3.50 per gallon including taxes for 15 gallons of gas. Federal and state gas taxes make up 14% of the total cost. How much do you pay in gas taxes?

2. A new car depreciates (loses value) by 9% immediately after it is purchased and driven from the lot. If a new car costs \$28,400, how much is it worth right after it is driven off the car lot?

3. A company expects a new sales employee to work 40 hours per week. The company offers the employee either \$25 per hour or a salary of \$500 per week plus a 7% sales commission. Each sales employee averages \$7,800 in sales each week. Which offer pays more?

Do you UNDERSTAND?

4. Error Analysis A basketball player made 88% of 125 free throw attempts. Your friend calculates how many free throws the player made below. Explain her error and find the correct number.

total = 88% • 125
= 88.0 • 125
= 11,000

5. Writing Your uncle offers to sell your guitar at his auction. He offers you \$75 or 50% of the final selling price. How would you choose? Explain.

9-3 Simple Interest

Common Core State Standards: 7.RP.2: Recognize and represent proportional relationships between quantities. **7.RP.3:** Use proportional relationships to solve multistep … percent problems. *Examples: simple interest ….*

Launch

Two banks offer different incentives to make a deposit at their bank. Bank A offers a $10 gift card for making a minimum initial deposit. Bank B offers cash back equal to 2% of your deposit at the end of the year.

Tell which line represents each bank's offer. Explain your reasoning.

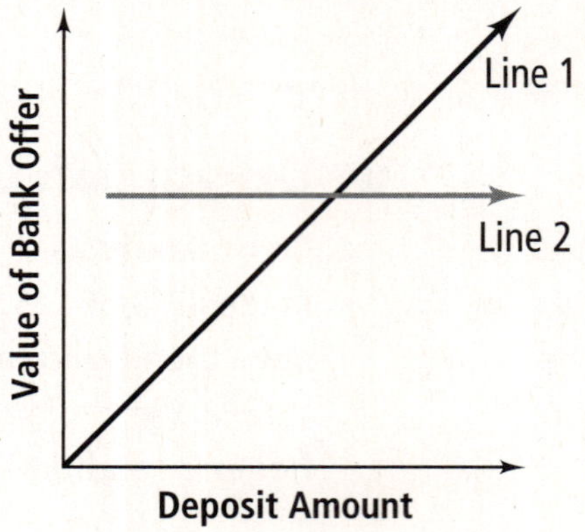

Reflect

What would you need to know to decide which offer to choose? Explain.

Close and Check

Focus Question

Why is simple interest called "simple"? When would you use simple interest?

Do you know HOW?

1. U.S. savings bonds pay 1.4% interest. You purchase $750 in savings bonds and hold them for $2\frac{1}{2}$ years. Circle the true statement(s).

A. $I = 1.4\%$

B. $p = 750$

C. $r = 26.25$

D. $t = 2.5$

2. You buy $2,500 of savings bonds at 1.7% interest. How many years will it take for your investment to equal $3,000? Round your answer to the nearest whole year.

3. Suppose after 15 months you earn $74.80 in interest on an investment that earns 1.6% interest. What was your principal investment?

Do you UNDERSTAND?

4. Reasoning You and your friend both have savings accounts that pay 3.5% interest. Do you both earn the same amount of money in interest? Explain how you know.

5. Error Analysis Your friend says she has $75 in her savings account that pays 3.5% interest. She finds the amount of interest earned in one year. Is she correct? Explain.

I = 75 • 3.5 • 1
I = 262.50

9-4 Compound Interest

Common Core State Standards: 7.NS.3: Solve real-world and mathematical problems involving the four operations with rational numbers.

Launch

A bank manager shows your friend a graph of different types of interest the bank can pay on her $100 deposit. The manager advises your friend to opt for 2% simple interest "because it's easy to compute and a good rate."

Tell which line represents simple interest. Explain whether your friend should listen to the bank manager.

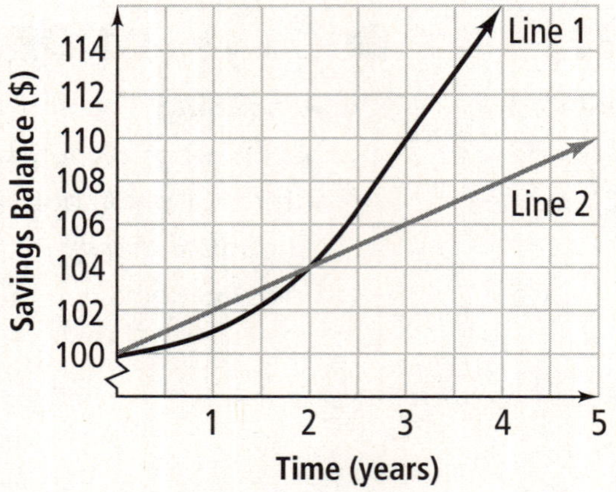

Reflect

What makes simple interest simple? How is the other interest line different? Explain.

Close and Check

Focus Question

How is compound interest different from simple interest? When do you use each kind?

Do you know **HOW?**

1. You invest \$750 in an account that earns 4.5%, compounded annually. Find the balance of the account after 2 years. Round your answer to the nearest cent.

2. A 10-year investment at 3.5%, compounded annually, totals \$4,250. Find the amount of the original deposit to the nearest cent.

3. You qualify for a 5-year loan of \$2,000. The interest rate is 9.5% with no late fees. How much more or less would you owe if interest is compounded quarterly rather than compounded annually?

Do you **UNDERSTAND?**

4. **Writing** Explain how can you use what you have learned about compound interest to develop a savings or investment plan.

5. **Error Analysis** Your friend can get a 3-year car loan for \$3,700 at 7.5% annual interest compounded quarterly. Explain the error she makes in calculating the amount of interest.

$$B = 3{,}700(1 + 0.01875)^4$$
$$= 3{,}985.40$$
$$I = 3{,}985.40 - 3{,}700$$
$$= 285.40$$

9-5 Percent Increase and Decrease

Common Core State Standards: 7.RP.2: Recognize and represent proportional relationships between quantities. **7.RP.3:** Use proportional relationships to solve multistep … percent problems. *Examples: … percent increase and decrease … .*

Launch

Two friends argue about which of their little town's populations grew the most between 2000 and 2009.

Write an argument to support each friend's point of view. Explain your reasoning.

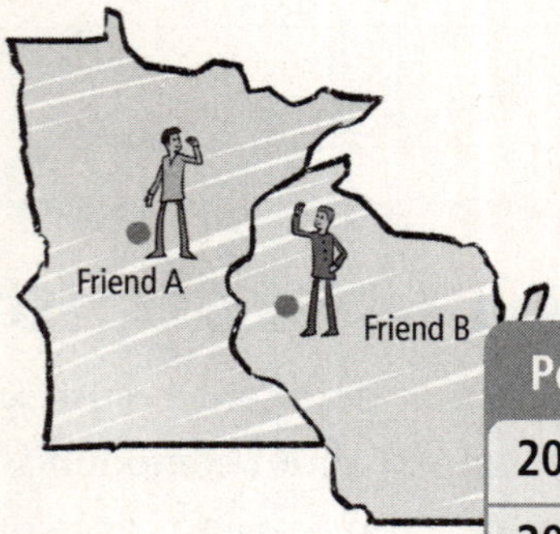

U.S. Census Bureau Data

Population data	Little Falls, MN	Little Falls, WI
2009 population	8,067	1,540
2000 population	7,719	1,334

Reflect

Which do you think tells more about the growth of a town — percent increase in population or increase in number of people? Explain.

Close and Check

Focus Question

How can you use a percent to represent change?

Do you know HOW?

1. The banded ribbon worm is a carnivorous aquatic worm. It measures about 2.5 ft when contracted and up to 25 ft when expanded. Find the percent increase between the contracted and expanded length of a banded ribbon worm.

2. The oceans' tide levels vary based on the phases of the moon. Find the percent decrease in tide levels when high tide is 4.25 ft and low tide is 0.75 ft above sea level.

3. The national debt in 2000 was about $5.7 trillion. In 2010, the nation debt had risen to about $13.6 trillion. Find the approximate percent of change in the national debt during that ten-year period.

Do you UNDERSTAND?

4. Reasoning Explain how you know whether a percent of change is a percent increase or a percent decrease.

5. Writing Give a real-world example of when it might be useful to calculate a percent of change. Would you expect the percent of change to be a percent increase or a percent decrease?

9-6 Markups and Markdowns

Common Core State Standards: 7.RP.3: Use proportional relationships to solve multistep … percent problems. *Examples: … markups and markdowns … .*

Launch

A sporting goods store holds a storewide clearance sale. You comb the ads for boxing items.

Order the ads from best deal to worst deal. Explain your reasoning.

Reflect

Should you always choose the item with the greatest change in price when shopping? Explain.

Close and Check

Focus Question

When are percent markups and percent markdowns used? How are they similar? How are they different?

Do you know HOW?

1. A car dealership pays $26,215 for a new car. They sell the car for $28,265. Find the percent markup on the car.

2. A computer is purchased by a store for $756 and offered to the customer for $1,200. At the end of the year, the store discounts the computer for quick sale. Find the greatest percent markdown possible without losing money.

3. Gaming Unlimited buys a gaming system for $249. It sells the system for $385. This week the system is on sale for 30% off. Find the amount of profit made on each gaming system sold.

Do you UNDERSTAND?

4. **Reasoning** Does a seller make a profit if the percent markdown on an item is equal to the percent markup? Explain using an example.

5. **Vocabulary** A $70 jacket is marked down to $52.50. Your friend says the markdown is 25%. You say the markdown is $17.50. Explain how both of you can be correct.

9-7 Problem Solving

Common Core State Standards: 7.RP.3: Use proportional relationships to solve multistep … percent problems. *Examples: simple interest, tax, markups and markdowns, gratuities and commissions, fees, percent increase and decrease … .*

Launch

Two friends agree to pay half each for their mostly excellent meatloaf dinner and most excellent 20% tip. Each friend has $8.50.

Do they have enough money to complete their excellent plan? If so, by how much? If not, tell what they should do.

Reflect

How do you use percents in your life outside of school? Provide one example.

Close and Check

Focus Question

How do percents help you compare, predict, and make decisions?

Do you know HOW?

1. You and 3 friends combine a snowboard purchase to save on shipping fees. Each board costs $82.50 after tax. The total bill is $392.70. Express the shipping fee as a percent rate to the nearest whole percent.

2. The number 450 is increased by 75%. The result is then decreased by 90%. What is the final number?

3. You receive a $50 gift card to your favorite store. If sales tax is 7.5%, what is the greatest amount you can spend without using any additional money?

Do you UNDERSTAND?

4. Writing A researcher finds that 11 out of 15 people work within 30 miles of their home. He says 73% of people work within 30 miles of their home. Which statement do you find more useful? Explain.

5. Reasoning A bookstore special-orders books for a fee of $1.50 per book. Online orders have a shipping charge of 10% of the total order. If 5 books cost $70.96, which is the better offer?

10-1 Expanding Algebraic Expressions

Common Core State Standards: 7.EE.1: Apply properties of operations as strategies to add, subtract, factor, and expand linear expressions with rational coefficients. **7.EE.2:** Understand that rewriting an expression in different forms in a problem context can shed light on the problem … .

Launch

Use the symbols, numbers, and a variable to make three equivalent expressions. Tell which properties (Commutative, Associative, and Distributive) you used. You can use each tile more than once.

( ) + • 7 −3 −21 *w*

Reflect

Your expressions are equivalent, but are they different in any way? Explain.

Close and Check

Focus Question

When would you want to expand an algebraic expression? What operation would you use? What does expanding an expression help you do?

Do you know HOW?

1. Circle the expression(s) that shows a sum or difference equivalent to $-0.9(3x - 2.6)$.

   A. $-2.7x - 2.34$ B. $-2.7x + 2.34$

   C. $-2.7x + 23.4$ D. $-27x - 23.4$

2. Write the expression in expanded form.

   $$(4.2z)(-5y - 3)$$

3. You charge $2.50 per hour for each child you babysit. You also earn an activity fee of $2.75 for each hour. You babysit an average of 10 hours a month. Write an expression using the product of two factors to find how much you will earn on average each month for any number of children *c*.

4. Simplify the expression you wrote in Exercise 3.

Do you UNDERSTAND?

5. **Writing** What does each factor in the expression in Exercise 3 represent? What does the expression itself represent?

6. **Error Analysis** A classmate says that the expression $-5r(6s)$ can be expanded to $-30r - 5rs$. Explain his error.

10-2 Factoring Algebraic Expressions

Common Core State Standards: 7.EE.1: Apply properties of operations as strategies to add, subtract, factor, and expand linear expressions with rational coefficients. **7.EE.2:** Understand that rewriting an expression in different forms in a problem context can shed light on the problem … .

Launch

Your friends name five expressions—all using the same variable *p*—equivalent to the one shown. They say there's even more equality to be expressed.

What five equivalent expressions could they have named? Explain your reasoning.

$12p + 3.6$

Reflect

Do you think there are only five expressions equivalent to $12p + 3.6$? Explain.

Close and Check

Focus Question

How does a common factor help you rewrite an algebraic expression?

Do you know HOW?

1. Write the factored form of the algebraic expression.

$$54f - 9g + 27h$$

2. Combine the like terms.

$$-17tr + 12tr$$

3. A video game store sells games for various prices. Sales tax is 7.5%. Let g be the price of a game. Use the expression to find the total cost of a video game.

$$g + 0.075g$$

4. A store advertises a sale of 15% off the total purchase price. Let p be the purchase price. Use the expression to find the final price.

$$p - 0.15p$$

Do you UNDERSTAND?

5. Writing How are the results of factoring the following expressions different?

$2b + 6b$ $\qquad$ $2b + 6$

6. Error Analysis A classmate says the expression cannot be rewritten because it does not contain any like terms. Do you agree? Explain.

$$3x + (4y - 2xy)$$

10-3 Adding Algebraic Expressions

Common Core State Standards: 7.EE.1: Apply properties of operations as strategies to add, subtract, factor, and expand linear expressions with rational coefficients. **7.EE.2:** Understand that rewriting an expression in different forms in a problem context can shed light on the problem … .

Launch

The twins hold a fundraiser for a local food pantry. People bring cash and food, so the twins struggle to state the total value of all items donated.

Write an expression to show the value of items donated. Explain your reasoning.

Reflect

Could the twins find out how much money all the donated items are worth? Explain.

Close and Check

Focus Question

When would you want to add algebraic expressions? How do properties of operations help you add expressions?

Do you know HOW?

1. Identify the parts of the expression.

$14d - 9 + 21k - 7dk + 2$

A. number of terms

B. the coefficients

C. the constant terms

2. Circle the expressions that are equivalent to $12r - 4$.

A. $(9r + 6) - (-3r + 10)$

B. $-4(3r + 1)$

C. $(6r - 2) + (6r - 2)$

D. $-2(-6r - 2)$

3. The length of a box is 2.75 times greater than the width. Write and simplify an algebraic expression for the perimeter of the box in terms of the width *w*.

Do you UNDERSTAND?

4. Reasoning Is the coefficient of *b* in the expression below 2 or −2? Explain.

$5c - 2b$

5. Error Analysis A classmate simplifies the expression in Exercise 1. Is the expression he wrote equivalent to the original expression? Explain.

$7dk(2 - 3 - 1) - 7$

10-4 Subtracting Algebraic Expressions

Common Core State Standards: 7.EE.1: Apply properties of operations as strategies to add, subtract, factor, and expand linear expressions with rational coefficients. **7.EE.2:** Understand that rewriting an expression in different forms in a problem context can shed light on the problem and how the quantities in it are related.

Launch

Your twin friends store the fundraiser items in a shed. Three raccoons break in and steal some of the food and money.

Write an expression that shows the value of the remaining fundraiser items in the shed. Explain your reasoning.

Reflect

How are adding and subtracting expressions alike? Explain.

Close and Check

Focus Question

When would you want to subtract algebraic expressions? How do properties of operations help you subtract expressions?

Do you know HOW?

1. Rewrite the expression without parentheses.

$4t - 4(3r - 2)$

2. Number the steps of simplifying the expression in the correct order.

$-3(-r + s) - 2(4r - 7s)$

- $3r - 8r - 3s - (-14s)$
- $3r - 8r - 3s + 14s$
- $3r - 3s - 8r - (-14s)$
- $-5r + 11s$

3. One friend buys a pair of shoes for \$54.98 and 3 t-shirts. Another friend buys a sweatshirt for \$26.49 and 5 t-shirts. Using one variable write a simplified expression to represent how much more one friend spent.

Do you UNDERSTAND?

4. Writing Explain a different method for simplifying the expression in Exercise 2 than the method shown.

5. Error Analysis A classmate says she prefers to remove the parentheses before solving the equation. Can she do that and still find the correct solution? Explain.

$(1.47a - 2.9) - (3.08a - 0.5)$

10-5 Problem Solving

Common Core State Standards: 7.EE.1: Apply properties of operations as strategies to add, subtract, factor, and expand linear expressions with rational coefficients. **7.EE.2:** Understand that rewriting an expression in different forms in a problem context can shed light on the problem . . . .

Launch

Two friends each write an expression to describe the total area, in square feet, of a three-panel mural. Each panel is a rectangle.

One friend wrote $6.7h + 12.4h + 5.9h$.

The other friend wrote $25h$.

Does one expression describe the area of the mural better than the other? Explain.

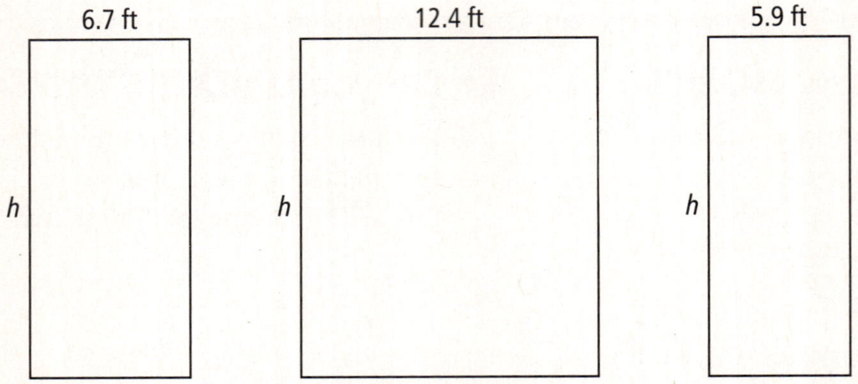

Reflect

Does it help to show the equivalent expressions in different ways? Explain.

Close and Check

Focus Question

How do different forms of an algebraic expression help you solve a problem?

Do you know HOW?

1. Write a difference of two products that is equivalent to $3x - 7y - 13$.

2. Write a product of two factors that is equivalent to $35x - 21$.

3. A homeowner wants to build a fence around her yard. Fencing costs $13.40 for each foot. Write and simplify an expression for the cost of the fencing.

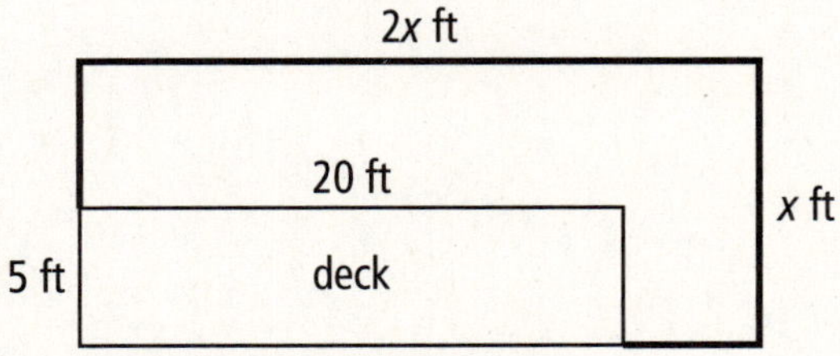

Do you UNDERSTAND?

4. Reasoning One student wrote an expression for Exercise 3 by using addition. Another student wrote an expression by using subtraction. Can both students be correct? Explain.

5. Reasoning If the dimensions of the yard in Exercise 3 were doubled, would the total cost of the fencing double? Explain.

11-1 Solving Simple Equations

Common Core State Standards: 7.EE.4: Use variables to represent quantities in a real-world or mathematical problem, and construct simple equations and inequalities to solve problems by reasoning about the quantities. Also, **7.EE.4.a.**

Launch

A shaky egg bagel baker just wants to keep things equal. What should he charge for one bagel to match his cross-town rival?

Write and solve an equation to help him out. Explain your reasoning.

Reflect

Can you represent this problem with more than one equation? Explain.

Close and Check

Focus Question

How can writing two equivalent expressions help you solve a problem?

Do you know HOW?

1. Solve the equation $g + 12 = 18$.

2. Solve the equation $4r = -1.6$.

3. Solve the equation $\frac{w}{2.5} = 9$.

4. Which equation(s) has the same solution as $\frac{d}{6} = 7.3$?

A. $d - 15.9 = 27.9$

B. $2d = 87.2$

C. $-49 + d = 5$

D. $\frac{d}{4} = 10.95$

Do you UNDERSTAND?

5. Vocabulary What does it mean to isolate the variable?

6. Error Analysis A classmate solves the equation shown below. Explain her error and find the correct solution.

$$5t = 65$$
$$5(5t) = 65(5)$$
$$t = 325$$

11-2 Writing Two-Step Equations

Common Core State Standards: 7.EE.4: Use variables to represent quantities in a real-world or mathematical problem, and construct simple equations and inequalities to solve problems by reasoning about the quantities. Also, **7.EE.4.a.**

Launch

The shaky mini-cheese bagel baker can't figure out how to calculate the price of each bagel for bagels one to twelve.

Write an equation the bagel maker could use to calculate the cost of each of the first twelve bagels. Explain your reasoning.

Reflect

Can you represent the value of the 13 bagels as 13 · *b*? Explain.

Close and Check

Focus Question

What kinds of problems call for two operations?

Do you know HOW?

1. An animal shelter houses 32 cats. The workers use 24 cups of cat food each day. Write an equation to find how many cups of food per cat the shelter uses each day.

2. An apartment rents for $725 per month plus a security deposit. The total cost for the apartment is $9,300 for the first year. Write an equation to find the security deposit amount.

3. Write an equation to represent the following description.

   The difference of seven times a number and 15 is 41.

Do you UNDERSTAND?

4. **Writing** Describe your strategy for rewriting a word problem in the form of an equation.

5. **Reasoning** Is there more than one way to set up an equation based on a word problem? If so, give an example using Exercise 1, 2, or 3.

11-3 Solving Two-Step Equations

Common Core State Standards: 7.EE.3: Solve multi-step real-life and mathematical problems posed with positive and negative rational numbers . . . . **7.EE.4.a:** Solve word problems leading to equations of the form $px + q = r$ . . . where p, q, and r are specific rational numbers . . . . Also, **7.EE.4.**

Launch

The shaky bagel baker decides to just divide by 13 to decide how much to charge for each bagel.

Does his method represent the per-bagel price his cross-town rival charges for bagels one to thirteen? Explain your reasoning.

Reflect

What's the most important thing about solving equations? Explain.

Close and Check

Focus Question

How is solving a two-step equation similar to solving a one-step equation?

Do you know HOW?

1. Write the modeled equation. Then solve it.

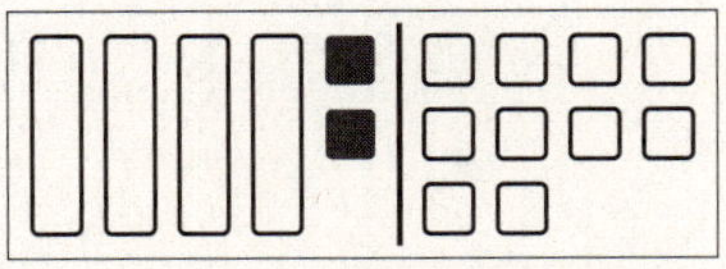

Equation:

Solution:

2. Solve the equation $24.8 = 6g + 10.4$.

Solution:

3. You open a savings account with \$30. You deposit an additional \$20 every week. Write and solve an equation to find how many weeks it will take you to save \$150.

Equation:

Solution:

Do you UNDERSTAND?

4. Reasoning Explain how to check the answer to Exercise 3.

5. Error Analysis Your friend says it will only take $4\frac{1}{2}$ weeks to save \$150 in the account from Exercise 3 because you have to subtract the original amount of the deposit, which is equal to $1\frac{1}{2}$ weeks. Do you agree? Explain.

11-4 Solving Equations Using the Distributive Property

Common Core State Standards: 7.EE.3: Solve multi-step real-life and mathematical problems posed with positive and negative rational numbers . . . . **7.EE.4.a:** Solve word problems leading to equations of the form $px + q = r$ . . . where p, q, and r are specific rational numbers . . . . Also, **7.EE.4.**

Launch

The shaky bagel baker boldly decides to charge 5¢ more per bagel than his rival does for whole-wheat bagels.

Write an expression to show how he could figure out a per-dozen price. Explain your reasoning.

Expression

Reflect

What is the difference between an expression and an equation?

Close and Check

Focus Question

When is it useful to model a situation in two different ways?

Do you know HOW?

1. Solve the equation.

$-3.2(5d - 7) = -17.6$

2. Circle the equation(s) that requires more than two operations to solve.

A. $\frac{2}{3}x = -15$

B. $3(5h + 9) = 57$

C. $4(8s) - 6 = 218$

D. $4.5(r + 1) = 27$

3. Three families each buy the same number of $15 tickets to the zoo. Each family also pays $5.50 for parking. The total cost is $196.50. Write and solve an equation to find how many tickets each family buys.

Equation:

Solution:

Do you UNDERSTAND?

4. Writing Write a possible real-world problem to match the equation in Exercise 2, letter D.

5. Error Analysis A classmate says the first step to solve the equation $12(3g - 9) = 99$ is to add 9 to both sides. Do you agree? Explain.

11-5 Problem Solving

Common Core State Standards: 7.EE.4: Use variables to represent quantities in a real-world or mathematical problem, and construct simple equations and inequalities to solve problems by reasoning about the quantities. Also, **7.EE.3, 7.EE.4.a.**

Launch

Use words to describe or a picture to model a real-world situation that relates to the equation shown. Your situation must somehow involve the secret ingredient, bagels. Go!

Reflect

Does describing an equation with words or modeling it with a picture help you solve an equation? Explain.

Close and Check

Focus Question

Real-world situations can be complicated or hard to understand. What can models and equations show better than words?

Do you know **HOW?**

1. At an arcade you buy 5 game cards and your friend buys 3 game cards. Your lunch costs $6 and your friend's lunch costs $4. Altogether, the two of you spend $50. Complete the bar diagram to find the cost of one game card.

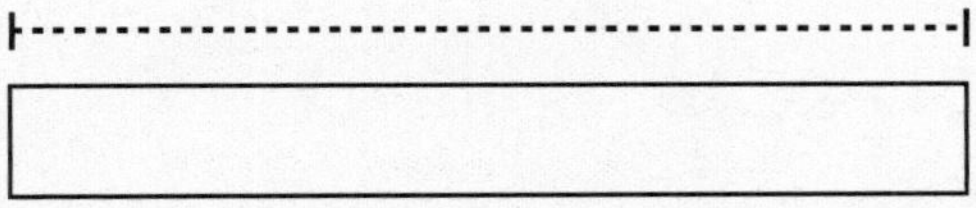

2. How much does each game card cost?

3. A ruby-throated hummingbird flies 9 miles in 20 minutes. Use the formula to find its average speed in miles per hour.

$$d = rt$$

Do you **UNDERSTAND?**

4. Writing Explain how formulas are helpful in problem solving.

5. Reasoning A classmate solves Exercise 3 by using division. Is this a reasonable method? Explain.

12-1 Solving Two-Step Equations

Common Core State Standard: 8.EE.7: Solve linear equations in one variable. **8.EE.7.b:** Solve linear equations with rational number coefficients, including equations whose solutions require expanding expressions using the distributive property and collecting like terms.

Launch

Two friends shovel snow on a winter Saturday. Some people pay them their fee by handing them cash. Some give them their fee in an envelope. They split the money they make evenly.

What is their shoveling fee? Explain how you know.

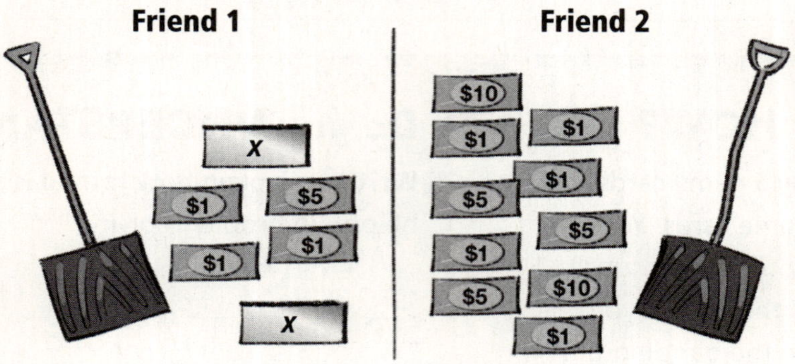

Reflect

Could you write an equation for this problem? How might that help?

Close and Check

Focus Question

What kinds of problems need two operations?

Do you know HOW?

1. Solve for x.

$$63 = 12x - 9$$

$x =$ ☐

2. A cell phone plan includes a monthly rate of $19.95 plus $0.55 per minute for international calls. The bill is $95.30. Write and solve an equation to determine how many minutes were spent on international calls.

3. A family buys 132 ft^2 of carpet for the guest bedroom and 270 ft^2 of carpet for the family room. They spend $1,201.98 on new carpet. What is the average cost per square foot for the new carpeting?

Do you UNDERSTAND?

4. Reasoning Which operation did you use first to solve Exercise 1? Explain.

5. Error Analysis A classmate solves the equation shown. Explain his error and tell how you would solve it.

$$1.25x + 7.4 = 10.4$$
$$100(1.25x) + 10(7.4) = 10(10.4)$$
$$125x + 74 = 104$$
$$125x = 30$$
$$x = 0.24$$

12-2 Solving Equations with Variables on Both Sides

Common Core State Standard: 8.EE.7: Solve linear equations in one variable. **8.EE.7.b:** Solve linear equations with rational number coefficients, including equations whose solutions require expanding expressions using the distributive property and collecting like terms.

Launch

Two friends mow lawns on a spring Saturday. Some people pay them their fee by handing them cash. Some people give them their fee in an envelope. They split the money they make evenly.

What is their lawn-mowing fee? Explain how you know.

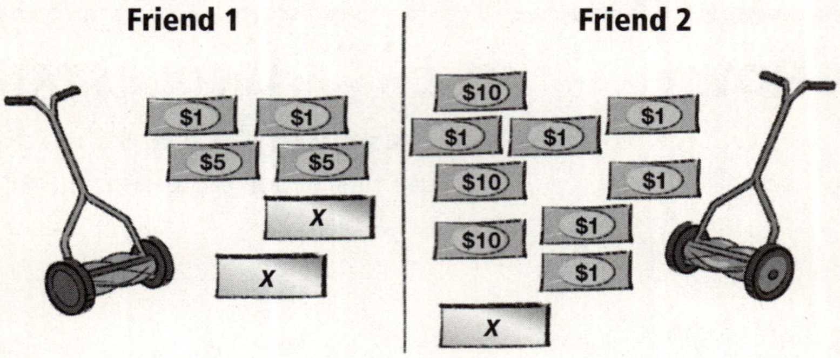

Reflect

In the snow-shoveling problem in Lesson 2-1, only one friend had an envelope. The other friend had all cash. Was this problem more difficult because both friends had envelopes? Explain.

Close and Check

Focus Question

Why do some equations have the same variable on both sides?

Do you know **HOW?**

1. What is the value of x when the expression $3x + 6$ equals the expression $-15 + 6x$?

$x =$ ☐

2. Two friends race. The first friend gets a head start and runs at a steady rate of 0.20 miles per minute. The second friend waits 1 minute and then runs at a steady rate of 0.25 miles per minute. How long will it take for the second runner to catch up with the first?

☐

3. Solve $72x + 436 = -96x + 1108$.

☐

4. You have \$12.50 in a savings account. You deposit \$7.25 more each week. Your friend has \$32.50 in a savings account. She deposits \$5.25 more each week. In how many weeks will the amount of money in the accounts be equal?

☐ weeks

Do you **UNDERSTAND?**

5. Reasoning If the two friends in Exercise 2 race for 4 miles at their constant rates, who will win the race? Explain.

6. Compare and Contrast How is solving an equation with the variable on both sides of the equation the same as and different from solving an equation with the variable on one side of the equation?

12-3 Solving Equations Using the Distributive Property

Common Core State Standard: 8.EE.7b: Solve linear equations with rational number coefficients, including equations whose solutions require expanding expressions using the distributive property and collecting like terms.

Launch

Match the equivalent expressions. Tell how you know your matches are correct.

$-3(-s + 5)$	$3s - 15$	$3(-s + 5)$
$-3(s - 5)$	$-3s + 15$	$3(s - 5)$

Reflect

Which expressions were the simplest to match? Which were the hardest to match? Explain.

Close and Check

Focus Question

How can you model a problem with an equation that uses the Distributive Property?

Do you know HOW?

1. Use the Distributive Property to solve $3(11r - 13) = -7r + 57 + 32r$.

2. Circle the correct solution to the equation $\frac{7}{9}x - 6 = 17$.

A. $\frac{9}{7}\left(\frac{7}{9}x\right) - 6 = \frac{9}{7}(17)$

$x - 6 = \frac{153}{7}$

$x = \frac{153}{7} + \frac{42}{7}$

$x = \frac{195}{7}$

B. $\frac{7}{9}x = 17 + 6$

$\frac{9}{7}\left(\frac{7}{9}x\right) = \frac{9}{7}(23)$

$x = \frac{207}{7}$

3. The width of a rectangle is 17 yd shorter than the length. The perimeter of the rectangle is 126 yd. Find the width of the rectangle.

Do you UNDERSTAND?

4. Error Analysis Explain the error made in the incorrect solution in Exercise 2.

5. Reasoning Write an equation for the perimeter of the rectangle in Exercise 3 in terms of the length ℓ. How is this equation different than an equation for the perimeter in terms of the width w?

12-4 Solutions – One, None, or Infinitely Many

Common Core State Standard: 8.EE.7: Solve linear equations in one variable. **8.EE.7.a:** Give examples of linear equations … with one solution, infinitely many solutions, or no solutions. Show which … is the case by successively transforming the given equation into simpler forms … .

Launch

Evaluate each expression using different values for s. Then, tell what you know about the expressions.

s	$3(4s + 8)$	$2(12 + 6s)$

Reflect

Could you have reached the same conclusion about the expressions without trying different values for s? Explain.

Close and Check

Focus Question

What does it mean if an equation is simplified to $0 = 0$? Do all problems have exactly one solution?

Do you know HOW?

1. Write *none, one,* or *many* to identify the number of solutions to each equation.

$\frac{2}{3}x + 15 = \frac{4}{6}x + 15$

$6 = 3^2$

$2.7y - 9 = 18$

2. Solve $5(12 - d) + d = 2d - 6$.

3. Solve $7t - (t + 5) = 6t + 5$.

4. Solve $\frac{2}{3}\left(9s - \frac{3}{2}\right) = s(0.45 + 5) + 1.2$.

Do you UNDERSTAND?

5. Writing Explain how to identify whether an equation has no solution, one solution, or infinitely many solutions.

6. Error Analysis A classmate solves the equation $8 + 2(8r - 2r) = 4(3r + 2)$. She says $r = 0$ is the only solution. Is she correct? Explain.

12-5 Problem Solving

Common Core State Standard: 8.EE.7: Solve linear equations in one variable. **8.EE.7.a:** Give examples of linear equations in one variable with one solution, infinitely many solutions, or no solutions … .

Launch

Two friends argue over how much to bill for a two-hour raking job. They charge their normal hourly rate plus $2.75 for lawn bags.

Write and solve equations to show how each friend could be correct. Then tell who you think is right and why.

Reflect

How did the money problem context affect the solution to this problem? Explain.

Close and Check

Focus Question

If you can describe a situation in two different ways, how do you use that information to solve a problem?

Do you know HOW?

1. A delivery driver earns \$7.50 per hour and \$2 per delivery. Each week, the driver spends \$28 on vehicle maintenance and \$86 on gas. If the driver works 40 hours per week, how many deliveries are needed each week to earn \$300 a week after expenses?

   ☐ deliveries

2. The total cost, after additional fees, for three tickets to the dinner theater is \$322.92. The fees include a 2% service charge and a 15% gratuity. What is the cost of one dinner theater ticket before the fees are added?

   ☐

3. Craft club members pay \$39 a year plus \$9 for each craft kit. Non-members can buy craft kits for \$12 each. How many kits will have to be bought for the price of membership and non-membership to be equal?

   ☐ kits

Do you UNDERSTAND?

4. **Writing** Two students solve the equation. Can both students be correct? Explain.

   $5(3r - 6) = 10r - 10$

Student A	Student B
$15r - 30 = 10r - 10$	$3r - 6 = 2r - 2$
$5r = 20$	$r = 4$
$r = 4$	

5. **Reasoning** Would Student B's method work if the equation were $5(3r - 6) = 11r - 14$? Explain.

13-1 Solving Inequalities Using Addition or Subtraction

Common Core State Standards: 7.EE.4: Use variables to represent quantities in a real-world or mathematical problem, and construct simple inequalities to solve problems by reasoning about the quantities. **7.EE.4.b:** … Graph the solution set of the inequality.

Launch

A superstar challenges a track team's top three runners to beat his 100-meter time. "You can take 5 seconds from your times and still not best it," he says. Two runners fail. One runner doesn't.

Show their possible times and how you know you're right.

Runner 1:

Runner 2:

Runner 3:

Reflect

How many possible times minus 5 seconds could beat the runner's record? Explain.

Close and Check

Focus Question

How is the solution to an inequality different from the solution to an equation?

Do you know HOW?

1. Use the symbol, $<$, $\leq$, $>$, $\geq$, $=$, or $\neq$, that best represents the statement.

I walked no more than 12 blocks.

b ☐ 12

2. Solve $12.5 + c > 27.3$.

3. Graph $r \geq -3$.

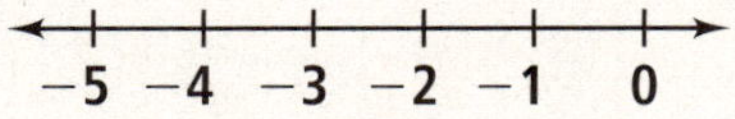

4. Write and solve an inequality to represent the statement.

$14\frac{3}{5}$ is less than $3\frac{1}{5}$ fewer than a number.

Inequality:

Solution:

Do you UNDERSTAND?

5. Reasoning Can the solution to an inequality ever be equal to only one value? Explain.

6. Error Analysis A classmate solves and graphs the inequality $-7 + k \leq 3$. Is her work correct? Explain.

$k \leq 10$

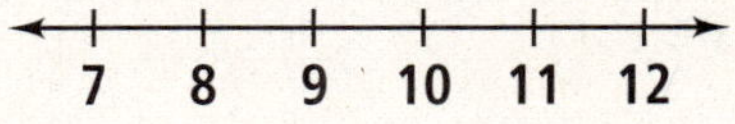

13-2 Solving Inequalities Using Multiplication or Division

Common Core State Standards: 7.EE.4: Use variables to represent quantities in a real-world or mathematical problem, and construct simple inequalities to solve problems by reasoning about the quantities. **7.EE.4.b:** ... Graph the solution set of the inequality.

Launch

The superstar runner says he can beat the track team's best 400 m time four straight times. "You can double my time each time I run, and I'll be fine," he says. The superstar succeeds three times and fails the fourth.

Show his possible times and how you know you're right.

Track Team Record

Run 1:

Run 2:

Run 3:

Run 4:

Reflect

Did the superstar have to run a specific time to back his claim about beating the track team's time? Explain.

Close and Check

Focus Question

The *concept of balance* plays a large role when you solve equations. What role does the *concept of balance* play when you solve inequalities?

Do you know HOW?

1. A rain forest receives up to 260 inches of rain each year. On average, how many inches of rain fall each month? Write and solve an inequality. Round your answer to the nearest tenth of an inch.

Inequality:

Solution:

Inches of Rain:

2. Solve $-3.7y \geq 9.62$.

3. Solve $\frac{s}{-4} < 14$.

4. Movie tickets cost at least $8. You want to buy as many tickets as possible with $36. Write and solve an inequality. Tell how many tickets you can buy.

Inequality:

Solution:

Tickets:

Do you UNDERSTAND?

5. Reasoning What values of x make the statement below false? Explain.

$$3x \geq 2x$$

6. Error Analysis A classmate solves the inequality $-5b > 40$. Her solution is shown below. Explain how to use substitution to determine if her solution is correct.

$$b > -8$$

13-3 Solving Two-Step Inequalities

Common Core State Standards: 7.EE.4: Use variables to represent quantities … and construct simple inequalities … . **7.EE.4.b:** Solve problems leading to inequalities of the form $px + q > r$ or $px + q < r$, where p, q, and r are rational numbers. Graph the solution and interpret it in the context … .

Launch

The superstar runner challenges the track team to a bowling match. "You can each double your score and include 10 more, and I'll still top the top score," he says.

All three team members who try beat the runner using his scoring method. Show their possible scores and explain your reasoning.

Track Team Bowler 1:

Track Team Bowler 2:

Track Team Bowler 3:

Reflect

Are there an infinite number of scores that could beat the superstar runner's boast? Explain.

Close and Check

Focus Question

What kinds of problems call for two operations?

Do you know HOW?

1. You have \$54 to take yourself and some friends to the movies. Movie tickets cost \$8.50 each. Write and solve an inequality to find how many tickets you can buy if you also want to spend \$11.50 on snacks at the concession stand.

   Inequality:

   Solution:

2. Write and solve an inequality to represent 19 less than the product of −7 and a number is greater than or equal to 23.

   Inequality:

   Solution:

3. Write and solve an inequality to represent the difference of 3 times a number and 18 is less than 63.

   Inequality:

   Solution:

Do you UNDERSTAND?

4. **Writing** Explain how solving an inequality by multiplying or dividing by a negative value affects the solution. Why is the solution affected this way?

5. **Vocabulary** Explain how to solve an inequality by finding equivalent inequalities.

13-4 Solving Multi-Step Inequalities

Common Core State Standards: 7.EE.4: Use variables to represent quantities in a real-world or mathematical problem . . . . **7.EE.4.b:** Solve problems leading to inequalities of the form $px + q > r$ or $px + q < r$, where p, q, and r are specific rational numbers . . . .

Launch

You and a friend spend Friday nights quizzing each other on math problems. Just as your friend races to show you the solution to $-2(x + 5.5) = 20$, you say, "I meant $-2(x + 5.5) > 20$."

Did your friend waste her time solving the equation? Explain.

Reflect

How is solving an inequality alike and different from solving an equation? Explain.

Close and Check

Focus Question

How is it possible for two different inequalities to describe the same situation? What does it mean for two inequalities to be equivalent?

Do you know HOW?

1. Solve $58 \leq 29(7 - r)$.

2. Graph the solution to Exercise 1.

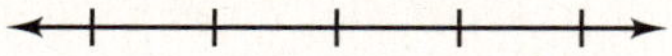

3. Solve $12.3g + 7.9g + 15.86 > 70.4$.

4. Graph the solution to Exercise 3.

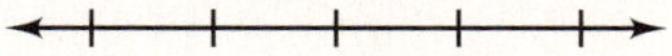

5. Your friend makes $15 each week babysitting. She makes $7.50 a week doing yard work. How many weeks will it take her to make more than $75?

weeks

Do you UNDERSTAND?

6. Writing Explain how to check the solution to Exercise 1.

7. Error Analysis A classmate writes the solution to $-10r - 2r - 2 < 22$. Use a counterexample to show that she is incorrect and explain her error.

$r < -2$

13-5 Problem Solving

Common Core State Standards: 7.EE.4: Use variables to represent quantities in a real-world or mathematical problem, and construct simple inequalities to solve problems by reasoning about the quantities. **7.EE.4.b:** Solve word problems leading to inequalities of the form $px + q > r$ or $px + q < r$.

Launch

The Friday night math club wants to beat last year's fund drive of $40.25. The superstar runner shows his support by buying two club mugs.

Write and solve an inequality to show how many more mugs the club needs to sell to beat last year's total. Explain your reasoning.

Reflect

Is an equation or an inequality better for solving this problem? Explain.

Close and Check

Focus Question

How can we describe problem situations that do not involve equal relationships?

Do you know HOW?

1. A credit card has a balance of \$5,245 plus an interest of 13% of the balance. Write an inequality to find how much the cardholder will need to pay to bring the balance below \$5,500.

2. For Exercise 1, what is the minimum amount the cardholder needs to pay to bring the balance below \$5,500?

3. Write a 1-step inequality and a 2-step inequality that each have the solution $x > -12$.

1-step:

2-step:

4. The revenue from your lemonade stand is $R = 2(g - 10) + 50$ where g is the glasses of lemonade you sell. The cost to keep the stand running is \$236. How many whole cups of lemonade do you have to sell to make a profit?

Cups:

Do you UNDERSTAND?

5. Writing Give an example of how writing an inequality can help you make a decision in real life.

6. Reasoning The bank charges a low-balance fee to customers when their checking accounts fall below \$100. A customer spends \$27.50 at the grocery store. Can writing an inequality help the customer avoid the fee? Explain.

14-1 Graphing Proportional Relationships

Common Core State Standards: 8.EE.5: Graph proportional relationships, interpreting the unit rate as the slope of the graph. Compare two different proportional relationships represented in different ways.

Launch

Make a graph based on the data in the table. Give the graph a title and label the axes so it's clear what the variables could represent.

Independent Variable	Dependent Variable
0	0
1	4
2	8
3	12
8	32

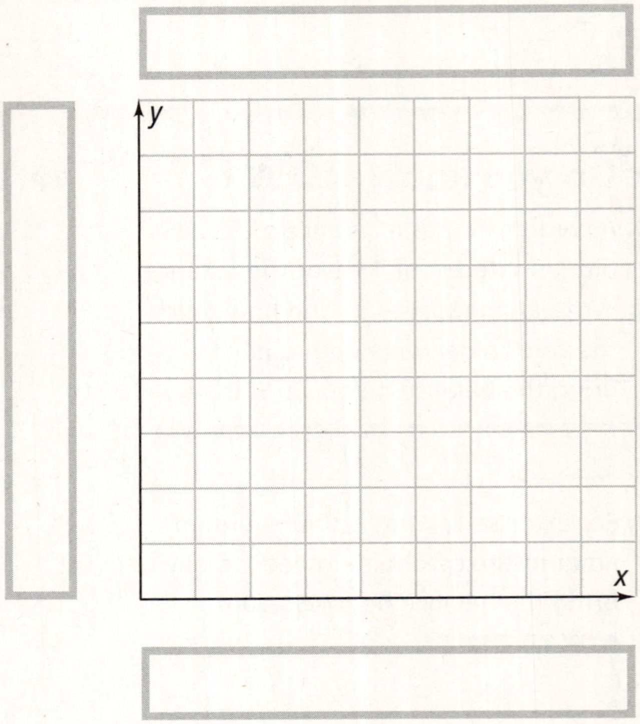

Reflect

Does the table represent a proportional relationship? Explain.

Close and Check

Focus Question

What does the graph of a proportional relationship look like? When and how can a graph of a proportional relationship be helpful?

Do you know HOW?

1. You earn \$4 in Bonus Bucks for each \$50 you spend. Complete the graph to model this situation.

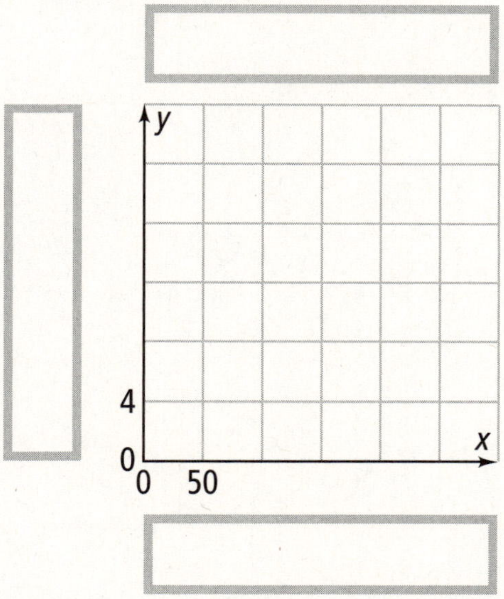

2. A scuba diver descends into the ocean from the surface at a rate of 65 feet per minute. Complete the table of the diver's position relative to the surface.

$$d = -65m$$

Minutes (m)	0	1	2
Depth (d)			

Do you UNDERSTAND?

3. Writing Based on the graph in Exercise 1, is the relationship between the amount spent and the amount of bonus bucks earned proportional? Explain.

4. Reasoning If the diver in Exercise 2 jumped off a boat into the ocean rather than descending from the surface of the ocean, would the relationship still be proportional?

14-2 Linear Equations: $y = mx$

Common Core State Standards: 8.EE.5: Graph proportional relationships, interpreting the unit rate as the slope of the graph. Compare two different proportional relationships represented in different ways. **8.EE.6:** … derive the equation $y = mx$ for a line through the origin … .

Launch

How are the lines similar? How are they different? Explain.

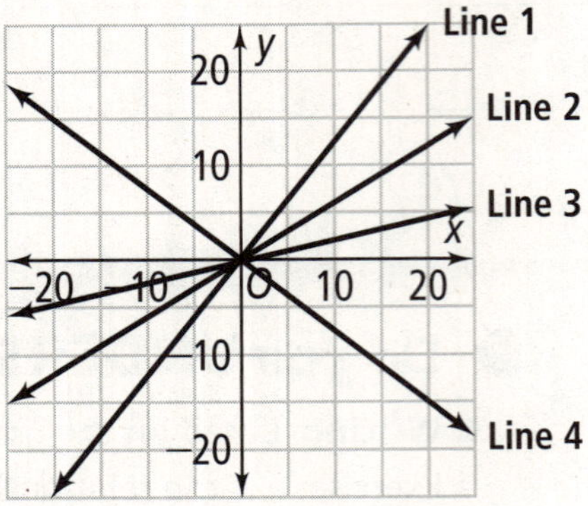

Similar:

Different:

Reflect

Is one line more different than the others? Explain.

Close and Check

Focus Question

What does it mean for an equation to be linear? What kind of relationships can be modeled by equations in the form $y = mx$?

Do you know HOW?

1. The graph shows the earnings e of an airplane mechanic for a number of weeks w at a constant rate r. Write an equation to model the situation shown.

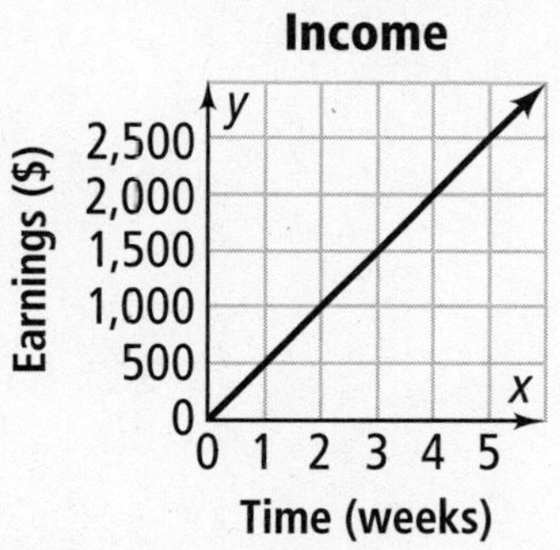

2. A machine manufactures a part in 11 minutes. A newer machine can manufacture the same part 1.5 minutes faster. Write an equation that models how many parts p each machine can manufacture in any number of minutes m.

Old Machine:

New Machine:

Do you UNDERSTAND?

3. **Writing** A diesel mechanic's earnings can be represented by the equation $e = 475w$. Who earns more, the airplane mechanic in Exercise 1 or the diesel mechanic? Explain.

4. **Reasoning** Are all proportional equations linear? Are all linear equations proportional? Explain.

14-3 The Slope of a Line

Common Core State Standards: 8.EE.5: Graph proportional relationships, interpreting the unit rate as the slope of the graph. Compare two different proportional relationships represented in different ways.

Launch

An architect diagrams a series of skyscrapers on a coordinate grid. Tell how they are alike and different.

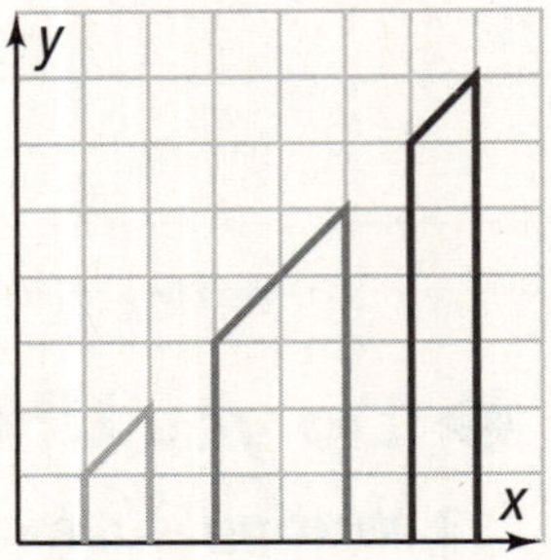

Alike:

Different:

Reflect

Is one building more different than the others? Explain.

Close and Check

Focus Question

What does the slope of a line tell you about the line?

Do you know HOW?

1. What is the slope of the line?

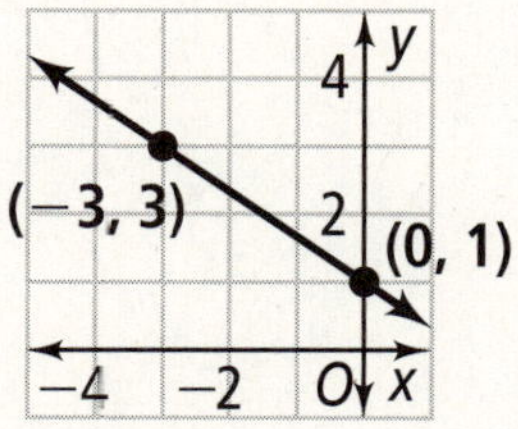

Slope:

2. What is the slope of the line that passes through the points (3, 3) and (1, −2)?

Slope:

3. Roof A has a rise of 11 and a run of 12. Roof B has a rise of 8 and a run of 9. Which roof is steeper?

4. Climber A climbs at a rate of 14 feet every 3 minutes. Climber B climbs 19 feet in 4 minutes. Which climber has the faster rate?

Do you UNDERSTAND?

5. Reasoning What is the slope of a horizontal line? Choose two points and show how you determined your solution.

6. Error Analysis A classmate finds the slope of a line containing the points (−7, 5) and (−3, 9). Explain the error she made in her calculations and find the correct slope.

$$\frac{9-5}{-7-(-3)} = \frac{4}{-4} = -1$$

14-4 Unit Rates and Slope

Common Core State Standards: 8.EE.5: Graph proportional relationships, interpreting the unit rate as the slope of the graph. Compare two different proportional relationships represented in different ways.

Launch

The graph shows the results of a plant-growing contest among three friends at a local plant club.

Which friend's plant grew the fastest? Explain how you know.

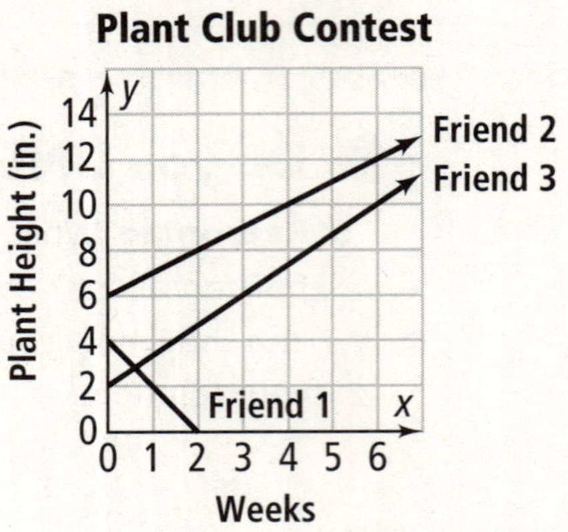

Reflect

Is one line more different than the others? Explain.

Close and Check

Focus Question

How are unit rates and slope related?

____

____

____

____

Do you know HOW?

1. A caterer is preparing meatloaf for a large party. She needs 3 eggs for 2 pounds of ground beef. Graph the ratio of eggs to ground beef.

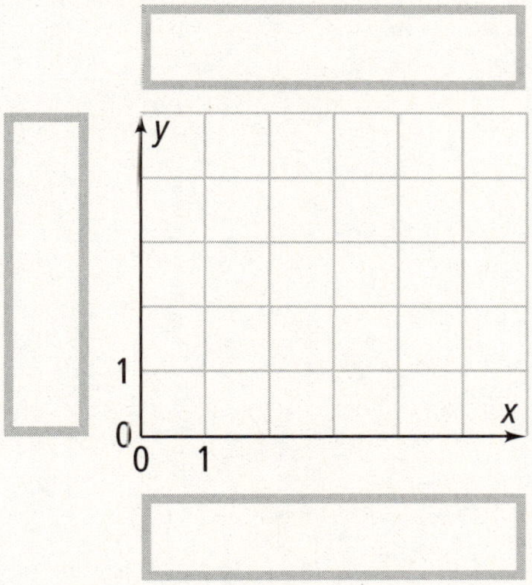

2. What is the slope of the line in the graph?

Slope: ☐

3. Write an equation for Exercise 1 to find the number of eggs y for any number of pounds of ground beef x. How many eggs will be needed for 18 pounds of ground beef?

Equation: ☐

☐ eggs

Do you UNDERSTAND?

4. Reasoning Your creative writing teacher says you will have 15 short stories due over the next 12 weeks. What is the slope of the graph of number of papers due? Explain whether the graph represents a proportional relationship.

____

____

____

____

5. Writing Explain how to graph a line if you only know one point on the line and the slope of the line.

____

____

____

____

____

____

14-5 The *y*-intercept of a Line

Common Core State Standards: 8.EE.6: ... derive the equation $y = mx$ for a line through the origin and the equation $y = mx + b$ for a line intercepting the vertical axis at b.

Launch

The graph shows the results of a plant-growing contest among three friends at a local plant club. The person with tallest plant after six weeks wins the contest.

Who won the contest? Do you think the contest was fair? Explain.

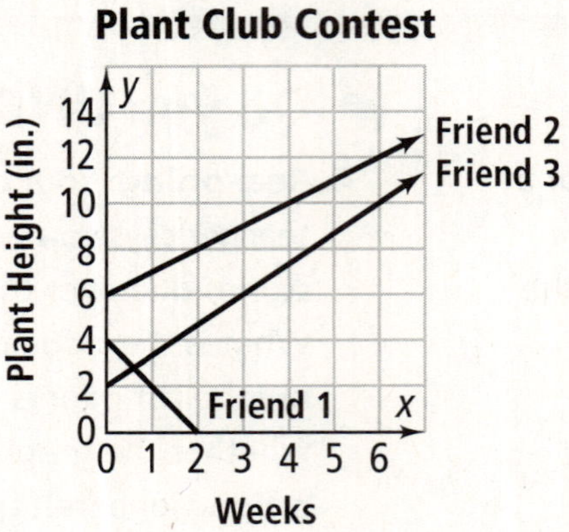

Reflect

What do the lines all have in common?

Close and Check

Focus Question

What is the y-intercept of a graph? What does the y-intercept tell you about the equation being graphed?

Do you know HOW?

1. You open a savings account with a $75 deposit. Then you deposit $25 each month. Complete the graph to model the situation.

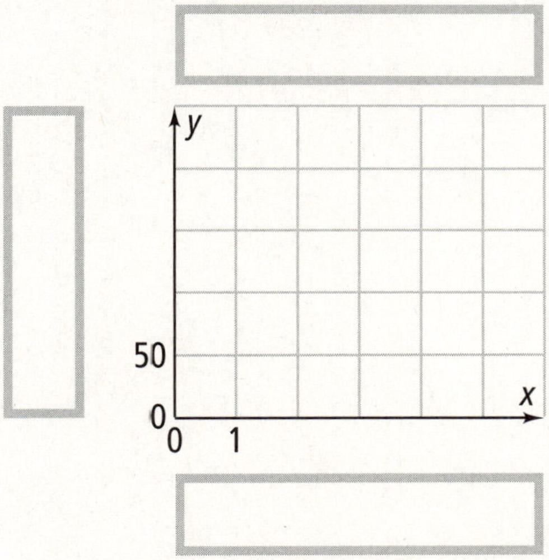

2. What does the y-intercept represent?

3. What is the slope of the line?

Slope:

4. What does the slope represent?

Do you UNDERSTAND?

5. Compare and Contrast What about the graph in Exercise 1 would change if the initial deposit had been 0? What would stay the same? Explain.

6. Error Analysis A classmate says a line with slope = 0 does not have a y-intercept. Do you agree? Explain.

14-6 Linear Equations: $y = mx + b$

Common Core State Standards: 8.EE.6: ... derive the equation $y = mx$ for a line through the origin and the equation $y = mx + b$ for a line intercepting the vertical axis at b.

Launch

Complete the table. Describe any patterns you see between the slope and y-intercept for each line and the equation.

Equation	Slope	y-intercept
$y = 2x + 1$		
$y = 2x + 3$		
$y = -\frac{1}{3}x + 6$		
$y = x$		
$y = 1$		

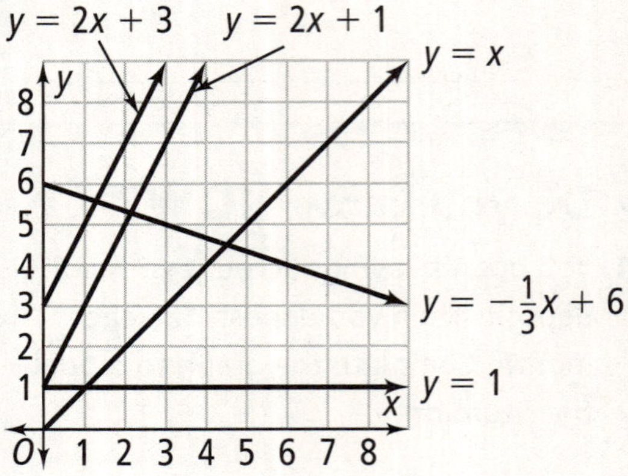

Reflect

Is it easier to spot the slope and y-intercept of a line from the graph or the equation of the line? Explain.

Close and Check

Focus Question

Previously you studied equations in the form $y = mx$. How are equations in the form $y = mx$ similar to equations in the form $y = mx + b$? How do you know when to use each form?

Do you know HOW?

Use the graph for Exercises 1–4.

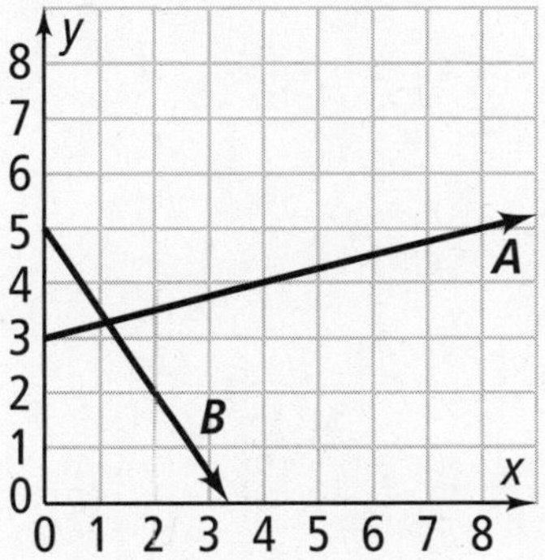

1. Write an equation in slope-intercept form for Line *A*.

2. Write an equation in slope-intercept form for Line *B*.

3. Graph and label Line *C* where $y = -\frac{2}{3}x + 7$.

4. Graph and label Line *D* where $y = \frac{7}{8}x + 1$.

Do you UNDERSTAND?

5. Reasoning You know the slope of a line and a point on the line that is not the *y*-intercept. Can you use a graph to write the equation of the line in slope-intercept form? Explain.

6. Writing Do the equations $y = \frac{5}{6}x + 2$ and $y = \frac{15}{18}x + 2$ represent two different lines? Explain.

14-7 Problem Solving

Common Core State Standards: 8.EE.5: ... Compare two different proportional relationships represented in different ways. **8.EE.6:** ... derive the equation $y = mx$ for a line through the origin and the equation $y = mx + b$ for a line intercepting the vertical axis at b.

Launch

Create your own graph and matching linear equation. Describe a situation that makes sense for each representation. Label your graph appropriately. Your situation must include the point (2, 4).

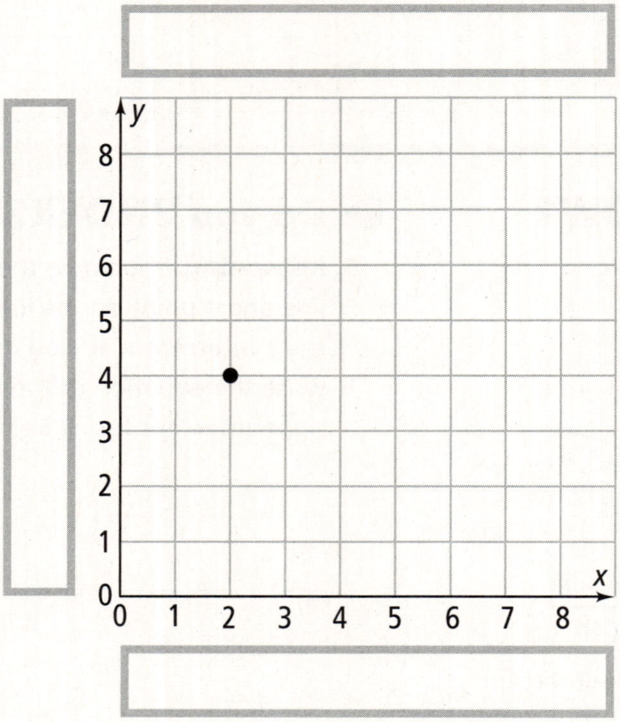

Equation:

Description of situation:

Reflect

What did you do first—write an equation, complete the graph, or describe the situation? Why?

Close and Check

Focus Question

You have studied the relationship between linear equations and proportional relationships. How and when can you use linear equations to solve problems?

Do you know **HOW?**

1. To make a multi-age 800-meter race fair, Runner 1 gets a 100-meter head start. He runs 350 meters every 2 minutes. Represent on the graph how Runner 1 runs the race.

Runner 1

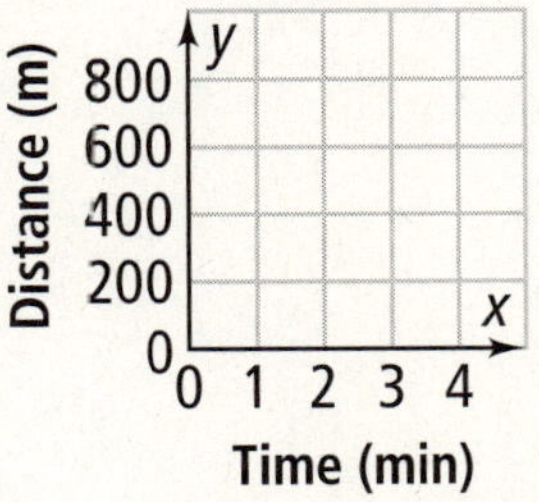

2. Runner 2 gets a 75-meter head start. Her rate is 210 meters per minute. Complete the table.

Time (min)	0	1	2	3	4
Distance (m)					

3. Runner 3 does not get a head start. He runs 750 meters every 3 minutes. Write an equation to represent Runner 3's distance y for x minutes.

Do you **UNDERSTAND?**

4. Writing Which runner from Exercises 1–3 is ahead after 1 minute? Will that runner win the race? Explain.

5. Reasoning Which is most helpful in problem solving, a graph, a table, or an equation? Explain.

15-1 Populations and Samples

Common Core State Standards: 7.SP.1: Understand that statistics can be used to gain information about a population by examining a sample of the population; generalizations about a population from a sample are valid only if the sample is representative of that population … .

Launch

The tumultuous town mayor decides to trash the way the town collects trash. The mayor vows to knock on every door and talk to each household to get new trash collection ideas.

Describe a situation where this approach would be a good idea and a situation where it would be a bad idea.

Reflect

When do you talk to everyone about an issue? Can the definition of "everyone" change depending on your issue?

Close and Check

Focus Question

When is it reasonable to use a small group to represent a larger group? When is it not reasonable?

Do you know HOW?

1. You are studying the nutritional value of all meals served at your school. Circle the samples.
   A. the nutritional value of all breakfasts served
   B. the nutritional value of meals served on Mondays
   C. the nutritional value of all meals served
   D. the nutritional value of all lunches served

2. You are studying the popularity of sports at your school. Circle the samples that are likely to contain a bias.
   A. students who play sports
   B. students who attend your school
   C. students who attend sporting events
   D. students who watch sports on TV

Do you UNDERSTAND?

3. **Reasoning** A shoe manufacturer surveys Midwest farmers about the popularity of work boots in the U.S. Can the manufacturer make a valid inference about boot popularity from the sample? Explain.

4. **Writing** Describe the population and representative sample of a study on high school graduates going to college. Explain how the study can limit bias.

15-2 Estimating a Population

Common Core State Standards: 7.SP.2: Use data from a random sample to draw inferences about a population with an unknown characteristic of interest. Generate multiple samples (or simulated samples) of the same size to gauge the variation in estimates or predictions. … . Also, **7.SP.1.**

Launch

A newspaper reporter arrives late to a game and sees a few remaining fans. The reporter knows nothing about the teams or the game but concludes that the home team lost. Describe how the reporter may have come to this conclusion.

Reflect

Could the reporter be wrong? How?

Close and Check

Focus Question

When can you use a small group to estimate things about a larger group?

Do you know HOW?

1. In a representative sample of 100 vehicles in a parking lot, there are 15 vans. There are 480 vehicles in the parking lot. Estimate how many of them are vans.

☐ vans

2. You want to find the number of red rubber bands there are in a bag of 540. The actual number of red rubber bands is 120. Which sample best represents the population?

A. 1 red, 2 green, 1 blue rubber band

B. 18 red, 28 green, 10 blue, 11 orange, and 23 purple rubber bands

C. 61 red, 92 green, 29 blue, 28 orange, and 60 purple rubber bands

3. The widget factory samples 75 widgets and finds 3 defective ones. If the factory produces 500 widgets a day, how many defective widgets can they expect to produce?

☐ defective widgets

Do you UNDERSTAND?

4. Reasoning You record the number of students in your class who have green eyes. Is this enough information to estimate the total number of green-eyed students in the school? Explain.

5. Error Analysis Three friends each visit 10 of the 60 area homes to find how many have pets. One friend finds 3 homes; the others find 7 and 5. They conclude that 15 of 60 homes have pets. Explain their error.

15-3 Convenience Sampling

Common Core State Standards: 7.SP.1: Understand that statistics can be used to gain information about a population by examining a sample of the population; generalizations about a population from a sample are valid only if the sample is representative of that population … .

Launch

The tumultuous town mayor wants to re-route the town bus routes. So, he goes to the two nearest bus stops and asks riders for their opinions.

Describe the good and not-so-good parts of this approach.

Reflect

Describe a situation where just asking friends for their opinions would be a good idea.

Close and Check

Focus Question

How do you sample in a way that is convenient? What are the advantages and disadvantages of convenience sampling?

Do you know HOW?

1. Suppose you are doing research on the most popular snack foods. Circle the examples of convenience sampling.

A. You ask your friends.

B. You ask each person shopping at a convenience store.

C. You give a survey to each household in your neighborhood.

D. You ask all the students who ride your bus.

2. You want to find out how many people support the school tax. Circle the representative sample.

A. You ask every adult in your extended family.

B. You ask the first 25 adults you see at the mall.

C. You ask the parents of your friends.

Do you UNDERSTAND?

3. Writing A new industrial plant moves into a city of 300,000 people. You want to know if the citizens support the industrial development. Describe a convenience sample and tell whether it would be a representative sample.

4. Reasoning A reporter finds that 9 out of the 10 people he interviews at a concert like the band. Use his data to estimate how many of the 40,000 people in the town like the band. Is it an accurate estimate? Explain.

15-4 Systematic Sampling

Common Core State Standards: 7.SP.1: Understand that statistics can be used to gain information about a population by examining a sample of the population; generalizations about a population from a sample are valid only if the sample is representative of that population . . . .

Launch

Your school holds a school-wide kickball tournament. Your gym teacher lines your class up and starts picking every third person to make up your class team.

Describe a possible benefit and a possible drawback of this sampling approach.

Reflect

How could the gym teacher make the sampling method better? Provide one idea.

Close and Check

Focus Question

How do you sample systematically? What are the advantages and disadvantages of systematic sampling?

Do you know HOW?

1. A moving company wants to survey their customers to find out what they like the most about the company's service. Circle the descriptions of systematic sampling.
   A. The company surveys every customer.
   B. The company chooses every 8th name from its alphabetized customer list to survey.
   C. The company sends a survey to every household.
   D. Each driver surveys every 5th customer.

2. Sixty people are in line for a show. Starting with the 3rd person, you ask every 5th person if they bought their ticket in advance. Nine people say yes. Based on the sample, how many people bought tickets in advance?

   ☐ people

Do you UNDERSTAND?

3. **Compare and Contrast** Describe a situation in which convenience sampling would be sufficient and a situation in which systematic sampling would be more appropriate.

4. **Writing** Fruit bars come in 5 flavors. Describe how to gather a systematic sample to find the least popular flavor in your grade.

15-5 Simple Random Sampling

Common Core State Standards: 7.SP.1: Understand that statistics can be used to gain information about a population … ; generalizations … from a sample are valid only if the sample is representative … .
7.SP.2: Use data from a random sample to draw inferences about a population … .

Launch

The tumultuous town mayor decides he can't talk to every household to get ideas for a new trash plan. So, he puts all the town's phone numbers into a large hat and chooses at random some numbers to call.

Describe one possible benefit and one possible drawback of choosing a sample this way.

Reflect

What makes the process of choosing phone numbers random in the problem?

Close and Check

Focus Question

How do you sample randomly? What are the advantages and disadvantages of simple random sampling?

Do you know HOW?

1. Circle the example of simple random sampling.

A. calling the first entry for each letter of the alphabet in the phone book

B. surveying the first 10 students to enter the classroom

C. choosing numbers randomly assigned to the population

2. The results of a simple random sample are shown in the table. There are 207 people in the population. Based on the results, estimate how many participants have 2 siblings.

# of Siblings	# of Sample Population
None	3
One	2
Two	8
Three	5

☐ participants

Do you UNDERSTAND?

3. Reasoning Could the simple random sample in Exercise 2 be biased? Explain.

4. Error Analysis A bag has 150 balloons. Your friend says the results of picking the first 10 balloons from the bag is an example of a simple random sample. Do you agree? Explain.

15-6 Comparing Sampling Methods

Common Core State Standards: 7.SP.1: Understand that statistics can be used to gain information about a population by examining a sample of the population . . . . Understand that random sampling tends to produce representative samples and support valid inferences.

Launch

The tumultuous town mayor decides to set an example for the town by buying recycling bins for city hall. He can choose among red, green, and blue bins but wants input from city hall workers.

Should he use convenience, systematic, or simple random sampling to get input? Tell which you would choose and describe your plan.

Reflect

Which sampling method do you use most in your life? Explain.

Close and Check

Focus Question

You have studied three sampling methods. For what situations is each type of sampling most effective?

Do you know **HOW?**

Name the sampling method described in Exercises 1-3.

1. The drama teacher wants to audition students for a play. She assigns each student a number as they enter the room. She then draws 6 numbers from a basket to choose the students.

2. The music teacher wants to know how many people support the marching band. He asks 50 people attending a football game whether they support the band.

3. A marketing analyst wants to know if coupons influence the products people purchase. She asks every 3rd person entering a grocery store.

Do you **UNDERSTAND?**

4. **Reasoning** You want to know how many times each year students in your school visit an amusement park. Which sampling method will you use? Explain.

5. **Error Analysis** A pet shop owner wants to know which tropical fish to stock. On weekday mornings, customers are asked about their favorite tropical fish. Explain why this is not the best sampling method to use.

15-7 Problem Solving

Common Core State Standards: 7.SP.1: Understand that … generalizations about a population from a sample are valid only if the sample is representative … . **7.SP.2:** Use data from a random sample to draw inferences … . Generate multiple samples … to gauge the variation in estimates or predictions … .

Launch

To build morale, the radio station manager and the owner each separately ask station workers what special food item should be added in the cafeteria. They both systematically sample every 5th worker by last name.

Explain how their recommendations could be so different.

Reflect

Can a sample ever be completely free of bias? Explain.

Close and Check

Focus Question

If you make a judgment about a population based on a sample, how accurate is that judgment? What determines how accurate that judgment is?

Do you know HOW?

1. A researcher attaches satellite tags to 36 sea turtles. Over the next 6 months she identifies 825 sea turtles in the same area. Nine of those turtles have satellite tags. Estimate how many sea turtles are in the area.

[ ] sea turtles

2. A bookstore owner wants to know which department to expand. Manager A surveys every 3rd teenager that comes in the store. Manager B surveys every customer on Monday evening. Manager C surveys 25% of the customers chosen at random from the store's mailing list. Identify each type of sampling and circle the one that is the least biased.

Manager A: [ ]

Manager B: [ ]

Manager C: [ ]

Do you UNDERSTAND?

3. Error Analysis Choose one of the managers' surveys from Exercise 2. Explain how you would change the sampling technique in order to gather more accurate information.

4. Reasoning How might the results of the survey in Exercise 2 vary if Manager B repeated the survey every evening for a week and compared each day's results? Explain.

16-1 Statistical Measures

Common Core State Standards: 7.SP.1: Understand that statistics can be used to gain information about a population by examining a sample of the population .... **7.SP.4:** Use measures of center and measures of variability for numerical data from random samples ... .

Launch

Ms. Adventure and Data Girl proposed different research studies to the local airline.

Which study should the airline fund? Explain.

Reflect

Which study could have a numerical result of 89.5? Explain.

Close and Check

Focus Question

What can you do to make data more useful? How does what you are looking for determine how data are best used and represented?

Do you know HOW?

Use the data set below for Exercises 1–4.

Monthly High Temperatures (°F) Anchorage, Alaska
15, 18, 25, 36, 47, 55,
59, 57, 48, 35, 22, 16

1. Find the mean monthly high temperature to the nearest degree.

2. Find the median of the data set.

3. Find the range of the data set.

4. Find the IQR of the data set.

Do you UNDERSTAND?

5. Reasoning Is the mean or the median a better representation of the temperature data of Anchorage, Alaska? Explain.

6. Error Analysis Your friend uses the mean temperature to decide which clothes to buy for her move to Anchorage. Do you agree with the measure she chose? Explain.

16-2 Multiple Populations and Inferences

Common Core State Standards: 7.SP.1: Understand that statistics can be used to gain information about a population by examining a sample .... **7.SP.4:** Use measures of center and measures of variability ... to draw informal comparative inferences about two populations .... Also, **7.SP.3.**

Launch

Data Girl plans out her research study for a local airline. The airline asks her to answer the following questions as part of her plan.

Provide a possible response for each question.

Who?

What?

Where?

When?

Why?

Reflect

Which "W" question was the hardest to provide an answer for? Explain.

Close and Check

Focus Question

When does a group represent one population? When does it represent more than one population? How can you tell?

Do you know HOW?

1. The local newspaper is writing an article on the county schools. Write **S** if the question applies to a single population and **M** if the question applies to multiple populations.

A. ☐ What percent of the total student population plays sports?

B. ☐ What are the schools' rankings in the region?

2. The line plots show the number of students who are in the marching band. Circle the valid inference.

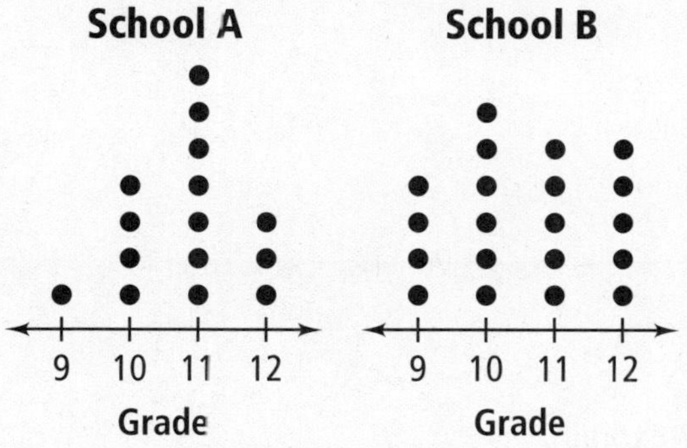

A. School A's band is more popular.

B. The number of band members from each grade is more evenly distributed in School B.

Do you UNDERSTAND?

3. Writing Write a question based on the line plots in Exercise 2 that represents more than one population. Explain why it represents more than one population.

4. Error Analysis Based on the line plots in Exercise 2, a classmate infers that School B has more students enrolled. Is this a valid inference? Explain.

16-3 Using Measures of Center

Common Core State Standards: 7.SP.4: Use measures of center … for numerical data from random samples to draw informal comparative inferences about two populations.

Launch

The lead local librarian and his lead assistant survey individual patrons on the number of e-books they read each week. The tablets show the survey results.

What inference should the librarians make based on the means of the data sets?

Reflect

Can you always draw a clear inference from data? Explain.

Close and Check

Focus Question

How can you compare two groups using a single number from each group?

Do you know HOW?

1. A city planner records the weight of a day's garbage from a random sample of households. Find the median weight of the garbage in each neighborhood.

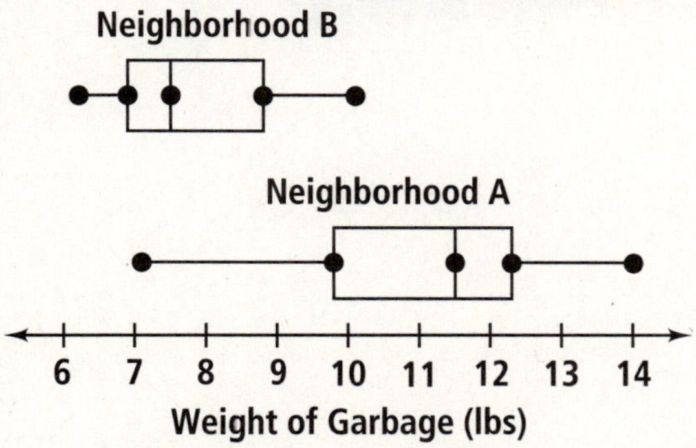

A: ______ B: ______

2. Next, the planner records the weight of a day's recycling from a random sample of households. Find the mean weight of recycling in each neighborhood to the nearest tenth.

Weight of Recycling (lbs)

Neighborhood A	Neighborhood B
2.4, 0.5, 5.8, 3.3, 1.4, 2.2, 1.2, 0, 2.7, 2.5, 1.9	4.8, 3.5, 6.9, 5.5, 6.3, 4.9, 5.1, 6.1, 8, 5.8, 5.2

A: ______ B: ______

Do you UNDERSTAND?

3. Writing Make a comparative inference based on the median values in Exercise 1. Support your statement.

4. Writing Make a comparative inference based on the mean values in Exercise 2. Support your statement.

5. Reasoning Based on the previous Exercises, describe one conclusion you can make about how the neighborhoods compare.

16-4 Using Measures of Variability

Common Core State Standards: 7.SP.4: Use … measures of variability for numerical data from random samples to draw informal comparative inferences about two populations.

Launch

The data show a random sampling of heights in inches of female athletes in two different Olympic sports.

What inference(s) can you make about the sport each group plays?

Athlete Group A

60, 53, 54, 62,
55, 61, 63, 57

Athlete Group B

72, 70, 69, 74,
73, 71, 71, 75

Reflect

Could someone else come up with a different inference on the sport of each group? Explain.

Close and Check

Focus Question

How else can you compare two groups using a single number from each group?

Do you know HOW?

1. Find the range of TV viewing time for each population.

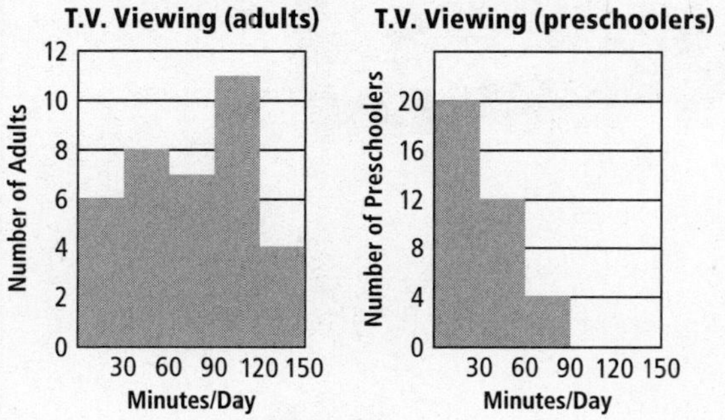

Adults:

Preschoolers:

2. Your friend surveys dog owners with different yard sizes. Find the IQR of each population.

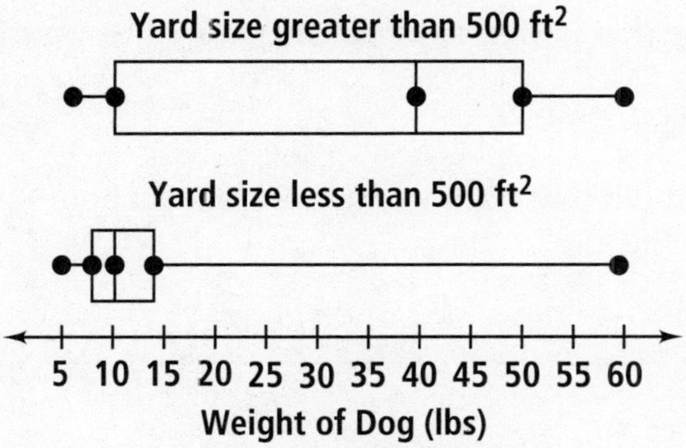

Yard > 500 ft^2:

Yard < 500 ft^2:

Do you UNDERSTAND?

3. Writing Write a comparative inference that you *cannot* make about the populations in Exercise 1 based on the ranges of the data. Explain.

4. Writing Make a comparative inference about the populations in Exercise 2 based on the IQR. Explain your inference.

16-5 Exploring Overlap in Data Sets

Common Core State Standards: 7.SP.3: Informally assess the degree of visual overlap of two numerical data distributions with similar variabilities, measuring the difference between the centers by expressing it as a multiple of a measure of variability . . . . Also, **7.SP.4.**

Launch

Each tablet shows a random sampling of heights in inches of male athletes in two different Olympic sports.

What inferences can you make about the sport played by each group based on the range and mean of heights?

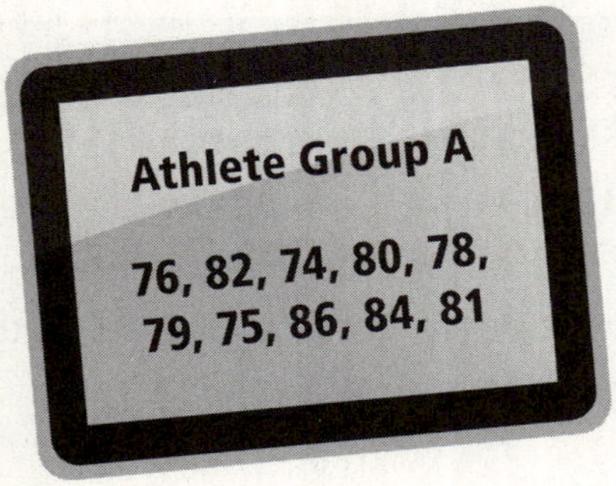

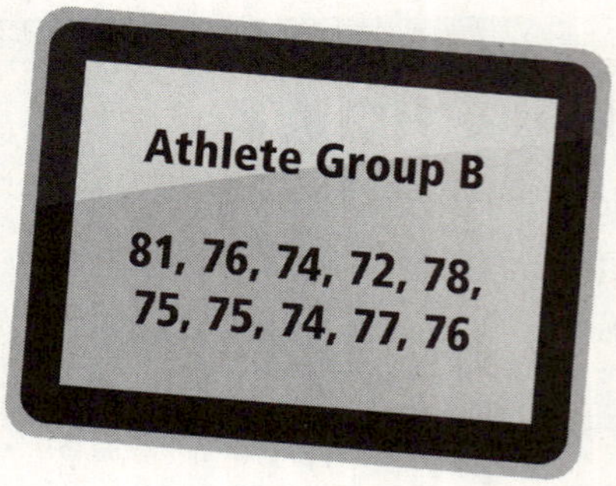

Reflect

The groups have heights in common. What impact did that have in your inferences about the sports of each group?

Close and Check

Focus Question

How do measures of center and variability help you determine how much two groups have in common?

Do you know HOW?

1. Find the mean absolute deviation to the nearest minute for the data set.

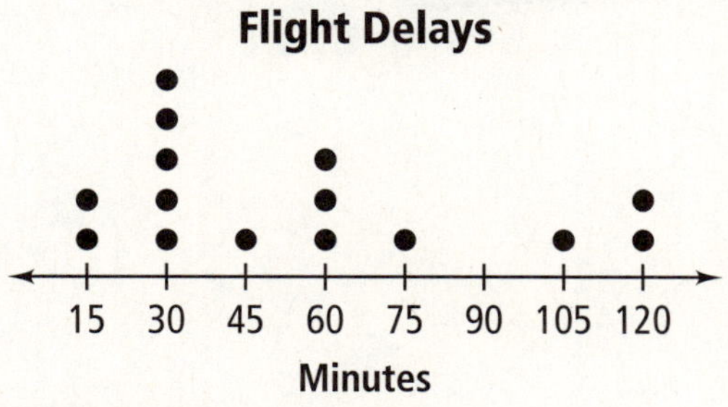

2. Express the difference between the grooming costs of Company A and Company B as a multiple of the mean absolute deviation of either company.

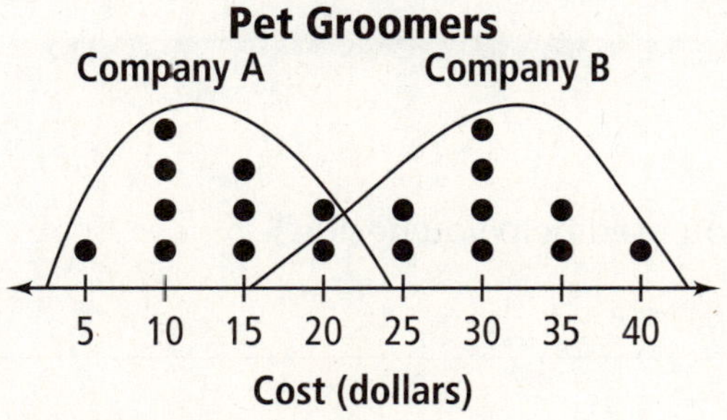

Do you UNDERSTAND?

3. Vocabulary Explain what the mean absolute deviation in Exercise 1 represents.

4. Reasoning Curve 1 has a mean of 30. Your friend correctly sketches a curve three mean absolute deviations from Curve 1. How could your friend be correct?

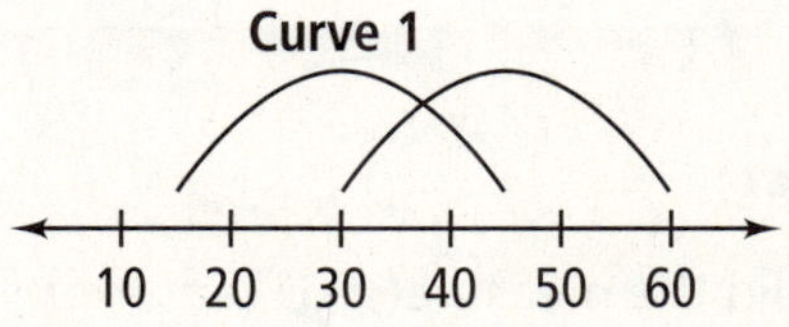

16-6 Problem Solving

Common Core State Standards: 7.SP.4: Use measures of center and measures of variability for numerical data from random samples to draw informal comparative inferences about two populations . . . .

Launch

The data sets show the monthly average high temperature from January to December in degrees Fahrenheit for two U.S. cities. You must choose to live in one of the cities.

Justify your choice based on at least one measure of center (mean or median) or variability (range, interquartile range, or mean absolute deviation).

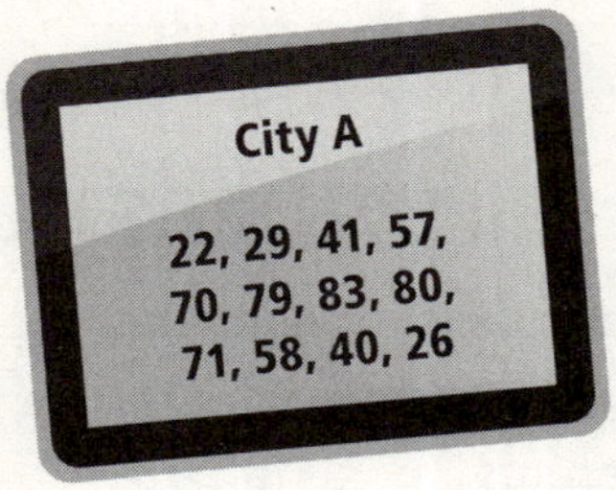

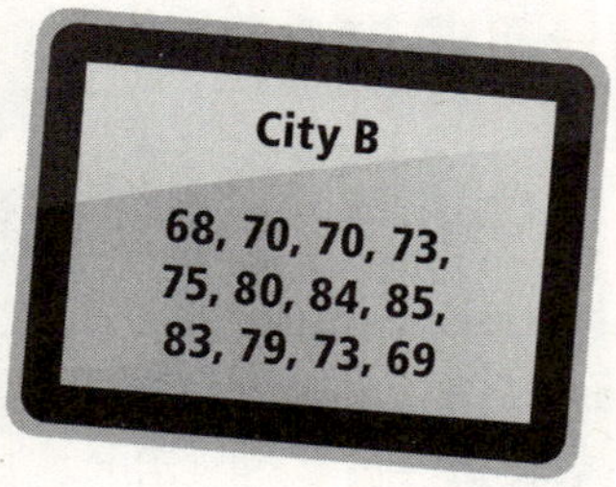

Reflect

How did the measure(s) of center or variability you used help you decide?

Close and Check

Focus Question

How can you use measures of center and variability of a random sample to make inferences, predictions, and decisions? Which measures work best and why?

Do you know HOW?

Use the data below to answer Exercises 1–3. Round your answers to the nearest hundredth.

Race Times (s)

Runner A: 12.52, 12.20, 8.89, 12.61

Runner B: 12.18, 12.13, 12.27, 12.15

1. Find the mean race time for each runner.

Runner A:

Runner B:

2. Find the median race time for each runner.

Runner A:

Runner B:

3. Find the IQR for each runner.

Runner A:

Runner B:

Do you UNDERSTAND?

4. Reasoning Based on the data from Exercises 1–3, which runner should be chosen to compete in the regional track meet? Explain.

5. Writing A study is conducted on two cities in different climates. What inference can you make? Explain.

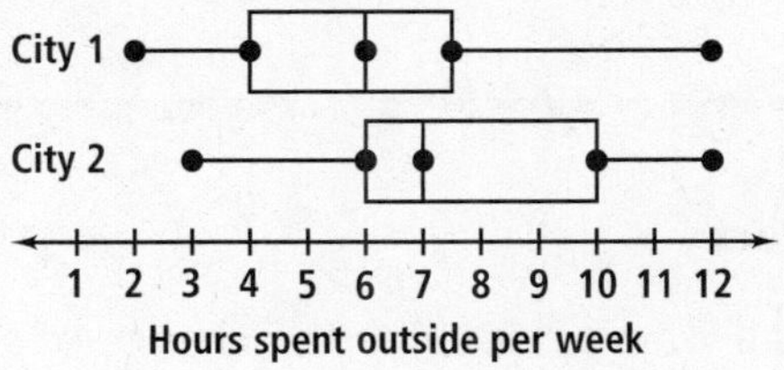

17-1 Likelihood and Probability

Common Core State Standards: 7.SP.5: Understand that the probability of a chance event is a number between 0 and 1 that expresses the likelihood of the event occurring . . . . **7.SP.6:** . . . predict the approximate relative frequency given the probability . . . .

Launch

To be annoying, your friend says "probably" to every question about the future. Come up with a better way to describe the chance of each of these events happening. Describe your method.

The Earth will go around the sun.	
Tigers will fly.	
It will rain this week.	
Your team will win the big game.	
You will write a best-selling novel.	

Reflect

Are all ways to describe the chance of something happening equally effective? Explain.

Close and Check

Focus Question

What are effective ways to describe the likelihood of an event?

Do you know HOW?

1. Choose a word from the following list to best describe the likelihood that there will be 365 days in a year: *impossible, unlikely, as likely as not, likely,* and *certain.*

2. The probability of a U.S. resident living in a state that begins with the letter M is 0.16. Write this probability as a fraction and as a percent.

fraction: percent:

3. There are 2,425 participants in a national phone survey that includes residents from every state. There is an 8% probability that a participant lives in a state that begins with the letter W. How many participants are expected to live in a state that begins with W?

participants

Do you UNDERSTAND?

4. Reasoning Would you rather know the likelihood of winning a prize in words or percents? Explain.

5. Writing Why is *maybe* not a good term to use when describing the probability of an event?

17-2 Sample Space

Common Core State Standards: 7.SP.7: Develop a probability model and use it to find probabilities of events. Compare probabilities from a model to observed frequencies; if the agreement is not good, explain possible sources of the discrepancy.

Launch

Your annoying friend designs a dart game for you to play. She says, "I get a point when a dart hits a composite number and you get a point when a dart hits a prime number."

Do you like her game? Who do you think will win? Explain.

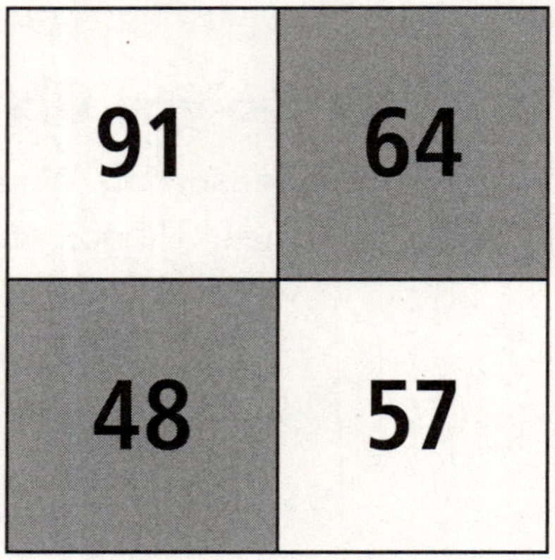

Reflect

Would you change the game above? If so, how?

Close and Check

Focus Question

What is the difference between an *action* and an *event*?

Do you know HOW?

Use the picture for Exercises 1 and 2.

1. Action: Choose one card.
   How many outcomes are in the sample space?

2. Action: Choose one card.
   Event: Choose a striped card.
   How many cards are in the event?

3. Number the following. Use 1 for *action*, 2 for *sample space* and 3 for *event*.

   Left, right, forward

   Pick right.

   Choose a direction.

Do you UNDERSTAND?

4. **Vocabulary** The cafeteria sells sack lunches with either a ham sandwich, turkey wrap, peanut butter sandwich, or corn dog. The lunches are not labeled. Determine the action, sample space, and event for buying a sack lunch.

5. **Error Analysis** In a certain game, players roll again if they roll a 6 on a number cube. Your friend says that rolling a 6 is an action, but you say it is an event. Explain who is correct.

17-3 Relative Frequency and Experimental Probability

Common Core State Standards: 7.SP.6: Approximate the probability of a chance event by collecting data on the chance process that produces it and observing its long-run relative frequency, and predict the approximate relative frequency given the probability . . . .

Launch

Lay your Companion page flat on your desk. Hold any coin about a foot directly above the circle on the page.

What is the probability that your coin will land completely inside the circle without touching the edge? Explain how you can find out.

Reflect

Could your probability be a lot different from your neighbor's? Explain why.

Close and Check

Focus Question

For some types of events there is more than one way to determine the probability. In what situations is conducting an experiment a good way to determine the probability of an event? How can you evaluate the reasonableness of an experimental probability?

Do you know HOW?

1. The table shows the results for rolling a number cube 100 times. What is the relative frequency for the event "roll a multiple of 3?"

Outcome	1	2	3	4	5	6
Frequency	22	14	23	19	10	12

2. Write the experimental probability for the event "roll a factor of 4" from the data above as a fraction, decimal, and percent.

3. A coin is tossed 50 times. What is the expected relative frequency of the coin landing on heads?

Do you UNDERSTAND?

4. **Reasoning** Assume the number cube in Exercise 1 is rolled 500 times. For which outcome listed would you not expect the experimental probability to change much? Explain.

5. **Writing** Your friend makes 3 free throws out of 5 attempts. Then she makes 1 basket and misses 2. Will your friend definitely make the next 2 shots? Explain.

17-4 Theoretical Probability

Common Core State Standards: 7.SP.7: Develop a probability model and use it to find probabilities of events. Compare probabilities … to observed frequencies … . **7.SP.7.a:** Develop a uniform probability model by assigning equal probability to all outcomes … .

Launch

Your annoying friend devises another game. Before she puts the tiles in the bag, she says, "I get a point if a negative number is picked and you get a point if a positive number is picked."

Is this game fair? Explain why or why not.

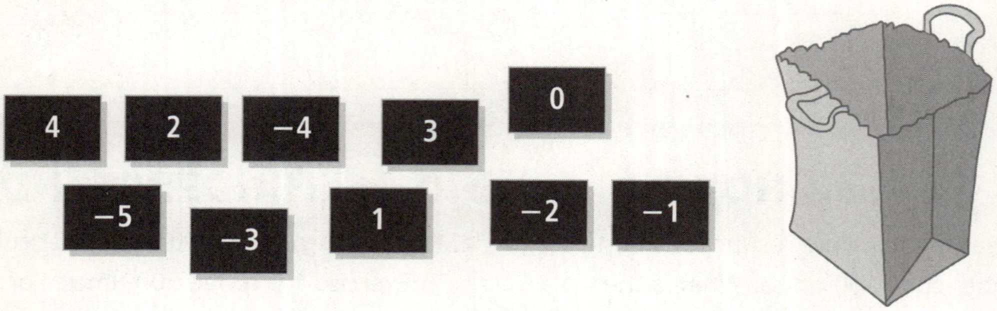

Reflect

What makes a game fair? Explain.

Close and Check

Focus Question

For some types of events there is more than one way to determine the probability. How do you tell the difference between a theoretical and an experimental probability?

____

____

____

____

Do you know HOW?

1. Suppose you chose a card at random. What is the probability of choosing a card with an even number and a ✿?

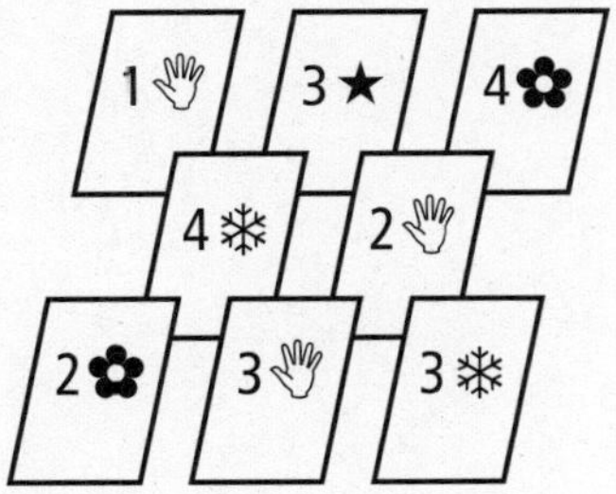

2. Circle the situation(s) that represents experimental probability.

A. Every 100th customer receives a door prize.

B. The gumball machine contains gumballs in six colors. You get a yellow gumball.

C. A survey finds that 4 out of 25 people have green eyes.

Do you UNDERSTAND?

3. Vocabulary A card from Exercise 1 is chosen at random 15 times.

✿	||||
❄	||||
★	|||
🖐	||||

Are the experimental probabilities and theoretical probabilities close? Explain.

____

____

____

____

4. Reasoning If a card were chosen at random another 100 times, what would you expect to happen to the comparisons between the theoretical and experimental probabilities?

____

____

____

____

17-5 Probability Models

Common Core State Standards: 7.SP.7.a: Develop a uniform probability model by assigning equal probability to all outcomes, and use the model to determine probabilities of events . . . . **7.SP.7.b:** Develop a probability model . . . by observing frequencies in data . . . . Also, **7.SP.7.**

Launch

Your annoying friend proposes another game as you wait for the bus. She says, "I get a point for every car that passes. You get a point for every truck. We each have a 1 out of 2 probability of getting a point."

Do you agree with your friend? Are you going to play by her rules? Explain.

Reflect

Can you always figure out if a game is fair before playing? Explain.

Close and Check

Focus Question

How do you choose the best type of probability model for a situation?

____

____

____

____

Do you know **HOW?**

1. Complete the probability model for the cards.

Action: Choose one card at random.

Sample space: Each card is one outcome.

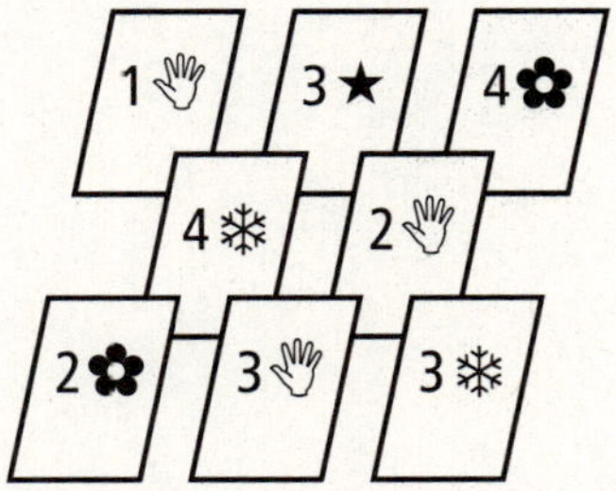

P(✿) = ☐ P(✋) = ☐

P(❄) = ☐ P(prime) = ☐

2. Circle the situation(s) for which you can use a uniform probability model.

A. A student will bring a backpack to school.

B. Tomorrow will be a school day.

C. The football team will win their next game.

Do you **UNDERSTAND?**

3. Error Analysis A student records the number of boys and girls who bring backpacks to school. What mistake does he make when finding probabilities?

Boys	$P(\text{yes}) = \frac{75}{143}$	$P(\text{no}) = \frac{21}{34}$
Girls	$P(\text{yes}) = \frac{68}{143}$	$P(\text{no}) = \frac{13}{34}$

____

____

____

____

4. Vocabulary Explain how to determine whether to use a uniform or an experimental probability model to predict outcomes.

____

____

____

____

17-6 Problem Solving

Common Core State Standards: 7.SP.7: … Compare probabilities from a model to observed frequencies; if the agreement is not good, explain possible sources of the discrepancy. **7.SP.7.b:** Develop a probability model … by observing frequencies in data … . Also, **7.SP.7.a.**

Launch

You are a basketball coach. You need to choose one player to take the shot that will determine the outcome of the game.

Which player should you choose? Support your choice by using the probability that the player chosen will make the winning shot.

Shooting Results

Player	Last Game	Last 5 Games	Last 10 Games
5	2 of 10	25 of 50	54 of 100
24	7 of 10	22 of 50	42 of 100

Reflect

Did the shooting results for the last game for each player match expectations? Explain.

Close and Check

Focus Question

What types of predictions and decisions can you make using probability?

Do you know HOW?

1. A dog has a litter of 6 puppies: 3 black, 2 brown, and 1 white. Circle the way you can assign the faces of a number cube to simulate randomly selecting a certain puppy.

A. Assign 1 and 2 to black, 3 and 4 to brown, and 5 and 6 to white.

B. Assign 1, 2, and 3 to black, 4 and 5 to brown, and 6 to white.

C. Assign 1 to black, 3 to brown, and 5 to white. Assign 2, 4, and 6 to represent roll again.

2. Every day, a widget company randomly samples 100 widgets and records how many are defective. Based on the week's data, write the probability that a widget will be defective as a fraction, decimal, and percent.

Day	1	2	3	4	5
Defective	2	3	3	2	2

Fraction Decimal Percent

Do you UNDERSTAND?

3. Reasoning In Exercise 1, is there an equal chance of randomly selecting a puppy of each color? Explain.

4. Writing Based on the percent of defective widgets you found in Exercise 2, would you feel confident buying a widget from this company? Explain.

18-1 Compound Events

Common Core State Standards: 7.SP.8: Find probabilities of compound events using organized lists, tables, tree diagrams, and simulation. **7.SP.8.b:** Represent sample spaces for compound events using methods such as organized lists, tables and tree diagrams … .

Launch

Draw lines to sort these tiles into two groups. Explain your groups.

Pick a number from 1–9.

Toss heads then tails.

Pick a number from 10–20.

Toss heads.

Spin red twice.

Spin red.

Group 1	Group 2

Reflect

Could you sort the tiles in more than one way? Explain.

Close and Check

Focus Question

What makes an event a compound event? What are the different types of compound events?

Do you know HOW?

1. How many steps or choices does the action of creating a parfait cup involve? Action: Choose a yogurt flavor, a type of fruit, and a topping.

Yogurt	Fruit	Topping
Plain	Blueberries	Granola
Vanilla	Strawberries	Nuts
Berry	Cherries	
	Bananas	

2. Are the events of creating a parfait cup in Exercise 1 dependent or independent?

3. In gym class, two students are chosen to pick teams for a game of soccer. Is the action of choosing team members a dependent or independent event?

Do you UNDERSTAND?

4. **Writing** Explain your answer to Exercise 3.

5. **Error Analysis** During a game, each player rolls a number cube and moves a game piece that number of spaces. A friend says each turn is a single independent event. Do you agree? Explain.

18-2 Sample Spaces

Common Core State Standards: 7.SP.8: Find probabilities of compound events using organized lists, tables, tree diagrams, and simulation. **7.SP.8.b:** Represent sample spaces for compound events using methods such as organized lists, tables and tree diagrams . . . .

Launch

A new car company allows you to design your own Car Model D online. Show all the different ways you can design the car. Explain how you know you've shown all the different ways.

Car Model D Options

Color

○ Red ○ Black ○ Silver

Doors

○ Two ○ Four

Transmission

○ Automatic ○ Manual

Reflect

Does it matter what order you list the different ways to design the car? Explain.

Close and Check

Focus Question

How do you know a sample space is complete? How do you know when you have accounted for all possibilities?

Do you know HOW?

1. How many possible combinations of parfait cups are there if one item is chosen from each list?

Yogurt	Fruit	Topping
Plain	Blueberries	Granola
Vanilla	Strawberries	Nuts
Berry	Cherries	
	Bananas	

2. A school offers three elective classes: art (a), band (b), and choir (c). Each student must choose a morning class and a different afternoon class. Make a tree diagram to show all possible class and time combinations.

Do you UNDERSTAND?

3. **Reasoning** The school in Exercise 2 adds an evening class time. Does the total number of combinations of classes change? Explain.

4. **Error Analysis** The table displays the outcomes for a sample space involving a spinner divided into colors. Your friend says the spinner was spun four times. Is she correct? Explain.

	R	B
R	R, R	R, B
B	B, R	B, B

18-3 Counting Outcomes

Common Core State Standards: 7.SP.8.a: Understand that … the probability of a compound event is the fraction of outcomes in the sample space for which the compound event occurs. **7.SP.8.b:** … For an event described in everyday language … , identify the outcomes … . Also, **7.SP.8.**

Launch

The new car company unveils two new models. Which car can you order in more ways? Explain your reasoning.

Car Model Q Options

Color

- ○ Silver ○ Black

Doors

- ○ Three ○ Four ○ Five

Transmission

- ○ Automatic ○ Manual

Car Model C Options

Color

- ○ Silver ○ Black ○ White
- ○ Green ○ Red ○ Tan

Doors

- ○ Two ○ Four

Transmission

- ○ Automatic

Reflect

How would your method work for counting the different ways you could order a car with even more choices such as 12 exterior colors, 4 Door Options, 3 transmission options, 2 engine types, and 6 interior colors?

Close and Check

Focus Question

How is the number of outcomes of a multi-step process related to the number of outcomes for each step?

Do you know HOW?

1. An online shoe store offers customized gym shoes. You have a choice of leather or canvas material; black, white, or gray shoe color; and red, pink, blue, green, or yellow lace color. How many different shoe choices are there?

2. Use a table to show all the possible outcomes of choosing a shape and a letter.

A B C D E

3. Based on the table in Exercise 2, how many outcomes are in this event?
Event: Choosing a polygon *or* a vowel.

Do you UNDERSTAND?

4. Writing Explain how you found the solution to Exercise 1.

5. Reasoning Explain how the number of possible outcomes for Exercise 3 would change if the event were choosing a polygon *and* a vowel.

18-4 Finding Theoretical Probabilities

Common Core State Standards: 7.SP.8: Find probabilities of compound events using organized lists, tables, [and] tree diagrams .... **7.SP.8.a:** Understand ... the probability of a compound event is the fraction of outcomes in the sample space for which the compound event occurs. Also **7.SP.6.**

Launch

An online shoe clerk unfortunately erases your order options on Shoe Model W. So, she sends you four different pairs and asks you to return any that don't match your order.

What are the chances you'll get the shoes you ordered? Explain.

Shoe Model W

Color

○ Silver ○ Black ○ Brown ○ Green

Size

○ 5	○ 6	○ 7	○ 8
○ $5\frac{1}{2}$	○ $6\frac{1}{2}$	○ $7\frac{1}{2}$	○ $8\frac{1}{2}$

Reflect

Will the chances be the same or different depending on which four different pairs the store clerk sent?

Close and Check

Focus Question

In what situations should you use an organized list, a table, or a tree diagram to find the probability of a compound event?

Do you know HOW?

1. Find the probability of rolling sequential numbers (for example; 1 then 2) in 2 consecutive rolls of a number cube.

P(2 sequential numbers) = ☐

or about ☐ %

2. Using a number cube and 4 marbles (red, blue, yellow, and green), what is the theoretical probability of rolling a specific number and choosing a specific marble without looking?

☐

3. For which compound event is the result closest to the result predicted by theoretical probability in Exercise 2?

Results of 100 Trials				
Event	(1, R)	(3, B)	(5, Y)	(6, G)
Count	6	2	4	3

☐

Do you UNDERSTAND?

4. Writing Explain how the theoretical probability in Exercise 2 changes if the action is rolling an even number and choosing a red or yellow marble.

5. Reasoning If 60 trials are conducted using the compound event described in Exercise 4, how many favorable outcomes would you expect to get? Explain.

18-5 Simulation with Random Numbers

Common Core State Standards: 7.SP.8: Find probabilities of compound events using organized lists, tables, tree diagrams, and simulation. **7.SP.8.c:** Design and use a simulation to generate frequencies for compound events . . . .

Launch

Describe a pick-a-number game where contestants have a 1 in 4 chance of winning. Your game must have two rounds and use all the tiles shown.

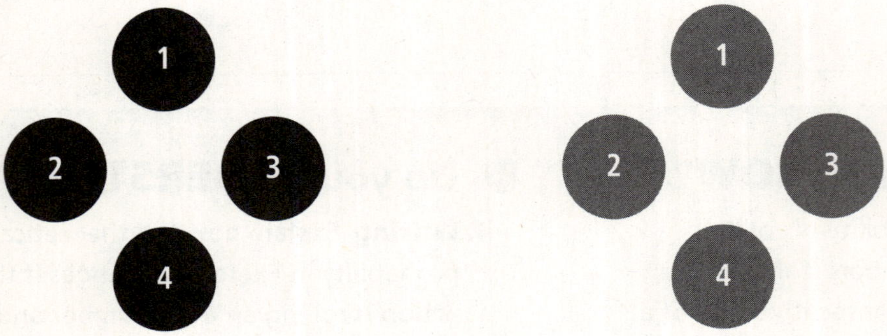

Reflect

What was most critical to you to design a game that worked?

Close and Check

Focus Question

How can you use random numbers to simulate real-world situations?

______

______

______

______

Do you know HOW?

1. A survey finds that 49 out of 84 students ride the school bus each day. Assign numbers to simulate the outcomes that a student chosen at random rides the school bus each day.

bus rider: ______

non-bus rider: ______

2. Circle the list of random numbers that simulates the survey results given in Exercise 1.

A. 3, 5, 9, 2, 11, 9, 5, 3, 8, 10, 12, 5

B. 12, 11, 7, 9, 4, 6, 3, 5, 7, 3, 9, 10

3. Eight students take a four-question quiz. Correct answers are assigned a 1, and incorrect answers are assigned a 2. Record the results of the quiz in the frequency table.

1111	2122	1112	1122
1112	1221	1211	1112

Quiz Results

Do you UNDERSTAND?

4. Writing Explain how you decided which numbers to assign in Exercise 1.

______

______

______

______

______

______

5. Reasoning According to Exercise 3, how many students got at least 3 items on the quiz correct? Explain how you found the solution.

______

______

______

______

______

______

18-6 Finding Probabilities by Simulation

Common Core State Standards: 7.SP.8: Find probabilities of compound events using organized lists, tables, tree diagrams, and simulation.

Launch

Your friend designs a game that involves drawing *makes* and *misses* blindly out of a bag to simulate a basketball free throw. He wants his game to have P(making two free throws) = 0.75.

Complete and explain the possible game rules using the items shown.

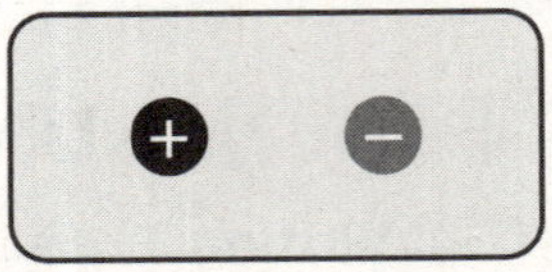

Reflect

Does your game guarantee a 75% probability of making two free throws? Explain.

Close and Check

Focus Question

In what situations should you use a simulation to find the probability of a compound event?

Do you know HOW?

1. A survey finds that 39% of households in a certain town own at least one dog. Assign a range of numbers to simulate each possible outcome.

Households that own at least one dog:

Households that do not own at least one dog:

2. Use the pairs of random numbers to find the experimental probability that exactly one of the next two people you meet will own a dog. Express the solution as a percent.

(72, 30)	(15, 38)	(67, 93)
(100, 2)	(80, 69)	(77, 89)
(88, 45)	(22, 51)	(57, 62)
(72, 59)	(74, 64)	(81, 97)

Do you UNDERSTAND?

3. **Writing** Describe one trial and tell what a favorable outcome would be for the simulation in Exercise 2.

4. **Reasoning** You decide to change the favorable outcome in Exercise 2 to *at least* one of the next two people you meet owning a dog. Would you expect the experimental probability to change? Explain.

18-7 Problem Solving

Common Core State Standards: 7.SP.7: Develop a probability model and use it to find probabilities of events. Compare probabilities from a model to observed frequencies .... **7.SP.8:** Find probabilities of compound events using organized lists, tables, tree diagrams, and simulation.

Launch

Design a three-spinner game in which contestants have a 30% chance of winning. Complete the spinners and describe the rules of the game.

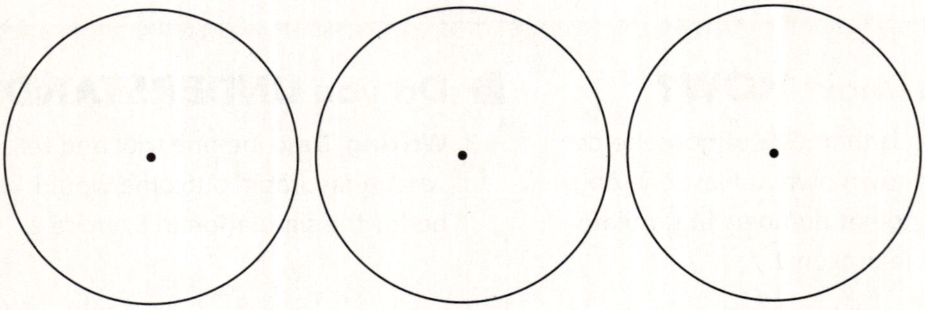

Reflect

What was the most challenging part of designing your game? Explain.

Close and Check

Focus Question

How do you choose a strategy for finding the probability of a compound event? Are there situations in which one strategy is better than another?

Do you know **HOW?**

1. You roll two number cubes 200 times. How many times should you expect to roll two number cubes that have an even sum?

2. You can travel from your house to a golf course by the roads shown. Any of the 3 intersections *A*, *B*, and *C* may be closed due to construction. Express the theoretical probability that there is an open path from your house to the golf course at any time as a fraction and as a percent.

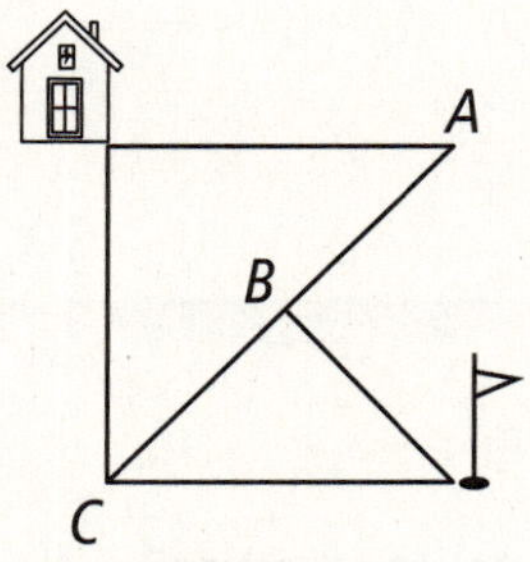

Fraction:

Percent:

Do you **UNDERSTAND?**

3. **Reasoning** Explain how you found the solution to Exercise 1.

4. **Writing** Explain how you could set up a simulation to find the experimental probability for Exercise 2.

19-1 Measuring Angles

Common Core State Standards: 7.EE.4: Use variables to represent quantities in a real-world or mathematical problem, and construct simple equations and inequalities to solve problems by reasoning about the quantities. Also, **7.EE.4.a** and **7.G.2.**

Launch

Compare Angle 1 and Angle 2. Tell which is greater.

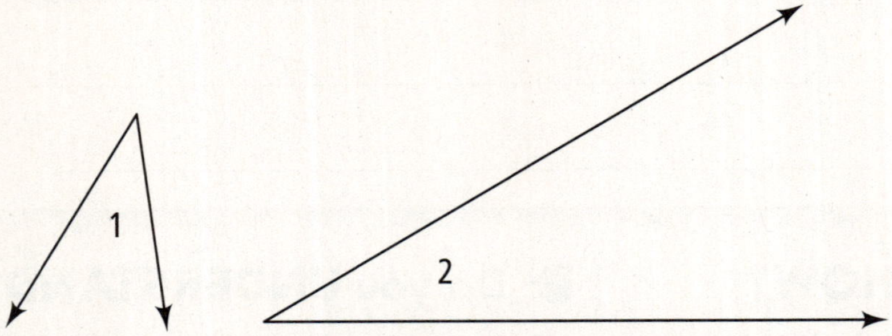

Show how you know using only paper and pencil.

Reflect

How does the length of the rays (or sides) in an angle relate to its measure?

Close and Check

Focus Question

All angles are formed by two rays. What makes angles different from each other?

Do you know HOW?

1. What is the measure of $\angle PQR$?

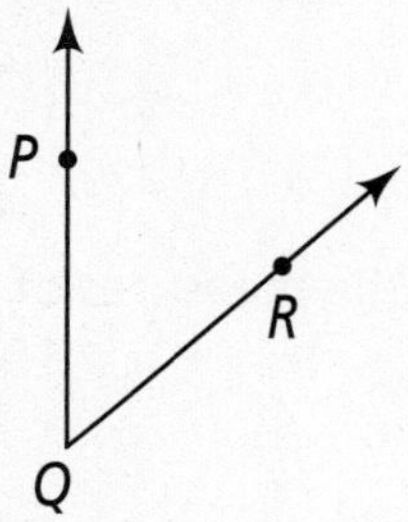

2. Label each angle *acute, right, obtuse,* or *straight.*

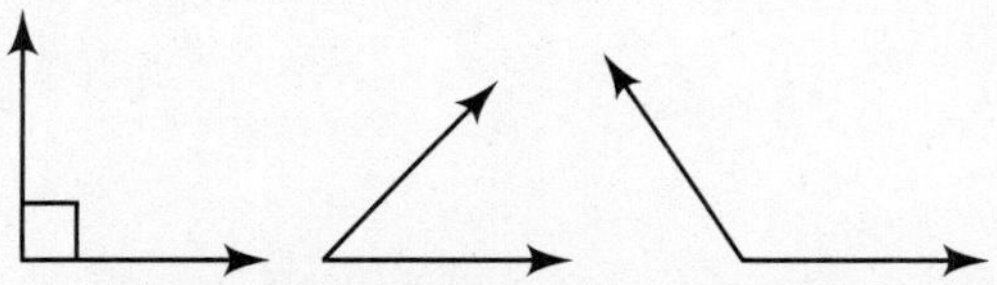

3. The measure of $\angle ABC$ is 70°. Find the value of x.

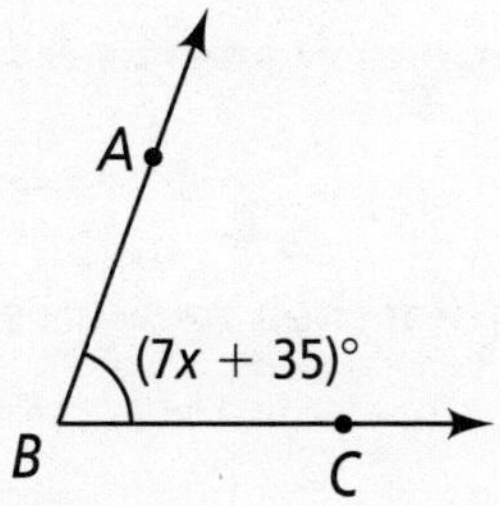

$x =$

Do you UNDERSTAND?

4. Error Analysis Your friend measures the angle below and says it is 30°. Explain his mistake and find the correct angle measure.

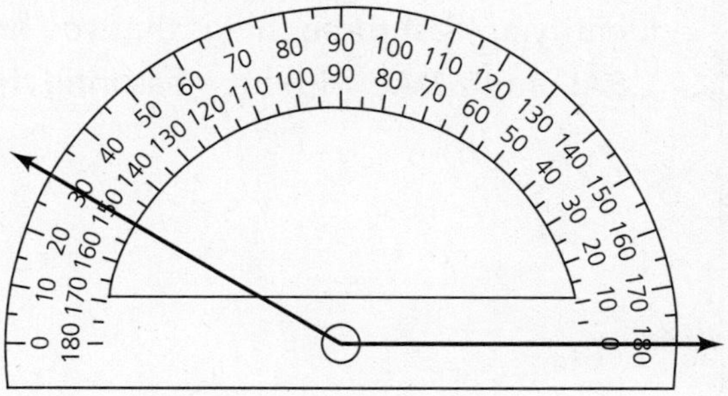

5. Reasoning Can the sum of an acute and a right angle be equal to the measure of a straight angle? Explain.

19-2 Adjacent Angles

Common Core State Standards: 7.G.5: Use facts about supplementary, complementary, vertical, and adjacent angles in a multi-step problem to write and solve simple equations for an unknown angle in a figure. Also, **7.G.2.**

Launch

∠*BAC* measures 100°.

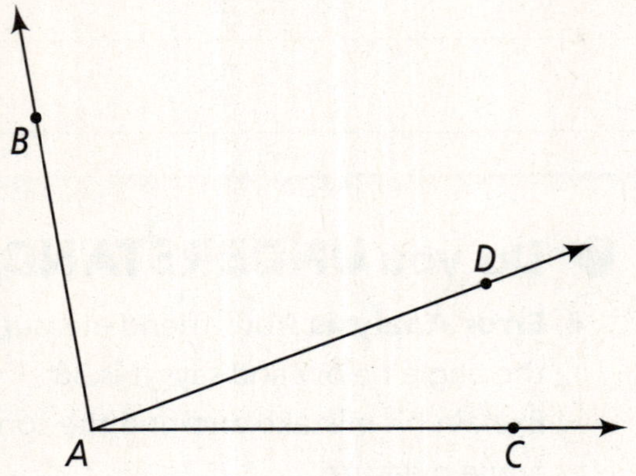

Identify at least three things that you know about the measures of ∠*BAD* and ∠*DAC* without measuring them.

Reflect

Do you need to measure both ∠*BAD* and ∠*DAC* to know both of their measures? Explain.

Close and Check

Focus Question

A whole is the sum of its parts. How can you apply this idea to angles?

Do you know HOW?

Use the diagram below for Exercises 1 and 2.

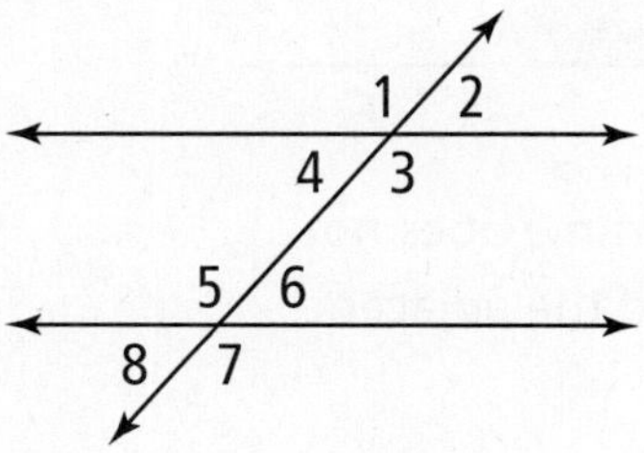

1. Name two angles adjacent to ∠2.

2. Name two angles adjacent to ∠5.

3. The measure of ∠*ABD* is 40°. What is the value of *x*?

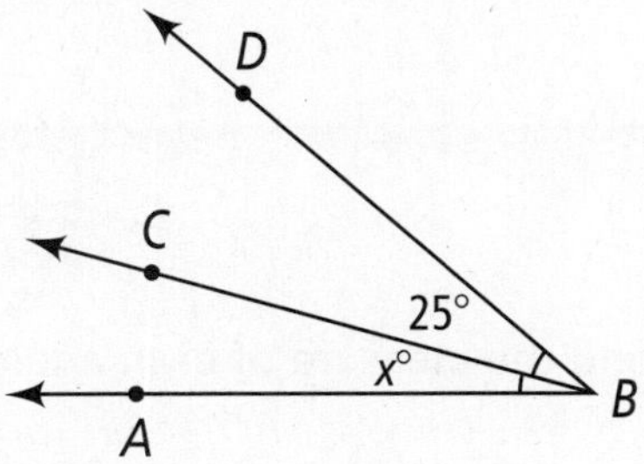

$x =$

Do you UNDERSTAND?

4. Vocabulary Explain why ∠1 and ∠3 from Exercise 1 are not adjacent angles.

5. Error Analysis The measure of ∠*JKL* is 125°. The equation $3x + 5 - 40 = 125$ was written to find the value of *x*. Is this correct? Explain.

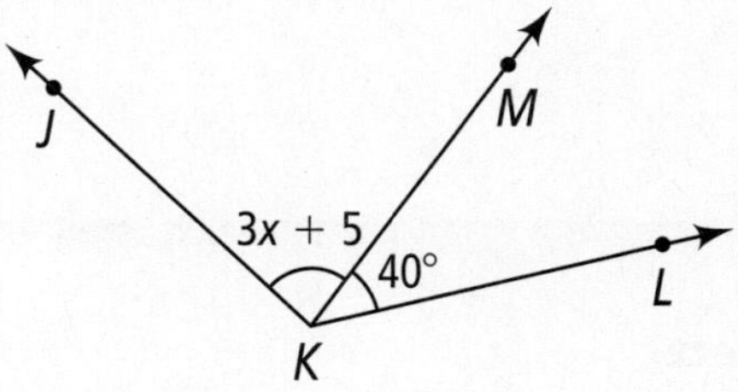

19-3 Complementary Angles

Common Core State Standards: 7.G.2: Draw (freehand, with ruler and protractor …) geometric shapes with given conditions … . **7.G.5:** Use facts about … complementary … angles in a multi-step problem to write and solve simple equations for an unknown angle in a figure.

Launch

You make two rectangular picture frames. Your pieces line up on the first frame but not on your second frame.

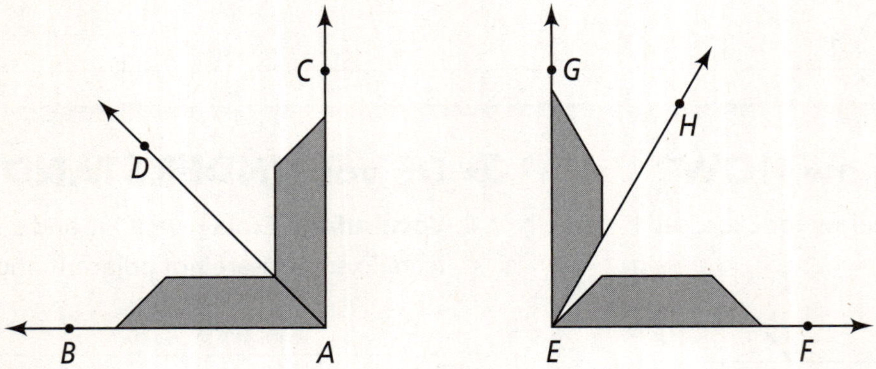

Explain why your first frame works and your second frame does not work. Explain what you know about frame angles and the adjacent angles in the frames.

Reflect

If $m\angle BAD$ and $m\angle DAC$ are equal, explain how you can find the measure of each angle.

Close and Check

Focus Question

What do you know about the measures of two angles that form a right angle?

Do you know HOW?

1. What is the measure of the complement for the angle below?

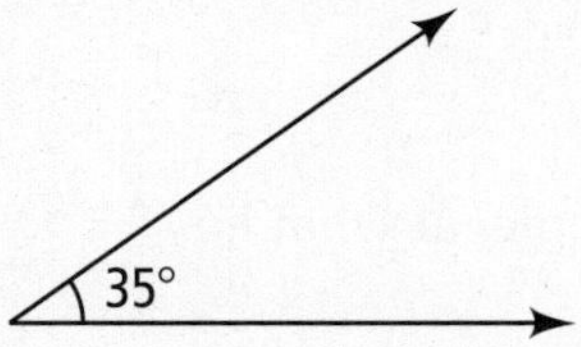

2. Name two complementary angles.

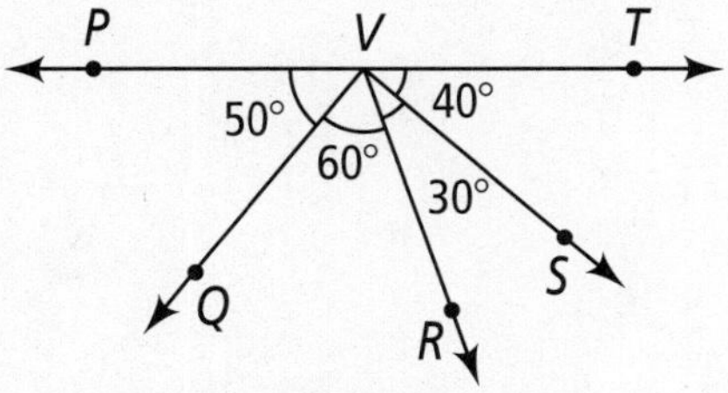

3. $\angle ABD$ and $\angle DBC$ are complementary angles. What is the value of x?

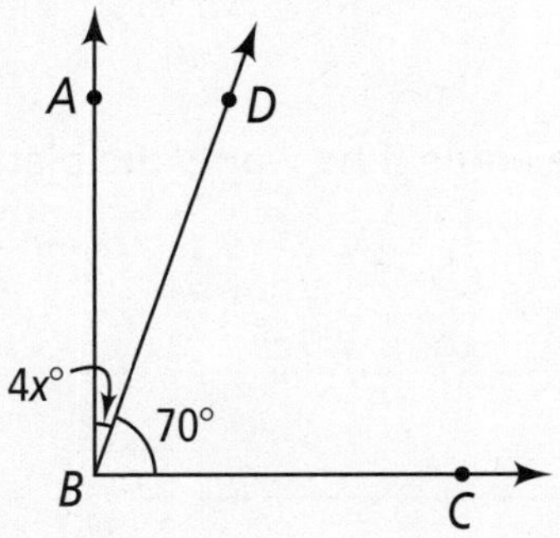

$x =$

Do you UNDERSTAND?

4. Reasoning Can two complementary angles form an obtuse angle? Explain.

5. Error Analysis Your friend says that the angles below are not complementary because they are not adjacent. Is she correct? Explain.

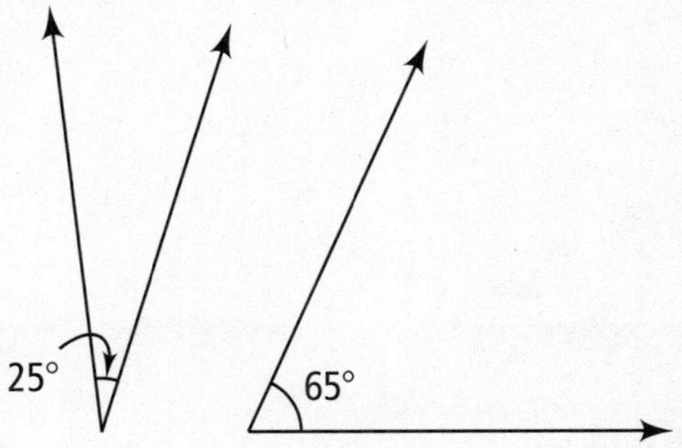

19-4 Supplementary Angles

Common Core State Standards: 7.G.2: Draw (freehand, with ruler and protractor …) geometric shapes with given conditions … . **7.G.5:** Use facts about supplementary … angles in a multi-step problem to write and solve simple equations for an unknown angle in a figure.

Launch

Hockey players want the blades of their sticks to lie flat on the ice.

If this player holds his hockey stick to the ice at a 45° angle, at what lie angle should his stick be? Explain how you know.

Reflect

Will a taller player need a stick with a greater or lesser lie angle if he wants the blade to lie flat on the ice? Tell how you know.

Close and Check

Focus Question

What do you know about the measures of two angles that form a straight angle?

Do you know HOW?

1. What is the measure of the supplement of the angle below?

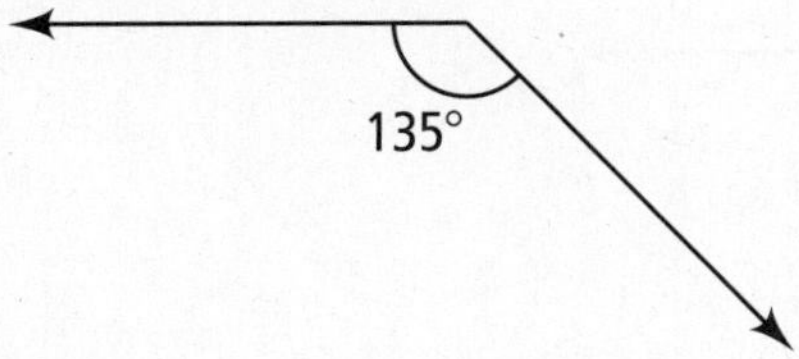

2. Suppose $m\angle PQR = 63.7°$. Find the measure of its supplement.

3. What is the value of x?

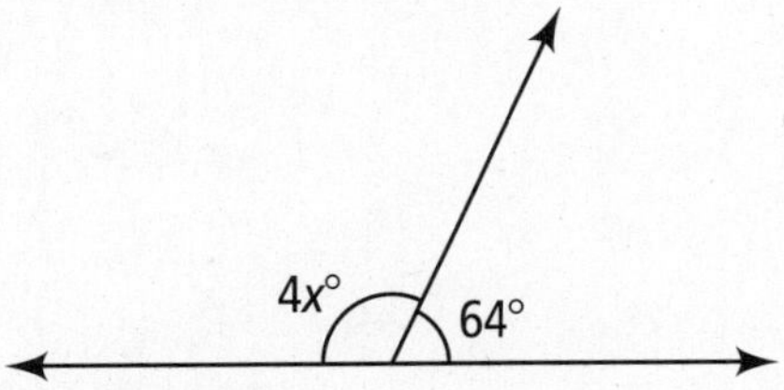

$x =$

Do you UNDERSTAND?

4. Reasoning What kinds of angles (acute, right, and obtuse) can form a pair of supplementary angles? Explain how you know.

5. Error Analysis A friend says that a straight line is a supplementary angle because it measures 180°. Do you agree or disagree with your friend? Explain.

19-5 Vertical Angles

Common Core State Standards: 7.G.5: Use facts about supplementary, complementary, vertical, and adjacent angles in a multi-step problem to write and solve simple equations for an unknown angle in a figure. Also, **7.G.2.**

Launch

Your friend claims to "know all the angles." She looks at Figure 1, laughs, and says, "All the angles are 90°."

So, you show her Figure 2 and tell her Angle 1 is 80°. She laughs and says she can find the other angle measures without measuring them.

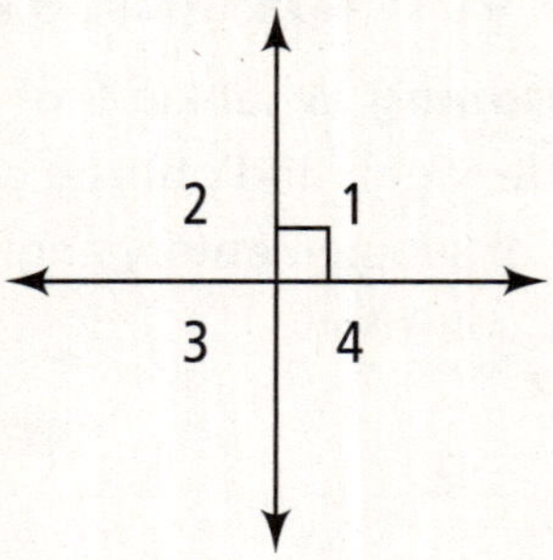

Figure 1

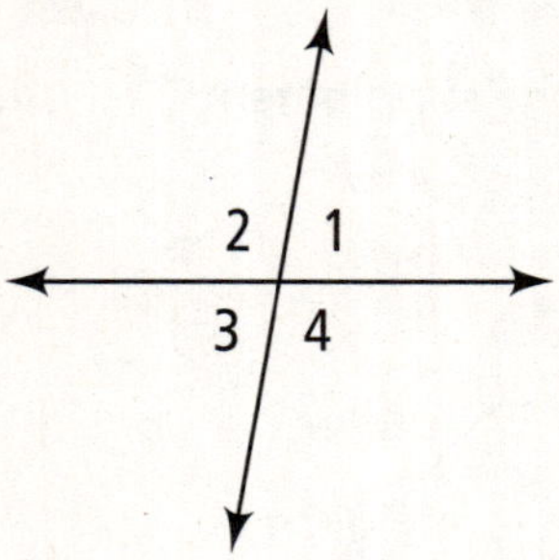

Figure 2

Explain how she could do this. Describe any patterns that you see.

Reflect

Did the patterns that you found in Figure 2 apply to the Figure 1? Explain.

Close and Check

Focus Question

Two intersecting lines form angles. How can you describe the relationship between the angles that are opposite each other?

Do you know HOW?

1. Name the angle that is vertical to ∠*ROQ*.

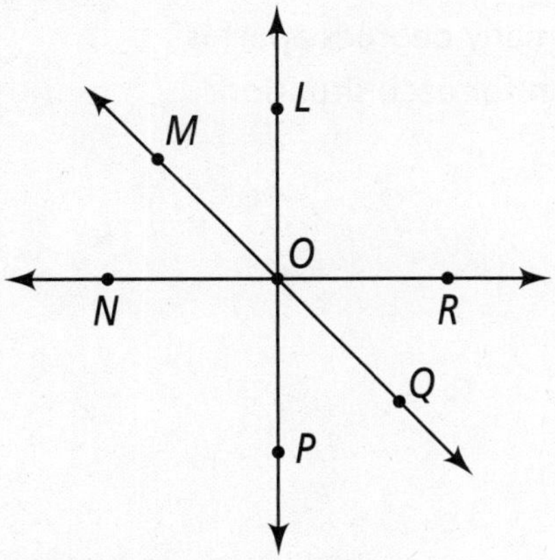

2. What is the value of *x*?

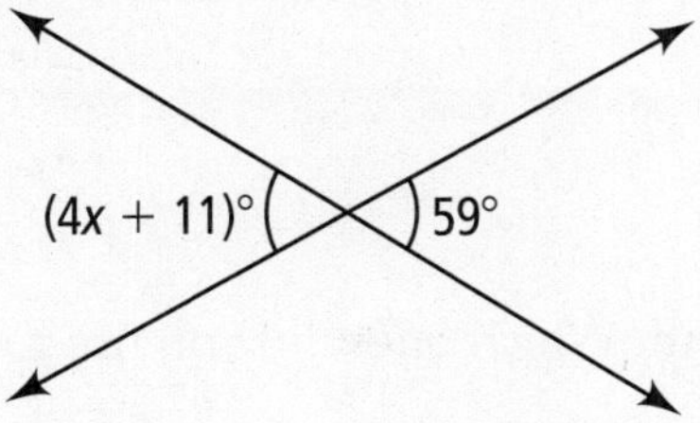

x =

Do you UNDERSTAND?

3. Writing In the diagram, ∠1 and ∠3 are vertical angles. Why aren't ∠2 and ∠4 vertical angles?

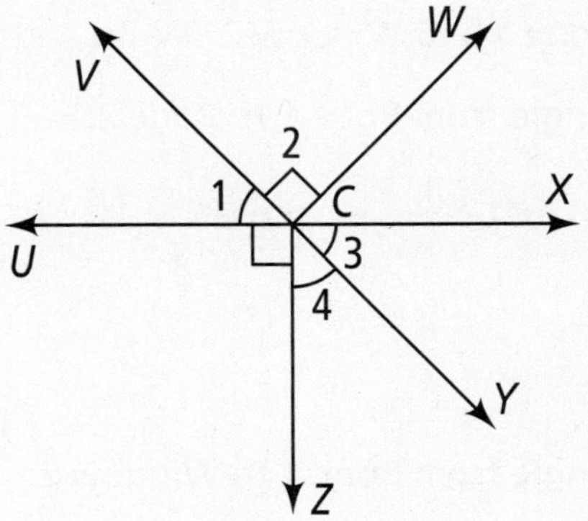

4. Reasoning If you know the measure of ∠4, how can you find the measure of ∠1?

19-6 Problem Solving

Common Core State Standards: 7.G.5: Use facts about supplementary, complementary, vertical, and adjacent angles in a multi-step problem to write and solve simple equations for an unknown angle in a figure.

Launch

A dog on a leash buries bones in strategic positions in the backyard. You watch from Window 2.

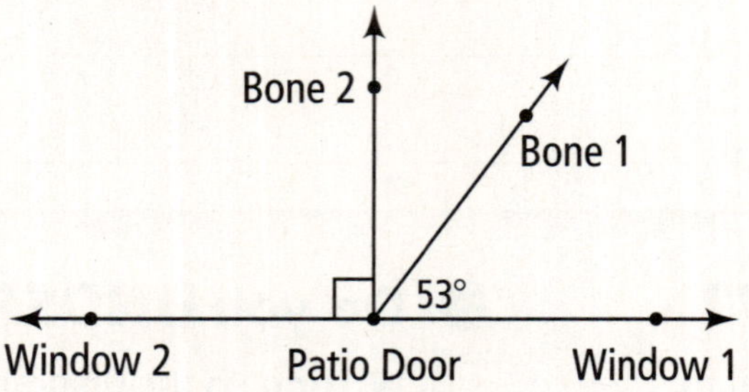

Look at the different angles formed by the leash and the house. How many degrees apart are Bones 1 and 2? How many degrees apart is Bone 1 and Window 2? Write and solve an equation for each situation.

Angle from Bone 1 to Bone 2:

Angle from Bone 1 to Window 2:

Reflect

Think about the different types of angles you know about. Which ones did you use to solve the problem?

Close and Check

Focus Question

You can use relationships between angles to break complex diagrams into smaller parts. How do you decide which relationships to use?

Do you know HOW?

1. Write True or False above each statement about the diagram.

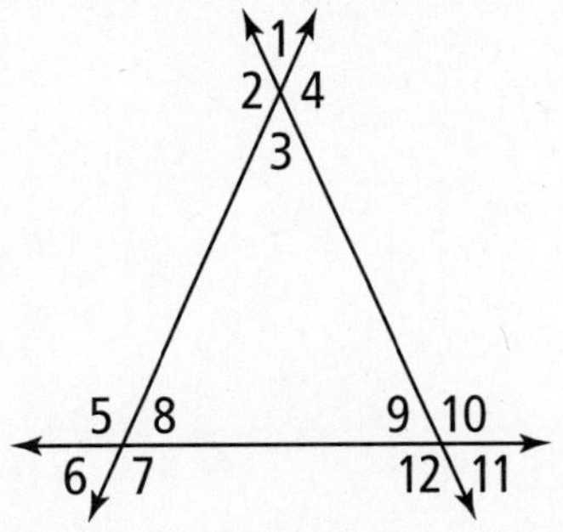

$m\angle 2 = m\angle 3$

$m\angle 1 = m\angle 3$

$m\angle 6 = m\angle 8$

$m\angle 5 + m\angle 8 = 180°$

2. What is the measure of $\angle 1$?

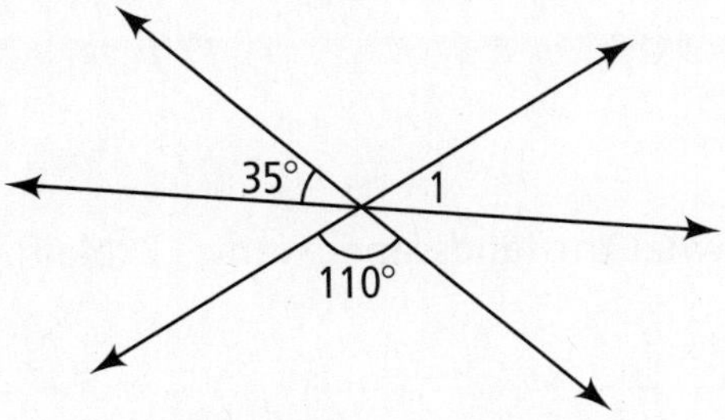

$m\angle 1 =$

Do you UNDERSTAND?

3. Reasoning In Exercise 1, $\angle 5$ and $\angle 12$ are congruent. Explain how to use the relationships between the angles in the triangle to find the $m\angle 1$?

4. Writing Explain how to find $m\angle 1$ in Exercise 1 if the $m\angle 5$ is 110°.

20-1 Center, Radius, and Diameter

Common Core State Standards: 7.EE.4: Use variables to … construct simple equations … . **7.G.4:** Know the formulas for the area and circumference of a circle and use them to solve problems … . Also, **7.EE.4.a** and **7.G.2.**

Launch

A landscaper wants to build a flower garden with a fountain in the center and a path on the outside. The landscaper wants the fountain to be same distance from anywhere on the path.

Draw the garden plan. Explain how it matches what the landscaper wants.

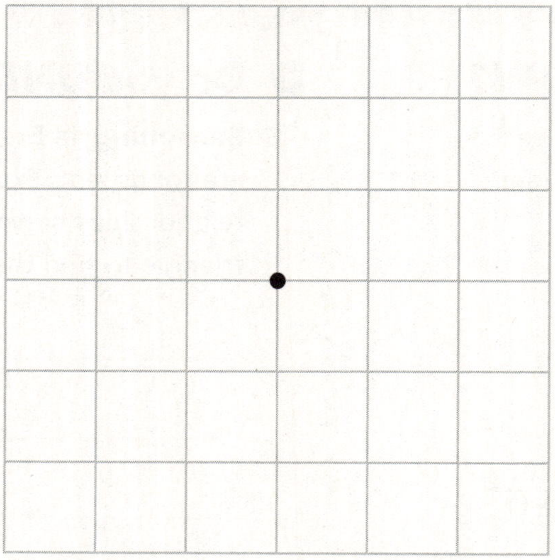

Reflect

Could the garden path be any shape and still match what the landscaper wants? Explain.

Close and Check

Focus Question

What are the relationships among the parts of a circle?

Do you know HOW?

1. How many radii are shown?

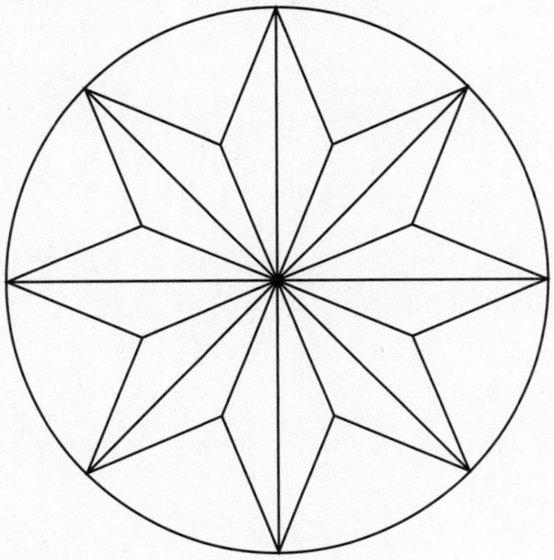

2. The radius of the circle above is 14.5 cm. Find the diameter.

3. The diameter of a circle is $7x + 5$ and the radius is 13. Find the value of x.

Do you UNDERSTAND?

4. Reasoning If the length of the radius of a circle is increased 3 times, what happens to the length of the diameter? Write an equation to show how you know.

5. Writing A circular path surrounds a dog park. The developers want to build a supply shed in the center of the park. How can they determine where to build the shed?

20-2 Circumference of a Circle

Common Core State Standards: 7.G.2: Draw … geometric shapes with given conditions … .
7.G.4: Know the formulas for the area and circumference of a circle and use them to solve problems … .

Launch

For each circle, describe any pattern you see between the distance around the circle and the length of its diameter.

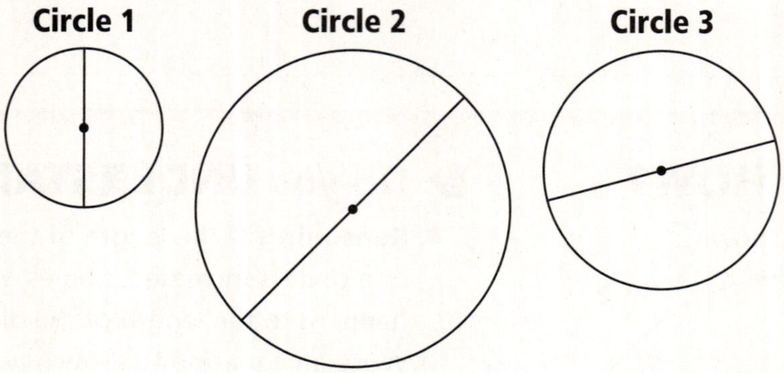

Reflect

What do you think will be the distance around a circle with a diameter of 100 cm? Explain.

Close and Check

Focus Question

How is the diameter of a circle related to the distance around a circle?

Do you know HOW?

1. Find the diameter and radius of a circle with a circumference of 16π in.

Diameter: Radius:

For Exercises 2–4, use 3.14 for π.

2. The distance across a circular reflecting pool is 12 m. Find the distance around the pool.

3. Find the diameter of a circle with a circumference of 62.8 yd.

4. A roundabout is a circular road built at a traffic intersection. One city has a roundabout that is 1.5 mi long. A statue sits in the center. Find the distance from the outer edge of the roundabout to the statue to the nearest hundredth.

Do you UNDERSTAND?

5. Compare and Contrast Two students find the circumference of a circle with a diameter of 16 ft. One student says the circumference is 50.24 ft. The other says it is 50.29 ft. Can both students be correct? Explain.

6. Writing Explain how to use a wheel's circumference to find its diameter.

20-3 Area of a Circle

Common Core State Standards: 7.G.4: Know the formulas for the area and circumference of a circle and use them to solve problems; give an informal derivation of the relationship between the circumference and area of a circle. Also, **7.G.2.**

Launch

Each grid square represents 1 ft by 1 ft. Estimate the area of the circle. Explain how you made your estimate.

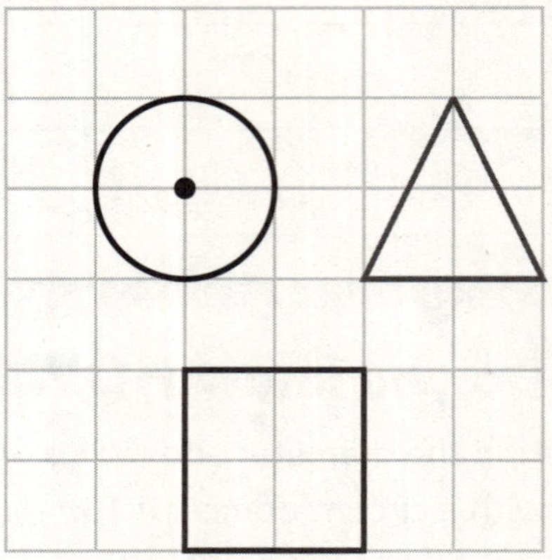

Circle	Square	Triangle

Reflect

Which shapes did you find the area of first? Why?

Close and Check

Focus Question

How are the areas of a circle and a parallelogram related?

Do you know HOW?

1. Find the area of a circle with a radius of 6.9 m to the nearest tenth. Leave your answer in terms of π.

2. The average crop circle is between 100 and 300 ft in diameter. Find the area of a crop circle that is 300 ft in diameter. Use 3.14 for π.

3. A baker makes a giant cookie for special occasions that is 16 in. in diameter. How many 4-in. diameter cookies would it take to equal the area of one giant cookie?

cookies

Do you UNDERSTAND?

4. Compare and Contrast What is the difference between the circumference and area of a circle?

5. Reasoning A round pizza has an area of 254.34 in.^{2}. Explain how to estimate the length and width of the square box needed to package the pizza.

20-4 Relating Circumference and Area of a Circle

Common Core State Standards: 7.G.4: Know the formulas for the area and circumference of a circle and use them to solve problems; give an informal derivation of the relationship between the circumference and area of a circle.

Launch

Does a greater distance around a shape always mean a greater area? Show one pair of rectangles and one pair of circles where greater distance around does not mean a greater area. If you can't show an example, explain why.

Rectangles **Circles**

Reflect

Besides size, can you change a circle's basic shape? Can you change a rectangle's basic shape? How might this relate to the problem above?

Close and Check

Focus Question

How are the area of a circle and the circumference of a circle related?

Do you know HOW?

1. A circle has a circumference of 38 yd. Find the approximate area of the circle. Use 3.14 for π.

2. The ratio of the area of a circle to the circumference of the circle $\left(\frac{A}{C}\right)$ is $\frac{7}{1}$. Find the circumference of the circle. Leave your answer in terms of π.

3. The ratio of the area of a circle to the circumference of the circle $\left(\frac{A}{C}\right)$ is $\frac{5}{1}$. Find the area of the circle. Leave your answer in terms of π.

4. The ratio of the area of a circle to the circumference of the circle $\left(\frac{A}{C}\right)$ is $\frac{6}{1}$. Find the circumference and area of the circle. Leave your answers in terms of π.

$C =$

$A =$

Do you UNDERSTAND?

5. Reasoning The ratio $\left(\frac{A}{C}\right)$ of a circle is $\frac{3}{1}$. Explain how to use this information to find the radius and circumference of the circle.

6. Error Analysis The ratio $\left(\frac{A}{C}\right)$ of a bike wheel is $\frac{4}{1}$. Your friend says $C = 8\pi$ and $A = 16\pi$. Explain and correct the error your friend made.

20-5 Problem Solving

Common Core State Standards: 7.G.4: Know the formulas for the area and circumference of a circle and use them to solve problems; give an informal derivation of the relationship between the circumference and area of a circle.

Launch

A T-shirt company plans a logo with green circles on yellow squares. Which logo has the most green? Explain.

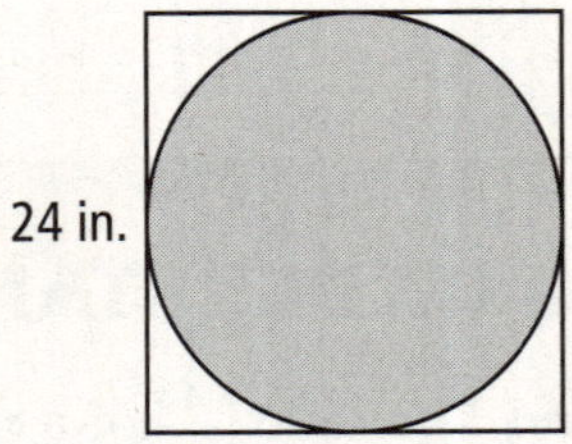

Plan A

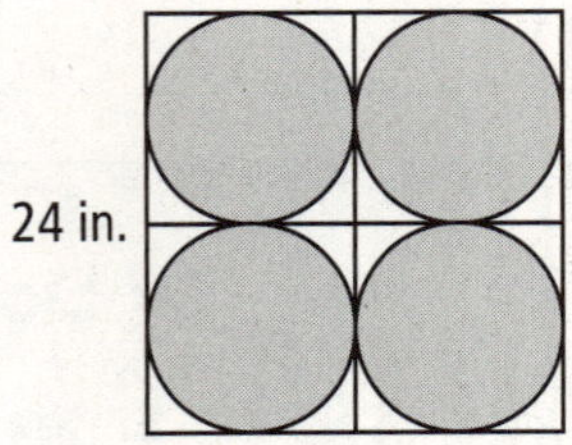

Plan B

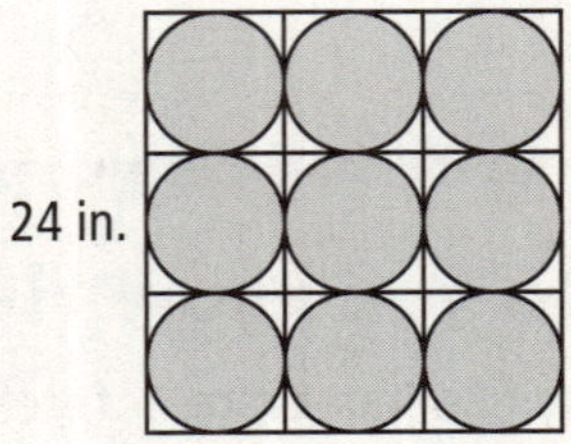

Plan C

Reflect

Which logo did you think had the most green before you found the areas? Why?

Close and Check

Focus Question

When do you use circumference to measure a circle? When do you use area?

Do you know **HOW?**

1. You buy a square tablecloth with a side length of 5 ft. You place it on a round table with a diameter of 4 ft. Find the area of the tablecloth that is hanging off the edge of the table. Use 3.14 for π.

2. The radius of each half circle is 2 cm. The length of the figure is twice the diameter of the half circles. Find the area of the figure. Use 3.14 for π.

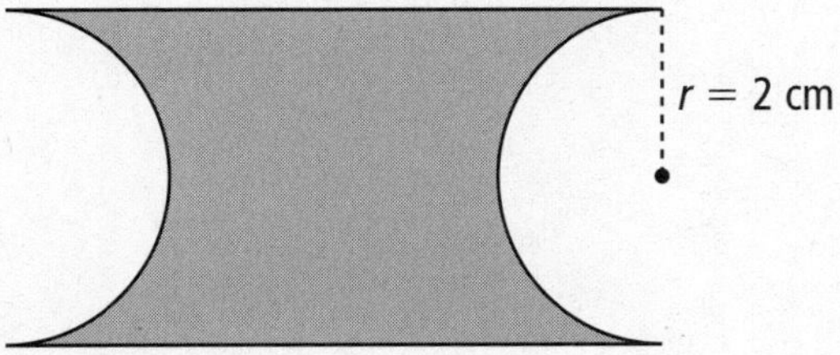

Do you **UNDERSTAND?**

3. Reasoning A fence encloses a circular area of 530.66 ft^2. Can the same fence be used to enclose a rectangular area with perimeter 90 ft? Explain how you know.

4. Error Analysis Your friend says that if you double a circle's radius, the circumference and area double as well. Explain his error.

21-1 Geometry Drawing Tools

Common Core State Standards: 7.G.2: Draw (freehand, with ruler and protractor, and with technology) geometric shapes with given conditions. Focus on constructing triangles from three measures of angles or sides, noticing when the conditions determine a unique triangle … .

Launch

A gift-shop owner sees the eight-sided sign she ordered from the local sign maker and says, "You got it wrong. I wanted an octagon like a stop sign."

Do you think the sign maker or the gift-shop owner was to blame for the wrong sign? Explain.

Reflect

If you ordered a sign for a shop, what would you do to make sure you received the correct sign?

Close and Check

Focus Question

Which geometry drawing tools are best for drawing which types of figures?

Do you know HOW?

1. Sketch a quadrilateral with one right angle and no parallel sides.

2. Use a ruler and a protractor to draw a trapezoid that has two right angles, two parallel sides, and one 55° angle. Let one side of the figure measure 3 cm and another side measure 2 cm.

Do you UNDERSTAND?

3. Writing You try to quickly explain the difference between equilateral and isosceles triangles to your cousin. Which geometry drawing tools should you use? Explain.

4. Error Analysis An architect sketches a diagram for a square room. Does the sketch provide enough information to the builders? Explain.

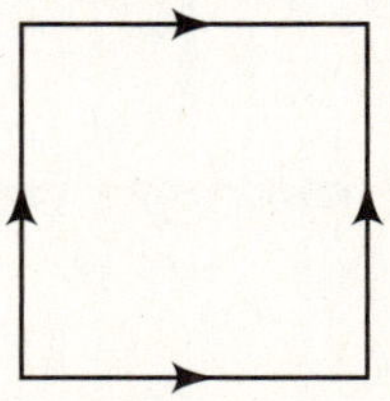

21-2 Drawing Triangles with Given Conditions 1

Common Core State Standards: 7.G.2: Draw geometric shapes with given conditions. Focus on constructing triangles from three measures of angles or sides, noticing when the conditions determine a unique triangle, more than one triangle, or no triangle.

Launch

The sign maker tries to sketch two possible triangle-shaped signs. Sign 1 has side lengths 2 ft, 3 ft, and 3 ft. Sign 2 has side lengths 1 ft, 1 ft, and 3 ft.

Draw the two signs and label the side lengths. Let 1 in. = 1 ft. Can the sign maker make both signs? Explain.

Sign 1	Sign 2

Reflect

What rule would you make about drawing triangles based on this problem?

Close and Check

Focus Question

What information do you need to draw a unique triangle?

Do you know HOW?

1. Draw triangle *DEF*, where $m\angle D = 45°$ and $DE = 4$ cm.

2. Given triangle *XYZ*, where $XZ = 10$ cm, $YZ = 7$ cm, and $m\angle XZY = 115°$, can you draw a *unique triangle, more than one triangle*, or *no triangle*?

3. For triangle *QRS* with the given conditions, can you draw a *unique triangle, more than one triangle,* or *no triangle*?
$QR = 15$ units, $RS = 10$ units, $ST = 5$ units

Do you UNDERSTAND?

4. Writing Is the triangle in Exercise 1 unique? Explain.

5. Error Analysis Your friend says that he can draw a unique triangle as long as he knows at least two sides and an angle. Explain the error in his reasoning.

21-3 Drawing Triangles with Given Conditions 2

Common Core State Standards: 7.G.2: Draw geometric shapes with given conditions. Focus on constructing triangles from three measures of angles or sides, noticing when the conditions determine a unique triangle, more than one triangle, or no triangle.

Launch

The sign maker again tries to sketch two triangle-shaped signs. Sign 1 has angle measures 45°, 45°, and 100°. Sign 2 has angle measures 30°, 60°, and 90°.

Draw the two signs and label the angle measures. Can the sign maker make both signs? Explain.

Sign 1	Sign 2

Reflect

What rule would you make about drawing triangles based on this problem?

Close and Check

Focus Question

What is the minimum number of side lengths and angle measures you need to draw a unique triangle?

Do you know HOW?

1. Given triangle *DEF*, where $m\angle D = 72°$, $m\angle E = 96°$, and $m\angle F = 17°$, can you draw a *unique triangle, more than one triangle,* or *no triangle*?

2. Given triangle *LMN*, where $LM = 23$ units, $m\angle NLM = 33°$, and $m\angle NML = 97°$, can you draw a *unique triangle, more than one triangle,* or *no triangle*?

3. For triangle *JKL*, two side lengths and the measure of the nonincluded angle are given. Can you draw a *unique triangle, more than one triangle,* or *no triangle*?

Do you UNDERSTAND?

4. Reasoning If you are given the length of $\overline{LN}$ instead of $\overline{LM}$ in Exercise 2, would your answer be the same?

5. Error Analysis A classmate says that if you know either three angle measures or three side lengths, then there is one unique triangle that can be constructed. Do you agree? Explain.

21-4 2-D Slices of Right Rectangular Prisms

Common Core State Standards: 7.G.3: Describe the two-dimensional figures that result from slicing three-dimensional figures, as in plane sections of right rectangular prisms and right rectangular pyramids.

Launch

A chef needs a piece of cheese for a new recipe. The chef makes a straight top to bottom slice from a block of cheese.

How are the attributes of the piece of cheese and the attributes of the block of cheese alike? How are they different? Explain your reasoning.

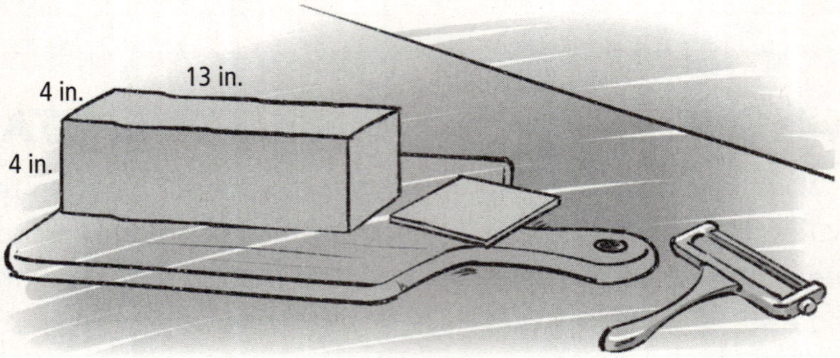

Alike:

Different:

Reflect

Does it matter to your solution where the chef makes the straight up and down slice? Explain.

Close and Check

Focus Question

How can the faces of a rectangular prism determine the shape and dimensions of a slice of the prism?

Do you know HOW?

1. What are the dimensions of the cross section formed by slicing the rectangular prism vertically as shown?

2. What are the dimensions of the cross section formed by slicing the same rectangular prism horizontally?

3. Draw the cross section that is formed by the vertical plane that intersects the front and back faces of the rectangular prism.

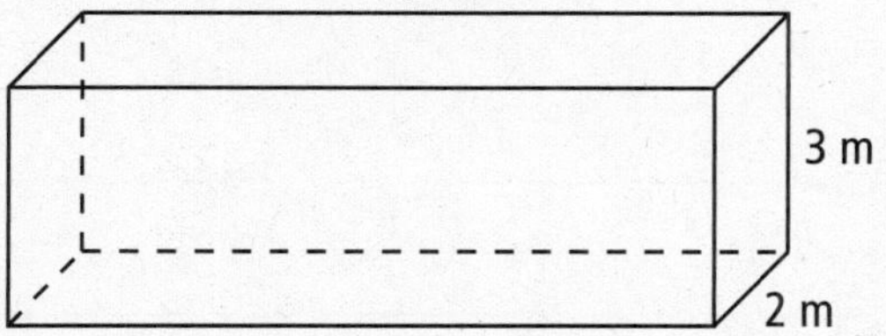

Do you UNDERSTAND?

4. Reasoning Draw the 3-D figure that would result from slicing a corner from the prism in Exercise 1. Describe the faces of the new figure and tell its name.

5. Writing Explain how could you change one of the dimensions of the rectangular prism in Exercise 3 without changing the size and shape of the cross section you drew.

21-5 2-D Slices of Right Rectangular Pyramids

Common Core State Standards: 7.G.3: Describe the two-dimensional figures that result from slicing three-dimensional figures, as in plane sections of right rectangular prisms and right rectangular pyramids.

Launch

A waiter slices his restaurant's world-famous meatloaf as shown for two diners to share.

Could the waiter's split be even? Is there a better way to make sure? Explain.

Waiter's Slice

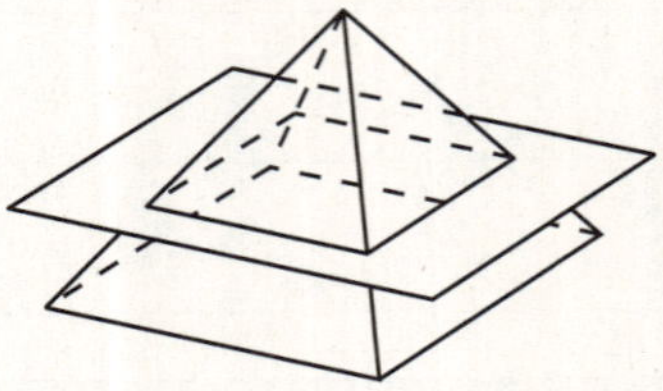

Reflect

Suppose the waiter's slice was perfectly horizontal to the square pyramid base. What two-dimensional shape would you see on the top of the bottom piece and the bottom of the top piece?

Close and Check

Focus Question

How can the faces of a rectangular pyramid determine the shape and dimensions of a slice of the pyramid?

Do you know HOW?

1. Would the area of a slice perpendicular to the base of a rectangular pyramid that passes through the vertex be *greater than, less than,* or *equal to* the area of a side of the pyramid?

2. A horizontal slice is made halfway up the rectangular pyramid. What is the shape of this cross section?

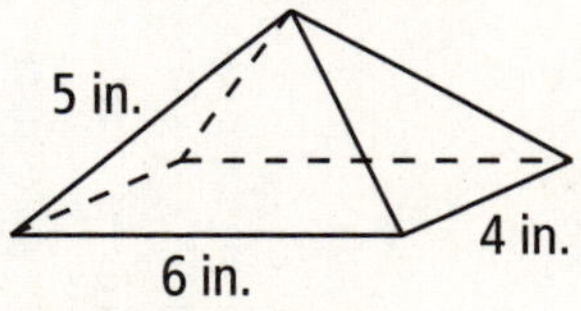

3. What are the dimensions of the cross section of the pyramid in Exercise 2?

Do you UNDERSTAND?

4. **Reasoning** Draw a slice from the rectangular pyramid that forms an isosceles trapezoid. Explain how you know your figure is correct.

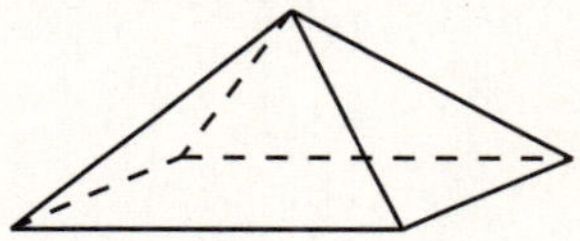

5. **Writing** Explain how you determined the answer to Exercise 3.

21-6 Problem Solving

Common Core State Standards: 7.G.2: Draw (freehand, with ruler and protractor, and with technology) geometric shapes with given conditions . . . . **7.G.3:** Describe the two-dimensional figures that result from slicing three-dimensional figures . . . . **7.G.6:** Solve real-world and mathematical problems involving area . . . .

Launch

Write detailed directions for someone else to draw a geometric figure. Test your directions by drawing the figure yourself.

Description	Drawing

Do you need to revise your directions? Explain.

Reflect

Was the description or the drawing the most difficult part of the problem? Explain.

Close and Check

Focus Question

Why might it be important to have precise descriptions for drawing or making figures?

Do you know HOW?

1. Label the top cross section **T**, the middle cross section **M**, and the bottom cross section **B**.

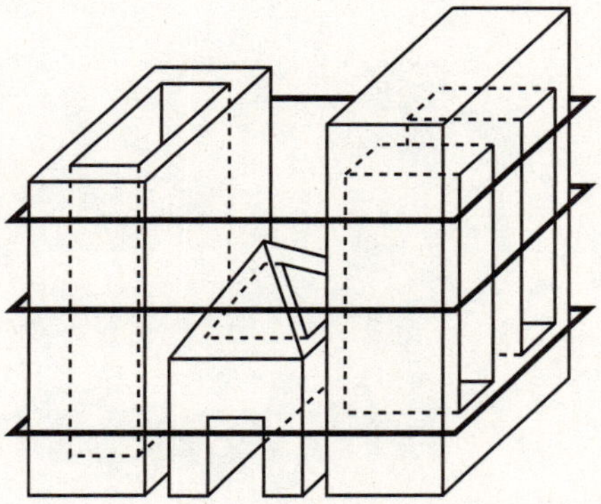

Do you UNDERSTAND?

2. Reasoning Two box makers want to slice the box so it has half the volume. One plans a 2 ft by 4 ft by 3 ft box. The other plans a 1 ft by 4 ft by 6 ft box. Explain which plan works.

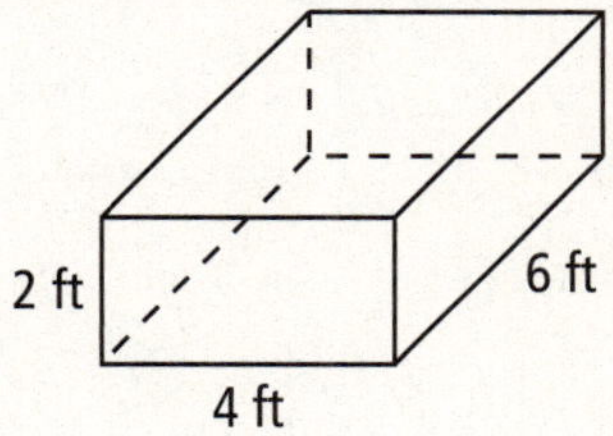

3. Writing Write a clearer description that their boss can use to explain that he wants a 2 ft by 2 ft by 6 ft box.

22-1 Surface Areas of Right Prisms

Common Core State Standards: 7.G.6 Solve real-world and mathematical problems involving area, volume and surface area of two- and three-dimensional objects composed of triangles, quadrilaterals, polygons, cubes, and right prisms.

Launch

One square foot of this cube-shaped sculpture takes you 10 minutes to polish. At this rate, how long will it take you to polish the whole thing? Justify your reasoning.

Reflect

Why do you need only the length of one edge to solve the problem?

Close and Check

Focus Question

How can you apply what you know about finding the surface area of a right rectangular prism to finding the surface area of any right prism?

Do you know **HOW?**

Find the surface area of each figure below.

1.

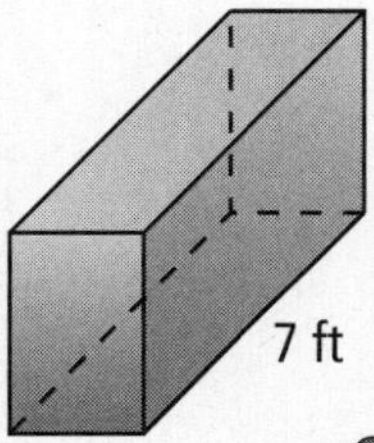

2.

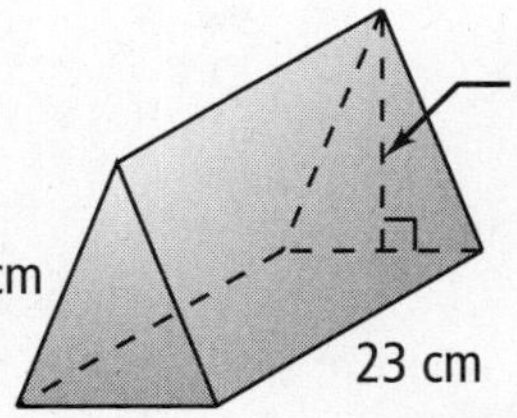

3.

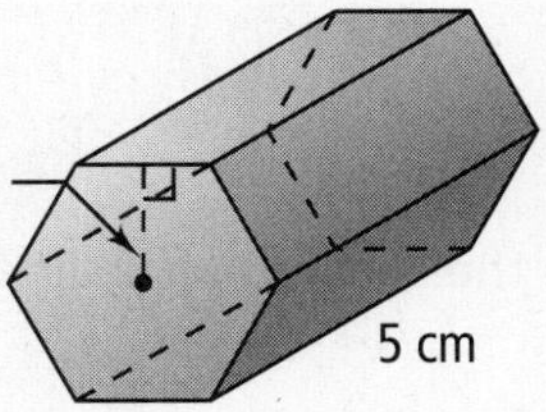

Do you **UNDERSTAND?**

4. Error Analysis Explain the mistake made below. What is the correct surface area?

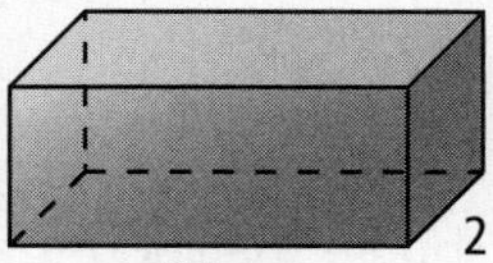

$S.A. = (2 + 2 + 2 + 2)(5) + 4$

$S.A. = (8)(5) + 4$

$S.A. = 40 + 4$

$S.A. = 44 \text{ in.}^2$

5. Writing If you turned the rectangular prism from Exercise 1, would the surface area change? Explain.

22-2 Volumes of Right Prisms

Common Core State Standards: 7.G.6 Solve real-world and mathematical problems involving area, volume and surface area of two- and three-dimensional objects composed of triangles, quadrilaterals, polygons, cubes, and right prisms.

Launch

In Germany, Ms. Adventure packs cube-shaped candles in a box to send home. She plans to wrap the box in brown paper for shipping.

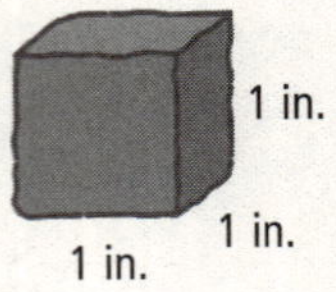

How many candles can she stack in each shipping box?

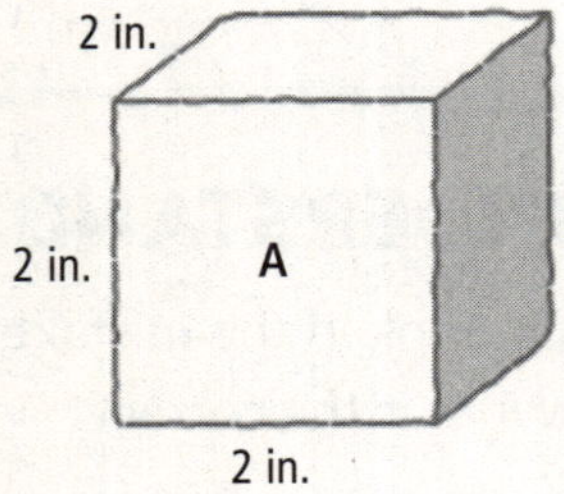

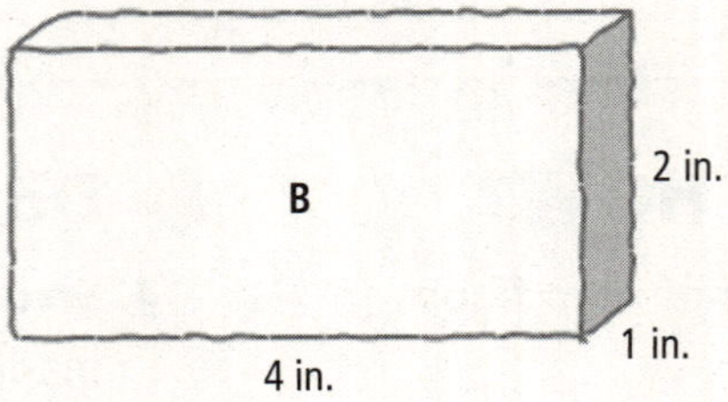

☐ candles ☐ candles

Which box should she choose? Explain your reasoning.

Reflect

Do boxes with the same amount of space inside always have the same surface area? Why is this important?

Close and Check

Focus Question

How can you apply what you know about finding the volume of a right rectangular prism to finding the volume of any right prism?

Do you know HOW?

Find the volume of each figure below.

1.

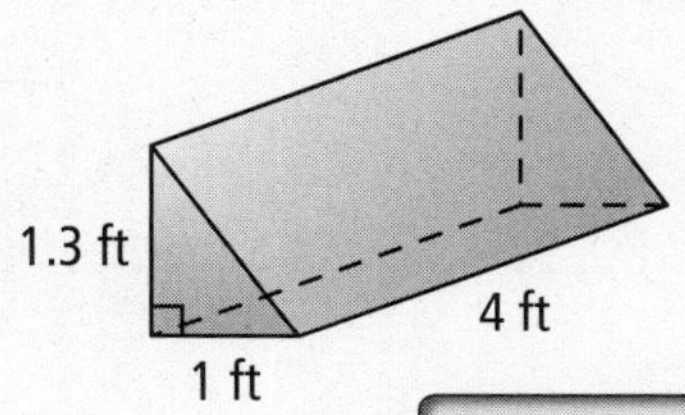

2.

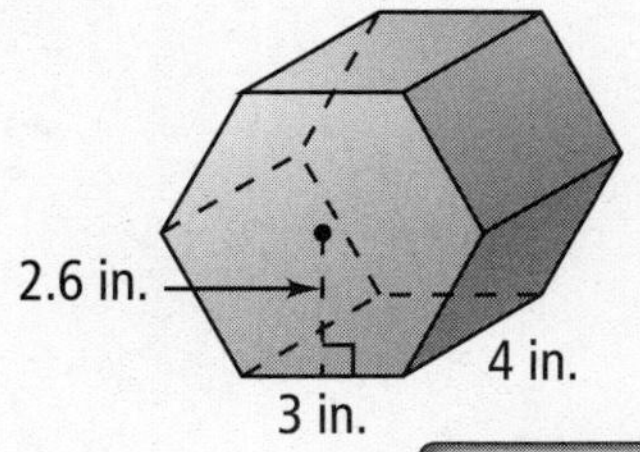

3. A shipping company packs ornaments in cubes that have an edge length of 4 inches. How many cubes can fit in a rectangular box that is 12 inches tall, 16 inches wide, and 20 inches long?

cubes

Do you UNDERSTAND?

4. Compare and Contrast Compare the volume of the triangular prism in Exercise 1 with the volume of the rectangular prism below.

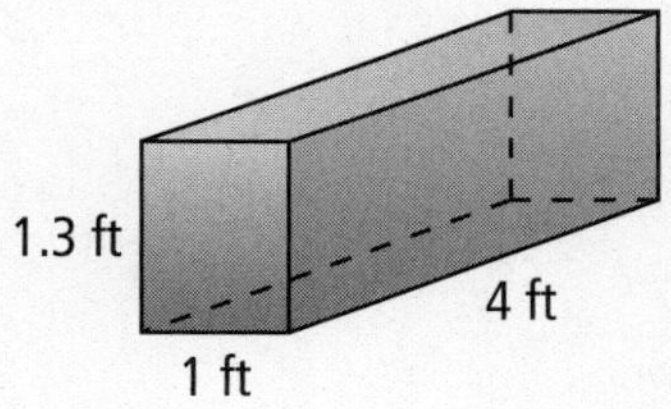

5. Writing Why can the formula for the volume of a rectangular prism be written as $V = Bh$ or $V = lwh$?

22-3 Surface Areas of Right Pyramids

Common Core State Standards: 7.G.6 Solve real-world and mathematical problems involving area, volume and surface area of two- and three-dimensional objects composed of triangles, quadrilaterals, polygons, cubes, and right prisms.

Launch

Ms. Adventure plans a cardboard model of the Red Pyramid she saw in Dashur, Egypt. She only has one piece of colored construction paper to cover her pyramid.

Does she have enough construction paper? Explain your reasoning.

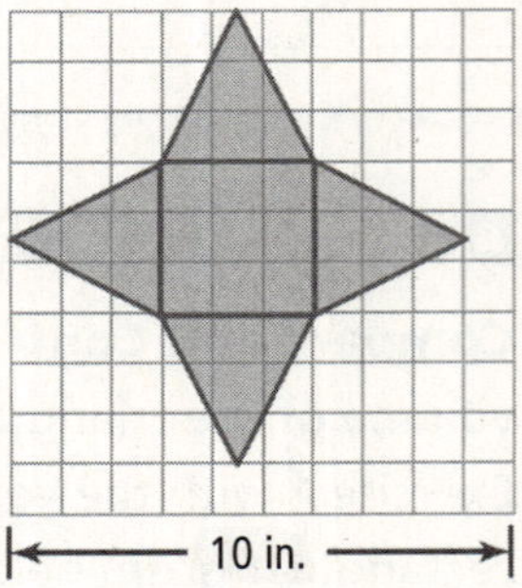

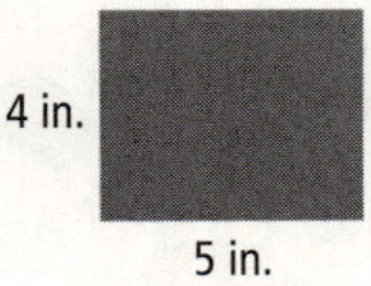

Reflect

Suppose you want to buy more than one piece of paper to cover an object. How would knowing the object's surface area help you decide how much paper to buy?

Close and Check

Focus Question

How can you apply what you know about finding the surface area of one right square pyramid to finding the surface area of any right pyramid?

Do you know HOW?

1. Circle the pyramid that has a surface area of 52 in.^{2}.

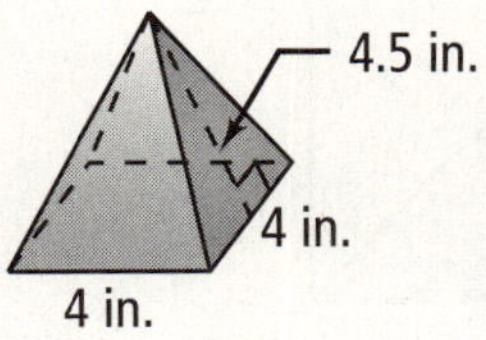

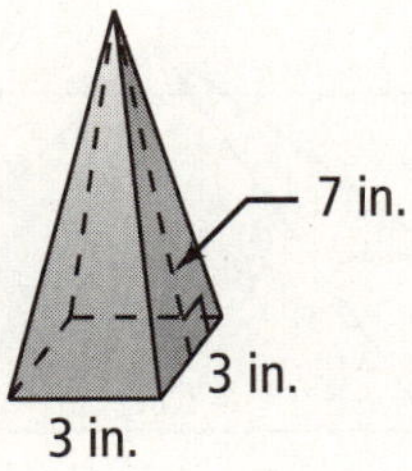

2. A paperweight is in the shape of a pyramid with an equilateral triangle for a base. Find the surface area of the paperweight.

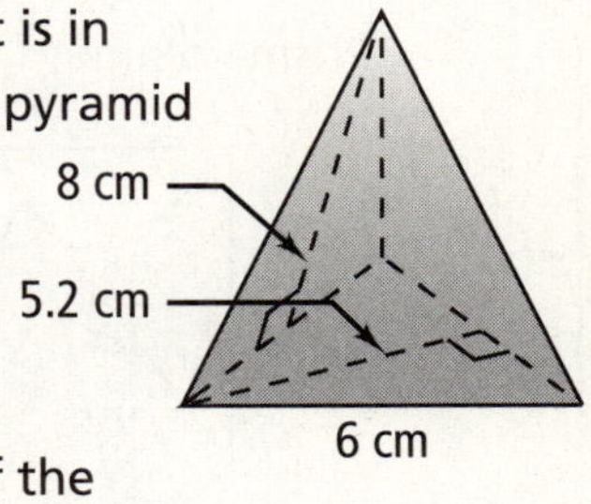

Do you UNDERSTAND?

3. Reasoning Is it possible to make a model of the pyramid below by using an 11-inch by 17-inch sheet of paper? Explain.

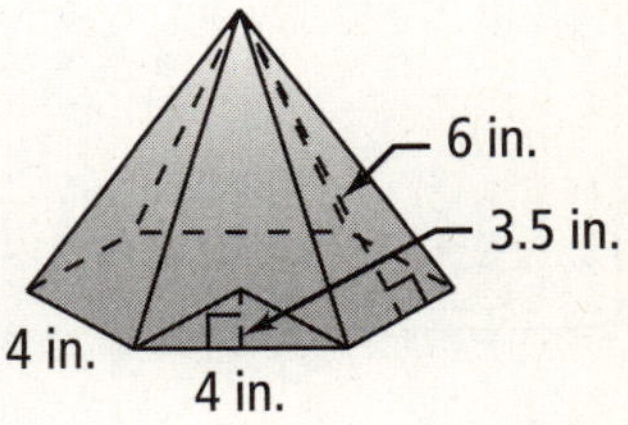

4. Error Analysis What mistake was made in the calculation? What is the correct surface area?

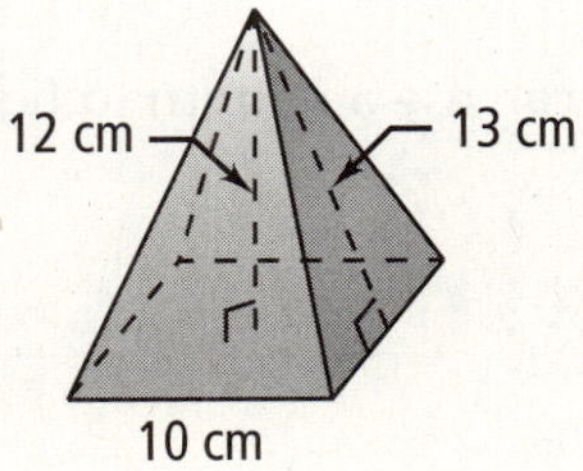

$S.A. = \frac{1}{2}(4 \times 10)(12) + (10)^2$

$S.A. = \frac{1}{2}(40)(12) + 100$

$S.A. = 240 + 100 = 340 \text{ cm}^2$

22-4 Volumes of Right Pyramids

Common Core State Standards: 7.G.6 Solve real-world and mathematical problems involving area, volume and surface area of two- and three-dimensional objects composed of triangles, quadrilaterals, polygons, cubes, and right prisms.

Launch

Look for a pattern in the volumes of the prism and pyramid pairs. Then find the volume of the fourth pyramid. Explain your reasoning.

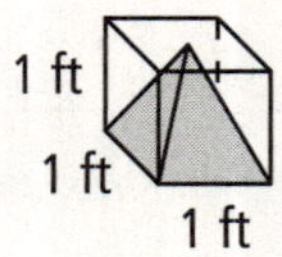

Pyramid volume: $\frac{1}{3}$ ft^3

Prism volume:

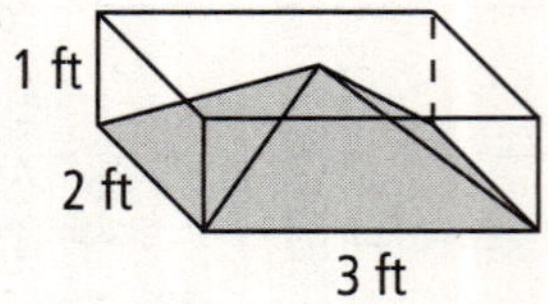

Pyramid volume: 2 ft^3

Prism volume:

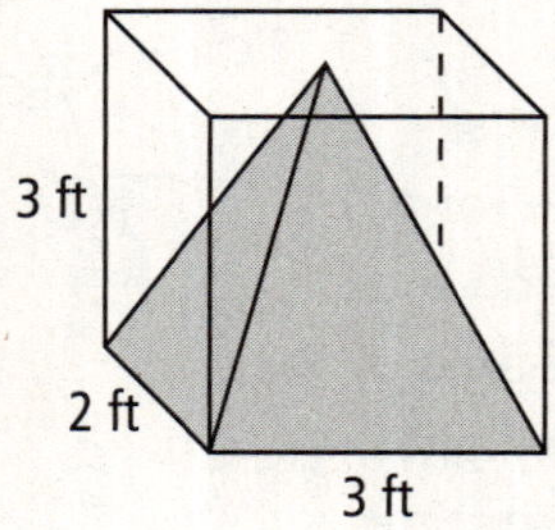

Pyramid volume: 6 ft^3

Prism volume:

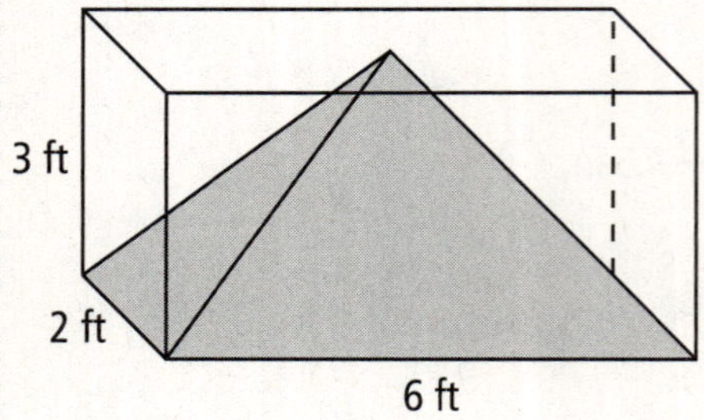

Pyramid volume:

Prism volume:

Reflect

Describe another situation where you can use a pattern to figure out something you don't know.

Close and Check

Focus Question

How can you apply what you know about finding the volume of one right square pyramid to finding the volume of any right pyramid?

Do you know HOW?

1. Circle the pyramid that has the greater volume.

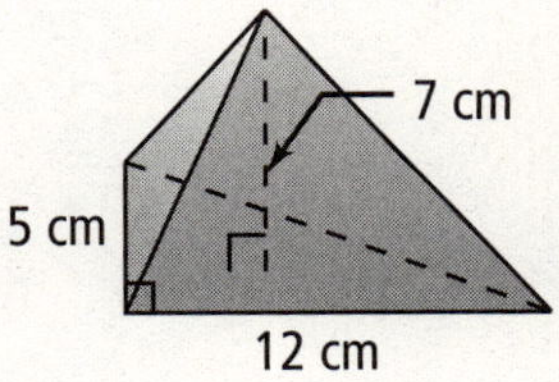

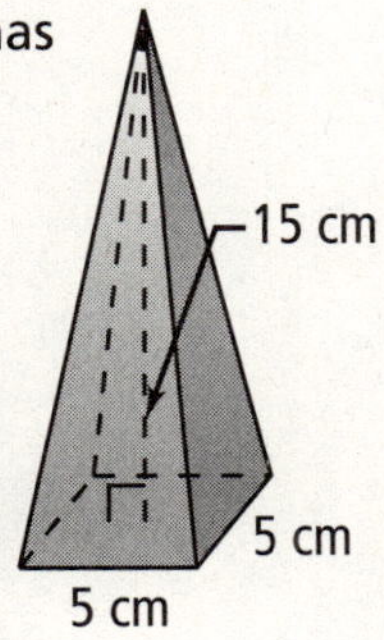

2. What is the volume of the pyramid below?

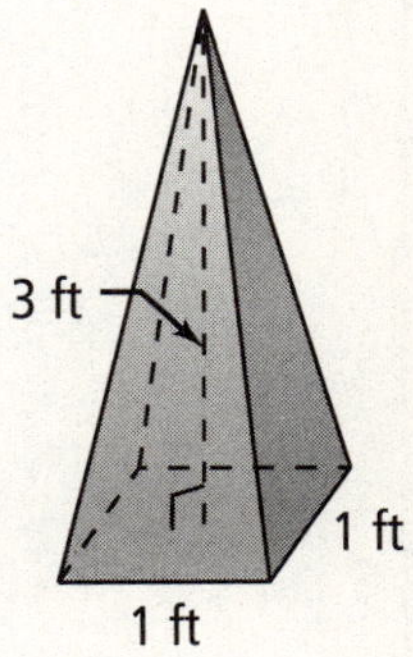

Do you UNDERSTAND?

3. **Compare and Contrast** What measures of a square pyramid do you need to calculate its surface area and volume?

4. **Error Analysis** Describe the mistake made when calculating the volume of the pyramid below. What is the correct volume?

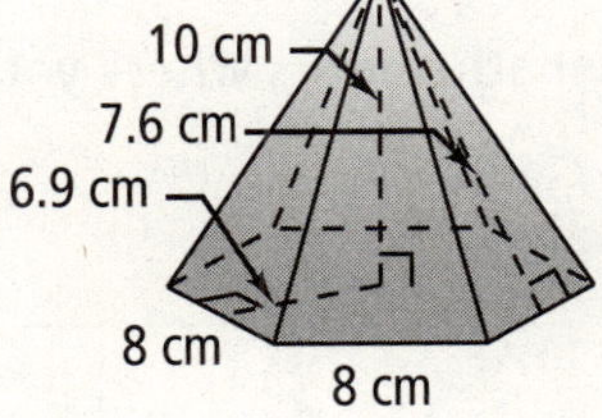

$V = \frac{1}{3}(165.6 \cdot 7.6)$

$V = \frac{1}{3}(1258.6)$

$V = 419.5 \text{ cm}^3$

22-5 Problem Solving

Common Core State Standards: 7.G.6 Solve real-world and mathematical problems involving area, volume and surface area of two- and three-dimensional objects composed of triangles, quadrilaterals, polygons, cubes, and right prisms.

Launch

On her trip to Morocco, Ms. Adventure finds a tea light lantern with the glass broken. How much glass will she need to fix the lantern? Explain your reasoning.

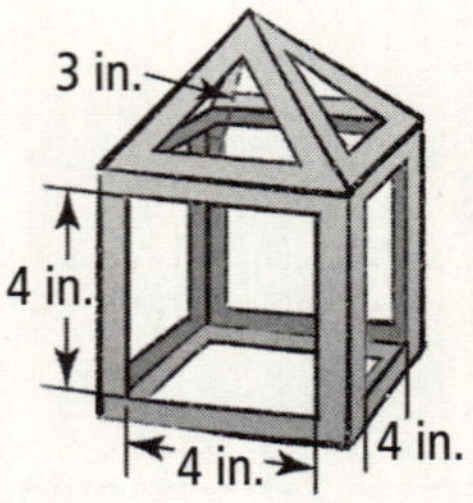

Reflect

Describe another situation in mathematics where you can break apart a problem into simpler parts to solve.

Close and Check

Focus Question

When do you use surface area to measure a three-dimensional figure? When do you use volume?

Do you know HOW?

1. A packaging company makes a rectangular box that is 9 inches long, 5 inches wide, and 5 inches tall. How many whole boxes can be made from a sheet of cardboard that is 20 inches by 33 inches?

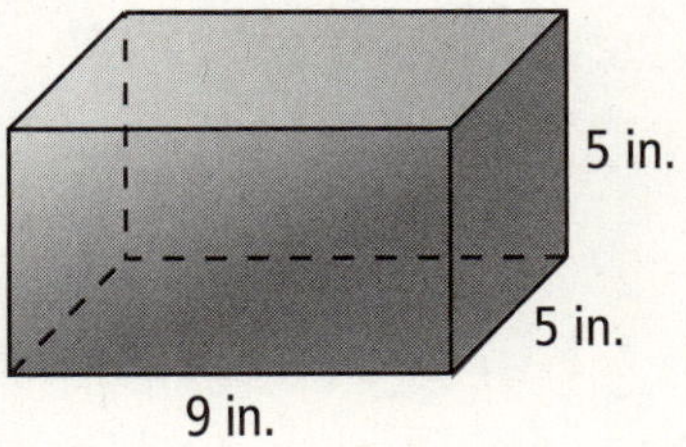

☐ boxes

2. A company is redesigning a box to hold pencil erasers. The volume of the box must be 24 cubic inches. What are the dimensions of the box that uses the least amount of material?

length = ☐

width = ☐

height = ☐

Do you UNDERSTAND?

3. **Reasoning** You want to find out how much wrapping you need to wrap a gift for your friend. Do you need to calculate the surface area or the volume of the gift? Explain.

4. **Writing** Describe how the volume and surface area change when all of the dimensions (length, width, and height) of a rectangular prism are doubled.

23-1 Translations

Common Core Standards: 8.G.1: Verify … properties of … translations: 8.G.1.a: Lines are taken to lines … segments to … segments … . 8.G.1.b: Angles … to angles … . 8.G.1.c: Parallel lines … to parallel lines. 8.G.3: Describe the effect of dilations … and reflections … using coordinates.

Launch

Your friend begins building a figure out of shapes. He traces a trapezoid, slides it, traces one side, and then strangely stops.

Complete the tracing of the trapezoid to show your friend's slide. Explain why your tracing shows the slide.

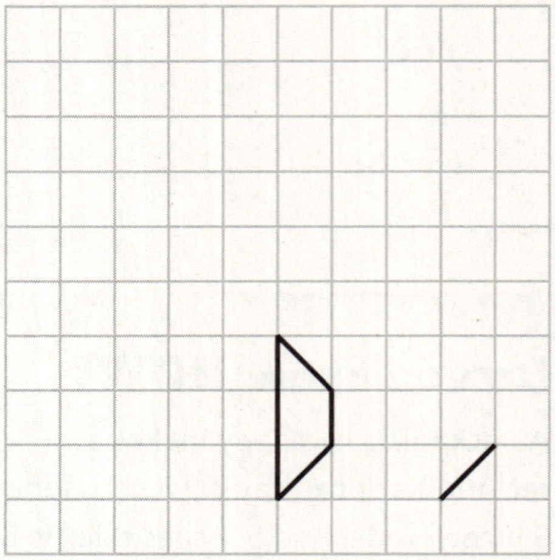

How my friend slid the trapezoid:

How my tracing shows the slide:

Reflect

Were there parallel line segments in the trapezoid before the slide? What about after the slide? Tell how you know.

Close and Check

Focus Question

What effect does a slide have on a figure?

Do you know HOW?

1. The vertices of $\triangle XYZ$ are $X(-4, 1)$, $Y(2, 2)$, and $Z(-1, -1)$. If you translate $\triangle XYZ$ 3 units left and 1 unit down, what are the coordinates of Y'?

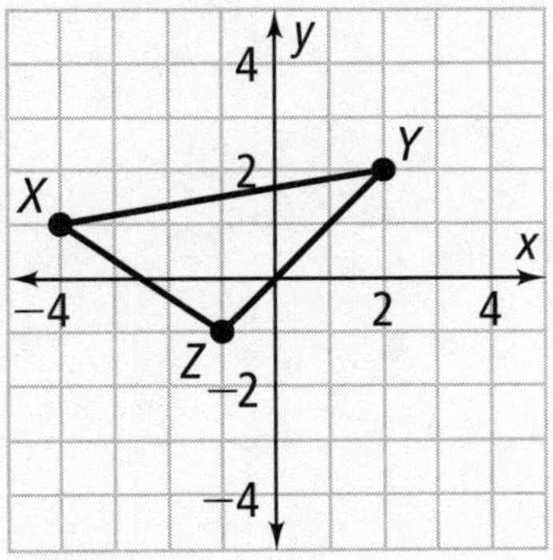

2. Use arrow notation to write a rule that describes the translation shown.

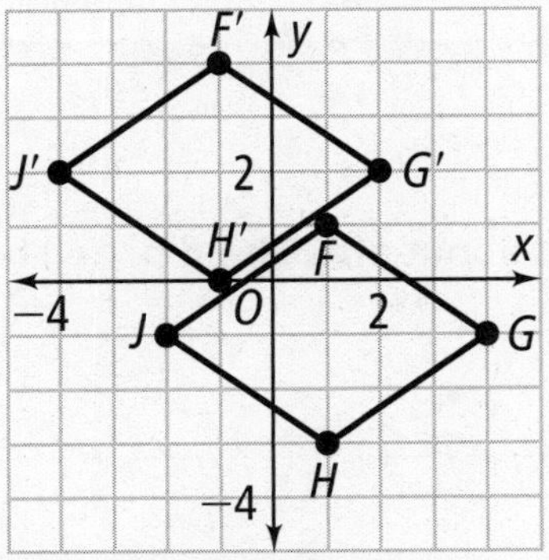

Do you UNDERSTAND?

3. Reasoning How do you know whether to add or subtract units from *x* and *y* when using arrow notation to describe a translation?

4. Error Analysis Explain the error in the translation below.

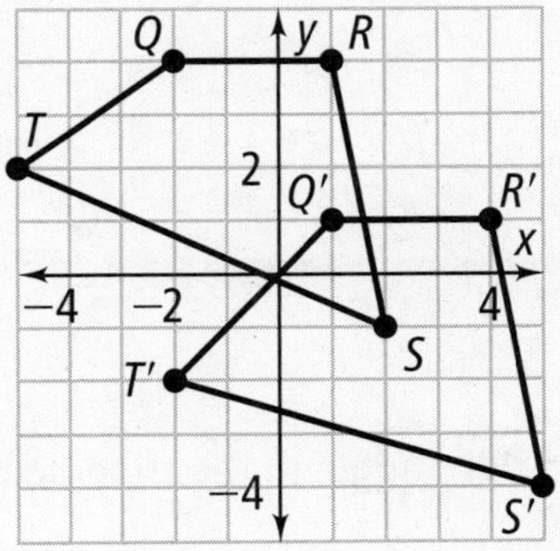

23-2 Reflections

Common Core Standards: 8.G.1: Verify … properties of … reflections … : **8.G.1.a:** Lines are taken to lines … segments to … segments … . **8.G.1.b:** Angles … to angles … . **8.G.1.c:** Parallel lines … to parallel lines. **8.G.3:** Describe the effect of dilations … and reflections … using coordinates.

Launch

Your friend continues the figure. He traces a triangle, flips it over his pencil, traces one side, and then suddenly ceases.

Complete the triangle tracing to show your friend's flip. Explain why your tracing shows the flip.

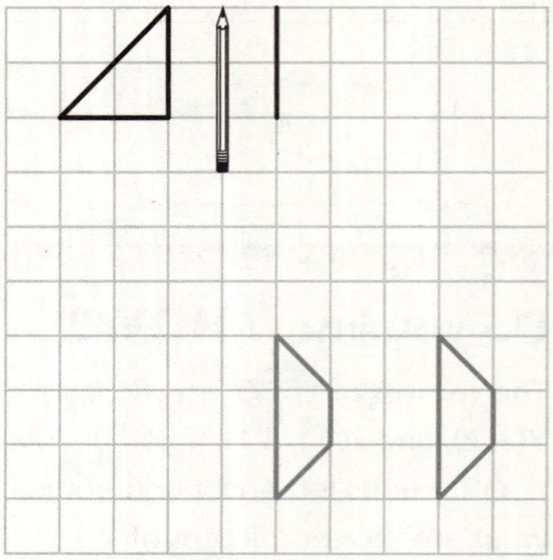

How my friend flipped the triangle:

How my tracing shows the flip:

Reflect

Is there a right angle in the triangle before the flip? What about after the flip? Tell how you know.

Close and Check

Focus Question

What effect does a flip have on a figure?

Do you know HOW?

1. The vertices of quadrilateral *QRST* are *Q*(−1, 3), *R*(2, 2), *S*(3, −2), *T*(1, −2). Graph quadrilateral *QRST* and quadrilateral *Q′R′S′T′*, its image after a reflection across the *x*-axis.

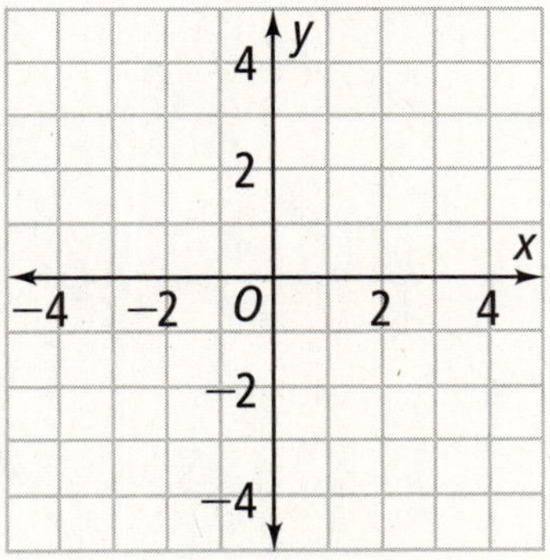

2. Use arrow notation to show how *QRST* maps to *Q′R′S′T′* from Exercise 1.

Q( ) → *Q′*( )

R( ) → *R′*( )

S( ) → *S′*( )

T( ) → *T′*( )

Do you UNDERSTAND?

3. Compare and Contrast How are translations and reflections the same and different?

4. Error Analysis A classmate says that the reflection across the *x*-axis of △*PQR* is △*P′Q′R′* where *P′*(−2, 1), *Q′*(−5, −2), and *R′*(2, −4). What error did he make? What should the vertices be?

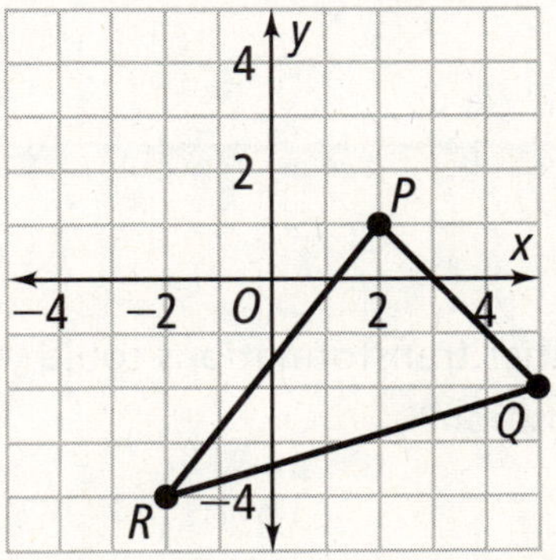

23-3 Rotations

Common Core Standards: 8.G.1: Verify … properties of rotations … : **8.G.1.a:** Lines are taken to lines … segments to … segments … . **8.G.1.b:** Angles … to angles … . **8.G.1.c:** Parallel lines … to parallel lines. **8.G.3:** Describe the effect of dilations … and reflections … using coordinates.

Launch

Your friend nearly completes his figure. He traces a square, turns it, traces one side, and then curiously quits.

Complete the turn and tracing of the square. Explain why your tracing shows your friend's turn.

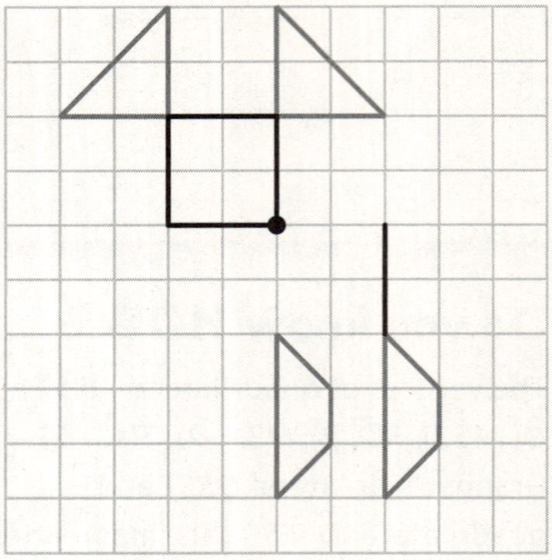

How my friend turned the square:

How my tracing shows the turn:

Reflect

What other transformations could your friend have used to move the square to the same position?

Close and Check

Focus Question

What effect does a turn have on a figure?

Do you know HOW?

1. Use arrow notation to show how $\triangle JKL$ maps to its image after a rotation 180° about the origin.

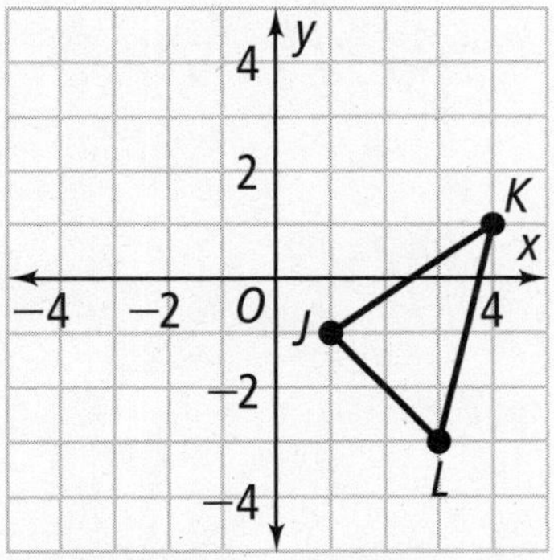

$J($ ______ $) \rightarrow J'($ ______ $)$

$K($ ______ $) \rightarrow K'($ ______ $)$

$L($ ______ $) \rightarrow L'($ ______ $)$

2. The vertices of parallelogram *WXYZ* are $W(-1, 1)$, $X(3, 2)$, $Y(3, -1)$, $Z(-1, -2)$. The vertices of its image, parallelogram $W'X'Y'Z'$, are $W'(-1, 1)$, $X'(3, 2)$, $Y'(3, -1)$, $Z'(-1, -2)$. What is the angle of rotation?

Do you UNDERSTAND?

3. Compare and Contrast How are reflections and rotations the same and different?

4. Reasoning Would the relationship between the vertices of any figure rotated 360° and its image always be true regardless of the point of rotation? Explain.

23-4 Congruent Figures

Common Core Standards: 8.G.2: Understand that a two-dimensional figure is congruent to another if the second can be obtained from the first by a sequence of rotations, reflections, and translations; given two congruent figures, describe a sequence that exhibits the congruence … .

Launch

Your neighbor drew three kites on the grid. She said they were all exactly the same. Do you agree? Explain how you know.

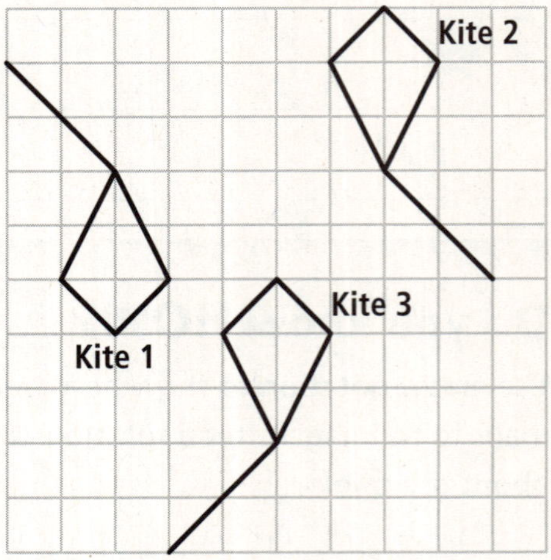

Reflect

How can two shapes be exactly the same but look different?

Close and Check

Focus Question

In what ways can you show that figures are identical?

Do you know HOW?

1. Use arrow notation to show how $\triangle ABC$ maps to its image after a reflection across the x-axis followed by a reflection across the y-axis.

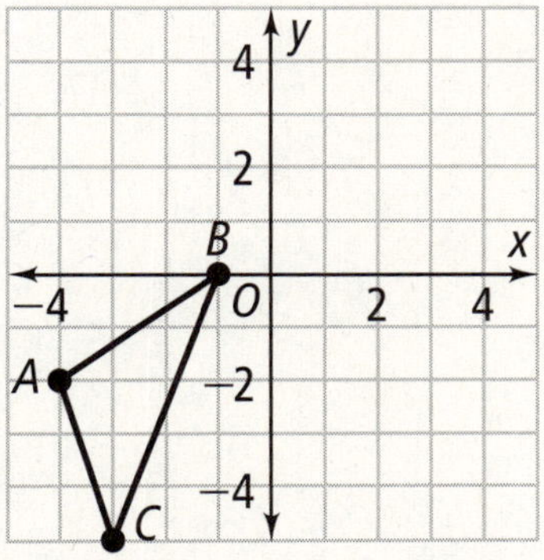

$A($ $) \rightarrow A'($ $)$

$B($ $) \rightarrow B'($ $)$

$C($ $) \rightarrow C'($ $)$

2. What are the vertices of $\triangle DEF$, the image of $\triangle ABC$ above, after a reflection across the y-axis followed by a 180° rotation clockwise around the origin?

$D($ $)$ $E($ $)$ $F($ $)$

Do you UNDERSTAND?

3. Reasoning Assume $\triangle ABC$ in Problem 1 is rotated 180° about point B. What other transformation(s) could you use to map $\triangle ABC$ to $\triangle A'B'C'$?

4. Writing Describe a sequence of rigid motions that maps $PQRST$ to $P'Q'R'S'T'$.

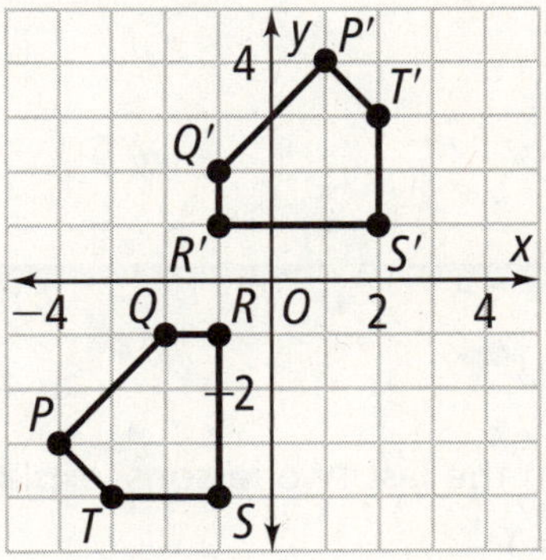

23-5 Problem Solving

Common Core Standards: 8.G.2: Understand that a two-dimensional figure is congruent to another if the second can be obtained from the first by a sequence of rotations, reflections, and translations; given two congruent figures, describe a sequence that exhibits the congruence … .

Launch

Draw and label three congruent figures. Each figure must be composed of more than one shape. Describe the moves needed to verify that the figures are congruent.

Reflect

Besides in the last two lessons, explain how you have used or could use congruence in your life.

Close and Check

Focus Question

How can you use what you know about transformations and congruence to solve problems?

Do you know HOW?

1. Given figure $ABCDEF \cong LMNPQR$, circle the sequence of rigid motions that maps $ABCDEF$ to $LMNPQR$.

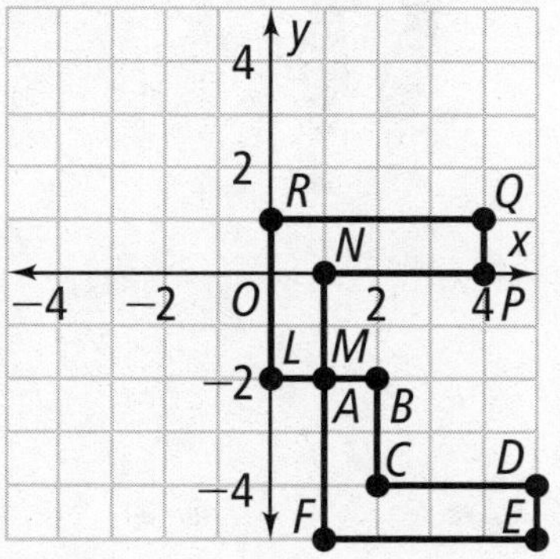

A. Reflection across x-axis, rotation 90° clockwise about point B', translation 1 unit right

B. Rotation 180° counterclockwise about point A', reflection across y-axis, translation 2 units left

C. Reflection across y-axis, rotation 180° clockwise about point A', translation 1 unit right

D. Rotation 90° counterclockwise about point C', translation 2 units left, reflection across $y = 1$

Do you UNDERSTAND?

2. Reasoning Given $\triangle PQR \cong \triangle STU$, explain how to find a possible coordinate for point T.

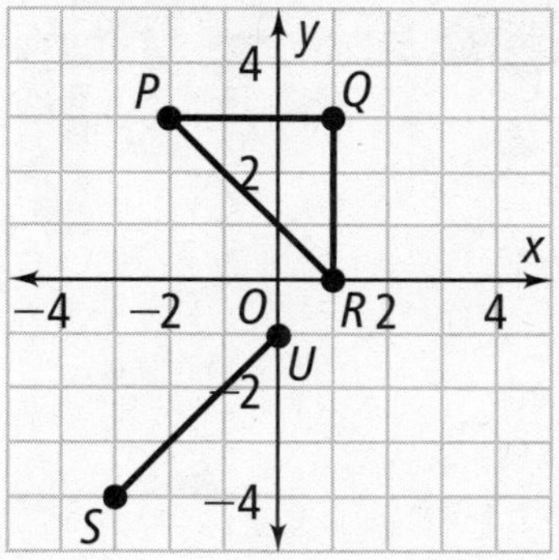

3. Writing Explain why there are two possible coordinates for point T.

24-1 Dilations

Common Core State Standards: 8.G.3: Describe the effect of dilations, translations, rotations, and reflections on two-dimensional figures using coordinates.

Launch

A modern art painter used an inch-grid canvas for a figure painting.

Did the artist paint the figure to scale? Explain.

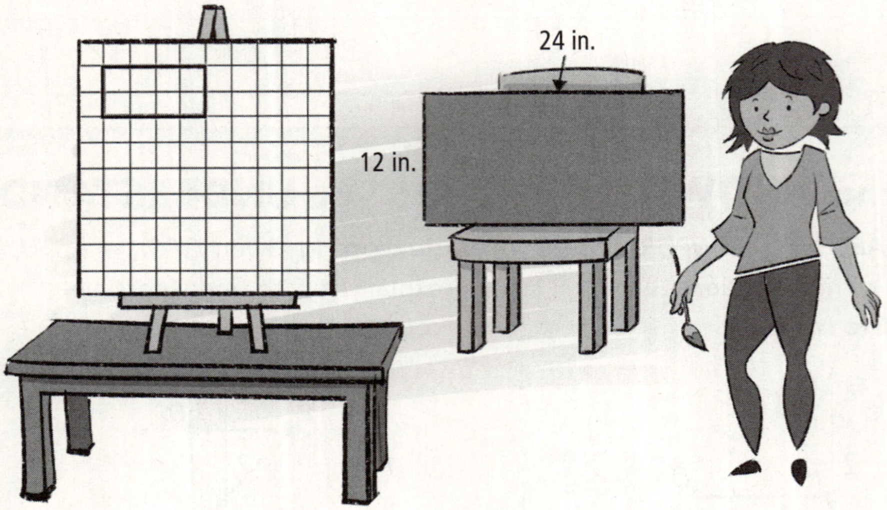

Reflect

Why did the artist have to scale the painting?

Close and Check

Focus Question

What effect does an enlargement have on a figure? What effect does a reduction have on a figure?

Do you know HOW?

1. Find the scale factor for the given dilation and tell whether the image is an enlargement or a reduction.

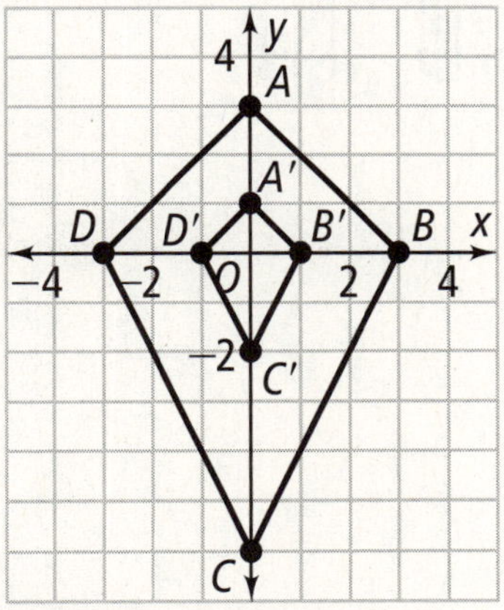

2. Parallelogram *QRST* has vertices at *Q*(−3, 1), *R*(2, 1), *S*(0, −2), and *T*(−5, −2). Find the coordinate of *Q′* after a dilation with the center at the origin and scale factor 5.

Do you UNDERSTAND?

3. Writing $\triangle XYZ$ has vertex *Y*(0, 0). The center of the dilation is at the origin. Describe the location of *Y′* after a dilation with scale factor $\frac{1}{5}$. Explain.

4. Error Analysis A classmate creates dilation *A″B″C″D″* for Exercise 1 with the origin at the center with scale factor 4. She says the coordinates are *A″*(0, 5), *B″*(5, 0), *C″*(0, −6), and *D″*(−5, 0). Explain her error.

24-2 Similar Figures

Common Core State Standards: 8.G.3: Describe the effect of dilations .... **8.G.4:** Understand that a ... figure is similar to another if the second can be obtained from the first by a sequence of ... dilations; given two similar ... figures, describe a sequence that exhibits the similarity between them.

Launch

The artist continues to paint the figure in different sizes on the inch-grid canvas. She stops and says, "One of these shapes clearly doesn't belong. I'd better start over."

Which shape does not belong? Explain your reasoning.

Reflect

Do shapes have to be the same size to belong together? Explain.

Close and Check

Focus Question

How can you show that figures are similar?

Do you know HOW?

1. Given trapezoid *QRST*, draw trapezoid *WXYZ* ~ *QRST* after a 90° clockwise rotation about the origin followed by a dilation with center (0, 0) and scale factor $\frac{1}{2}$.

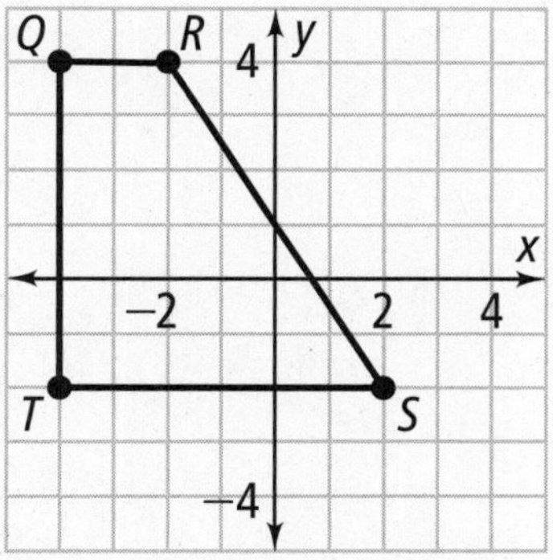

2. What would be the coordinates of *JKLM* ~ *QRST* after a reflection across the *y*-axis and a dilation with the center at the origin and scale factor 2?

J( )

K( )

L( )

M( )

Do you UNDERSTAND?

3. Writing How would the figure in Exercise 1 change if trapezoid *QRST* were translated up 1 unit and right 3 units followed by a dilation with center (0, 0) and scale factor 1? Explain.

4. Compare and Contrast How are a pair of congruent figures and a pair of similar figures alike? How are they different?

24-3 Relating Similar Triangles and Slope

Common Core State Standards: 8.G.3: Describe the effect of dilations .... **8.G.4:** Understand that a ... figure is similar to another .... **8.EE.6:** Use similar triangles to explain why the slope *m* is the same between any two distinct points on a non-vertical line in the coordinate plane ....

Launch

A museum displays the artist's right triangle series. The series features right triangles painted in proportion on each painting. One painting is a fake. Which is it? Explain how you know.

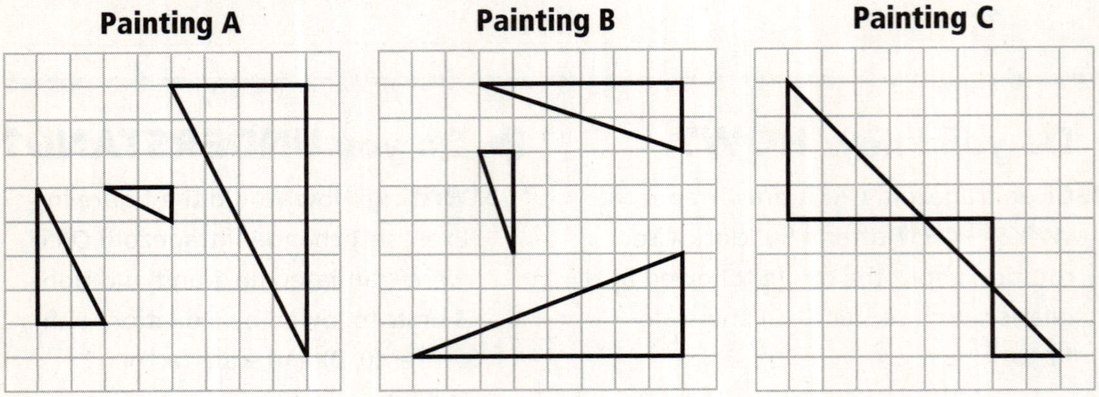

Reflect

For which painting was it easiest to find equivalent ratios? Explain.

Close and Check

Focus Question

How are similar triangles and slope related?

Do you know HOW?

1. Consider the image $\triangle XYZ$ after a dilation with center (0, 0) and scale factor 2. What is the ratio of the rise to the run of the image triangle?

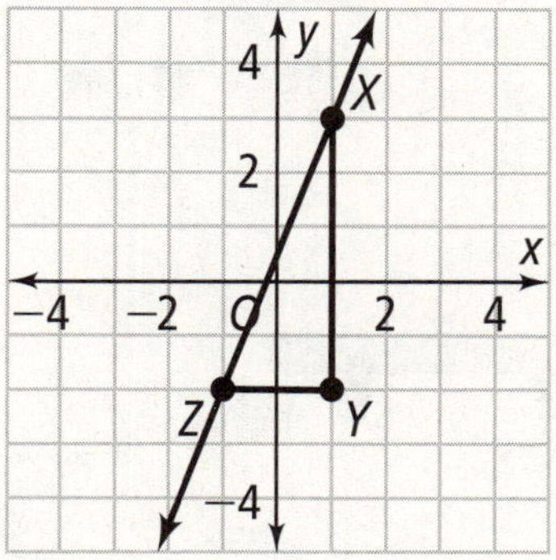

2. What is the slope of the image of $\triangle XYZ$ in Exercise 1 after a 180° rotation about point Y and a dilation with center (0, 0) and scale factor $\frac{1}{3}$?

Do you UNDERSTAND?

3. Writing Explain how you can use slope to check the accuracy of a dilation.

4. Error Analysis Your friend uses the slope triangle below to write the equation of the line: $y = \frac{1}{3}x + 3$. Explain his error and write the correct equation.

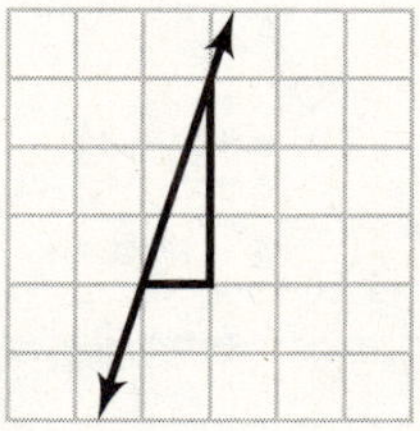

24-4 Problem Solving

Common Core State Standards: 8.G.3: Describe the effect of dilations . . . . **8.G.4:** Understand that a . . . figure is similar to another if the second can be obtained from the first by a sequence of . . . dilations; given two similar . . . figures, describe a sequence that exhibits the similarity between them.

Launch

Use the criteria to draw your own modern art figure painting on the grid. Give your painting a name.

Explain how your work of art meets the criteria.

Criteria

- Three of the figures are similar.
- Has at least one dilation.
- Has at least one translation, rotation, or reflection.

Title of Painting:

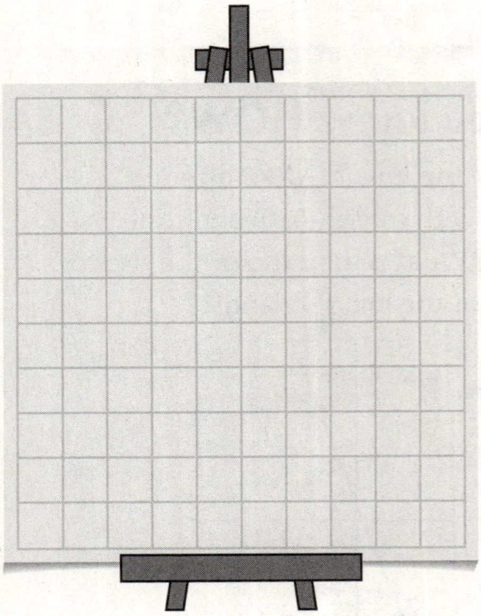

Reflect

How did you choose your painting's name?

Close and Check

Focus Question

How can you use what you know about transformations and similarity to solve problems?

Do you know HOW?

1. Given $\triangle ABC \sim \triangle EFG$, circle the possible coordinate pair(s) for point G after a dilation only.

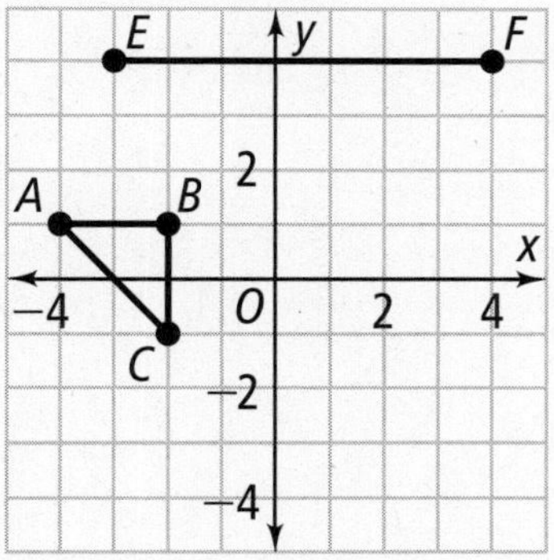

A. (4, −3) B. (−3, −3)

C. (−3, 11) D. (4, 11)

2. A landscaper makes a scale drawing of a triangular flowerbed. The side lengths of the drawing 3 cm, 4 cm, and 5 cm. If the scale is 2 cm = 7 m, what are the dimensions of the actual flowerbed?

3 cm =

4 cm =

5 cm =

Do you UNDERSTAND?

3. Reasoning Explain how scale drawings and indirect measurements are similar. Give an example of how one is used in real life.

4. Error Analysis A friend is 5.5 ft tall and her shadow is 8 ft long. The shadow of a building is 160 ft long. Explain her error in calculating the height of the building. What is the actual height?

$\frac{5.5}{160} = \frac{8}{x}$; $x = 27$ ft

25-1 Angles, Lines, and Transversals

Common Core State Standards: 8.G.5: Use informal arguments to establish facts about the angle sum and exterior angle of triangles, about the angles created when parallel lines are cut by a transversal, and the angle-angle criterion for similarity of triangles … .

Launch

Which angles have equal measures? Justify your reasoning.

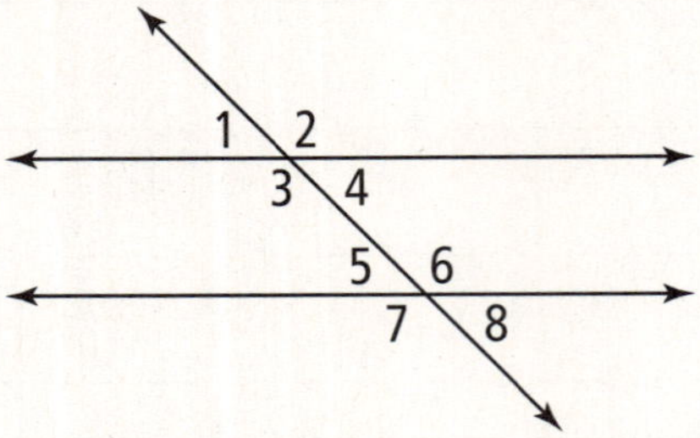

Reflect

Where have you seen angles like these in the real world? Explain.

Close and Check

Focus Question

If a line intersects two parallel lines, what are the relationships between the angles formed by the lines?

Do you know HOW?

Use the diagram to complete Exercises 1–4.

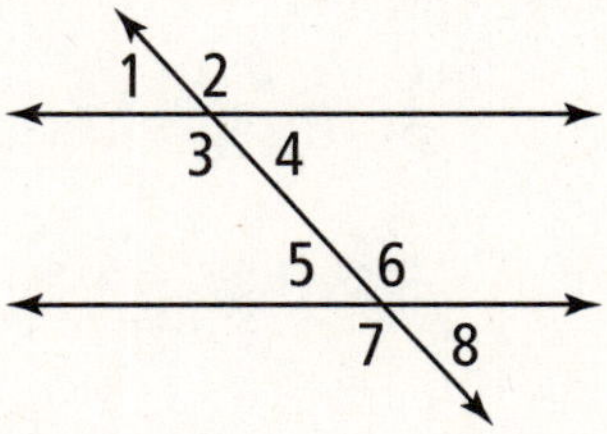

1. Name the pairs of corresponding angles.

2. Name the pairs of alternate interior angles.

3. If $m\angle 4 = 50°$, what is $m\angle 8$?

4. If $m\angle 6 = 130°$, what is $m\angle 3$?

Do you UNDERSTAND?

5. Reasoning How many different angle measures are there in the diagram? Explain.

6. Vocabulary What must be true about two lines cut by a transversal if corresponding angles are congruent and alternate interior angles are congruent? Explain.

25-2 Reasoning and Parallel Lines

Common Core State Standards: 8.G.5: Use informal arguments to establish facts about the angle sum and exterior angle of triangles, about the angles created when parallel lines are cut by a transversal, and the angle-angle criterion for similarity of triangles . . . .

Launch

Decide whether $\overline{AB}$ and $\overline{CD}$ are parallel. Justify your reasoning.

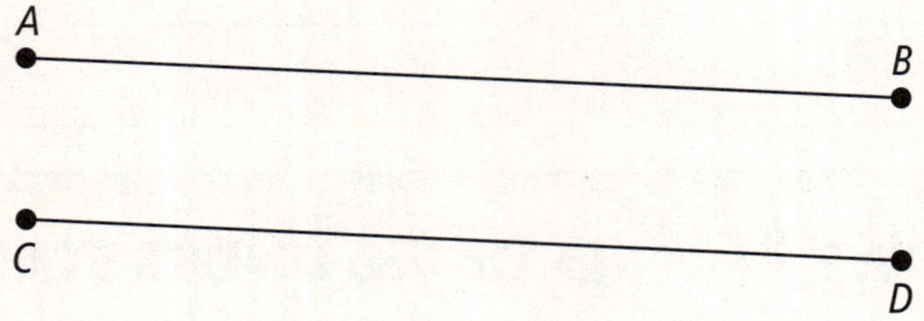

Reflect

What tools or materials did you use to solve the problem? Explain your choice.

Close and Check

Focus Question

How can you use congruent angles to decide whether lines are parallel?

Do you know HOW?

Use the diagram to complete Exercises 1–3.

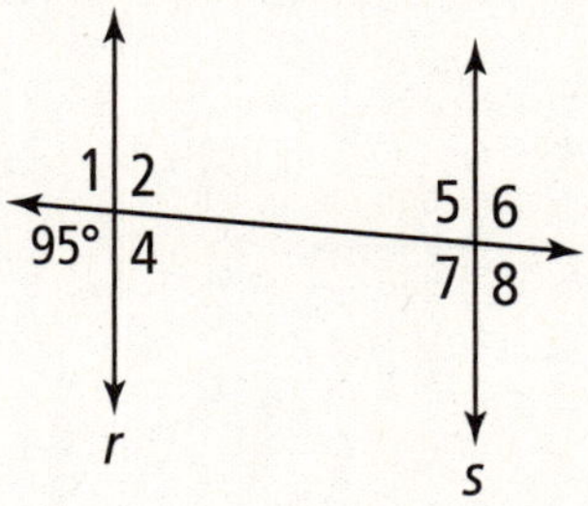

1. For what value of $m\angle 7$ is $r \parallel s$?

2. Write **T** if the statement is true and **F** if the statement is false.

If $m\angle 8 = 95°$, then $r \parallel s$.

If $m\angle 5 = 85°$, then $r \parallel s$.

If $m\angle 6 = 95°$, then $r \parallel s$.

3. If $\angle 7 \cong \angle 2$, then $r \parallel s$ because if ______ angles are congruent, then lines are ______.

Do you UNDERSTAND?

4. Vocabulary Explain how deductive reasoning is used to prove an argument.

5. Reasoning Explain why two lines cannot be assumed to be parallel just because they look parallel.

25-3 Interior Angles of Triangles

Common Core State Standards: 8.G.5: Use informal arguments to establish facts about the angle sum and exterior angle of triangles, about the angles created when parallel lines are cut by a transversal, and the angle-angle criterion for similarity of triangles . . . .

Launch

Which is greater—the measure of a straight angle or the sum of the measures of the angles of a triangle?

Use copies of the triangle to justify your reasoning. You cannot use a protractor.

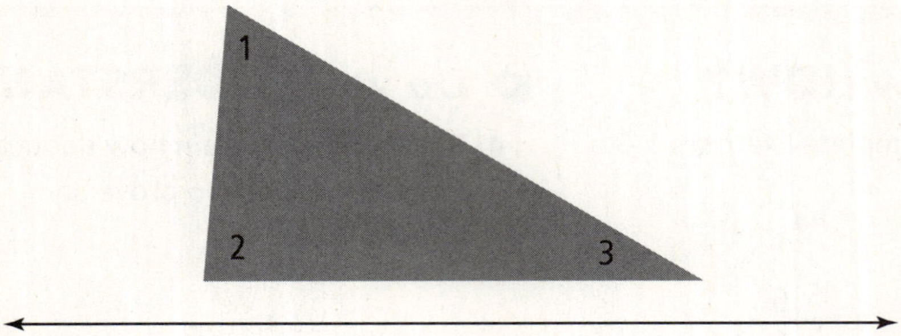

Reflect

Do the angle measures of the triangle you use to compare to the straight angle matter? Explain how you could determine the answer.

Close and Check

Focus Question

How is a straight angle related to the angles of a triangle?

Do you know HOW?

Use the diagram to answer Exercises 1–3.

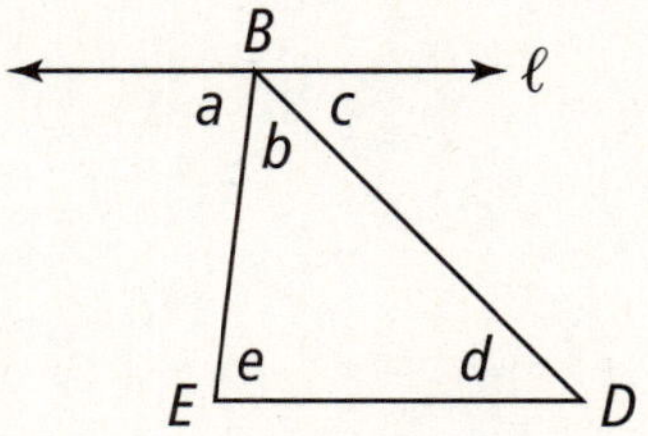

1. Find $m\angle b$, if $m\angle a = 83°$, and $m\angle c = 45°$.

   $m\angle b =$ ▢

2. Find $m\angle d$, given line $\ell \parallel \overline{ED}$, $m\angle a = 83°$, and $m\angle c = 45°$.

   $m\angle d =$ ▢

3. Find $m\angle e$, given line $\ell \parallel \overline{ED}$, $m\angle a = 83°$, and $m\angle c = 45°$.

   $m\angle e =$ ▢

4. What is the value of x when $m\angle b = 10x - 3$, $m\angle d = 5x + 6$, and $m\angle e = 8(x + 2)$?

   $x =$ ▢

Do you UNDERSTAND?

5. **Reasoning** Use deductive reasoning to justify the solution to Exercise 2.

6. **Writing** Make a conjecture about the relationship between the two triangles. Justify your reasoning.

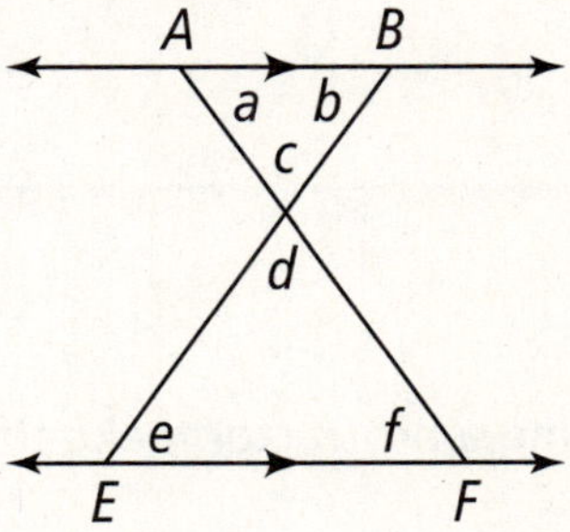

25-4 Exterior Angles of Triangles

Common Core State Standards: 8.G.5: Use informal arguments to establish facts about the angle sum and exterior angle of triangles, about the angles created when parallel lines are cut by a transversal, and the angle-angle criterion for similarity of triangles … .

Launch

State how the sum of the measures of angles 1, 2, and 3 compares to the sum of the measures of angles 4, 5, and 6. You cannot use a protractor. Justify your reasoning.

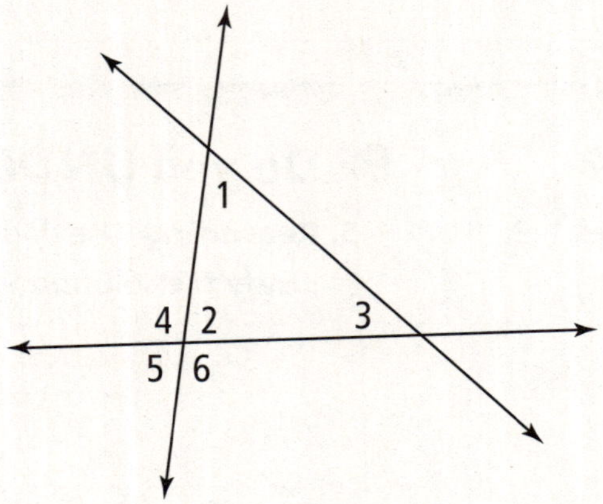

Reflect

Would using a protractor make this problem easier? Explain.

Close and Check

Focus Question

What is the relationship between the exterior and interior angles of a triangle?

Do you know HOW?

Use the diagram to solve Exercises 1–4.

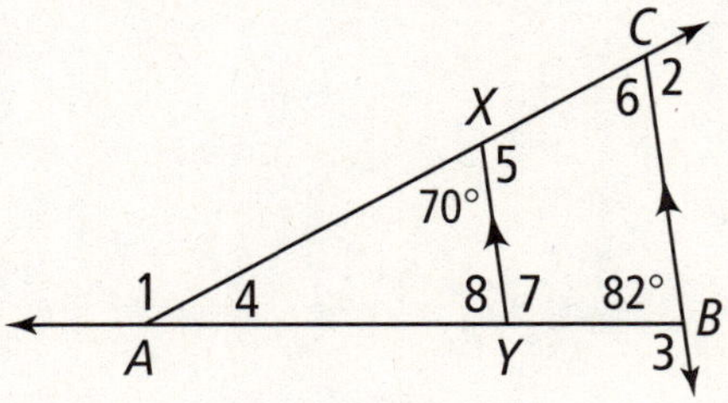

1. Find $m\angle 1$.

2. Find $m\angle 2$.

3. Find $m\angle 3$.

4. Find $m\angle 6$.

5. Given $m\angle 2 = 14x + 9$, and $m\angle 3 = 5x$, what is $m\angle 2$?

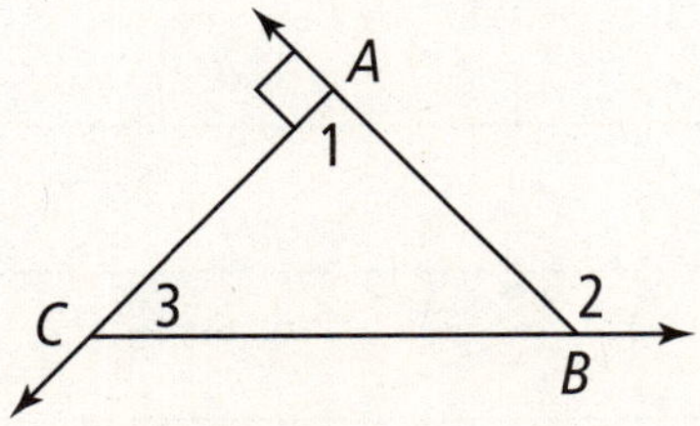

$m\angle 2 =$

Do you UNDERSTAND?

6. Reasoning How does the sum of the exterior angles of a triangle relate to the sum of the interior angles? Explain.

7. Writing Explain how you found the solution to Exercise 5.

25-5 Angle-Angle Triangle Similarity

Common Core State Standards: 8.G.4: Understand that … figure is similar to another if the second can be obtained from the first by … dilations … . **8.G.5:** Use informal arguments to establish facts about … the angle-angle criterion for similarity of triangles … . Also, **8.G.3.**

Launch

Is there a relationship between the triangles? Explain. You can use a protractor, a ruler, and copies of the triangles.

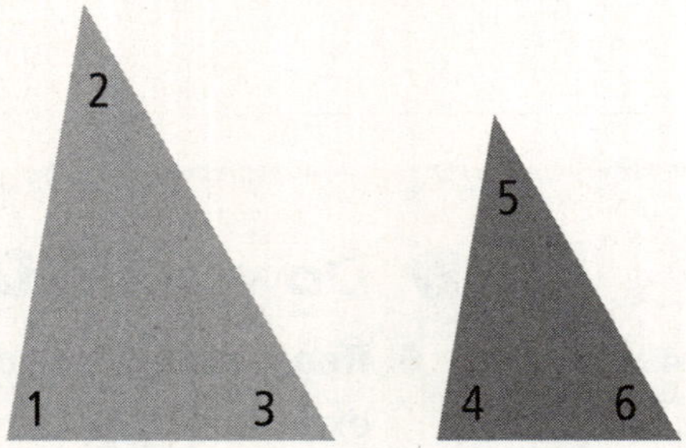

Triangle 1 **Triangle 2**

Reflect

Could you make another triangle related to either triangle? Explain.

Close and Check

Focus Question

How can you use angle relationships to decide whether two triangles are similar?

Do you know HOW?

1. Which pair of triangles are similar?

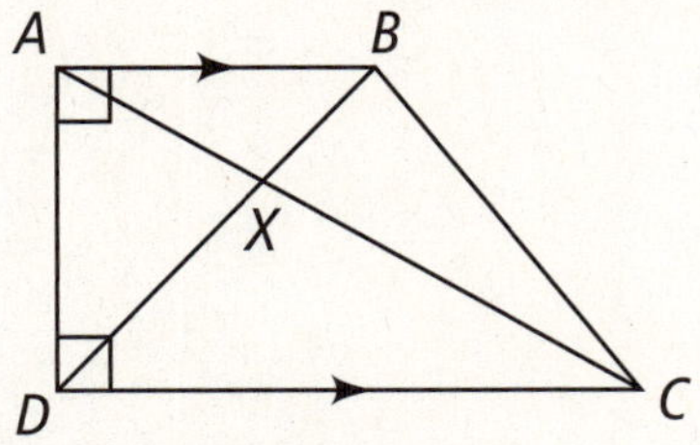

2. Use the diagram. Write **T** if the statement is true and **F** if the statement is false.

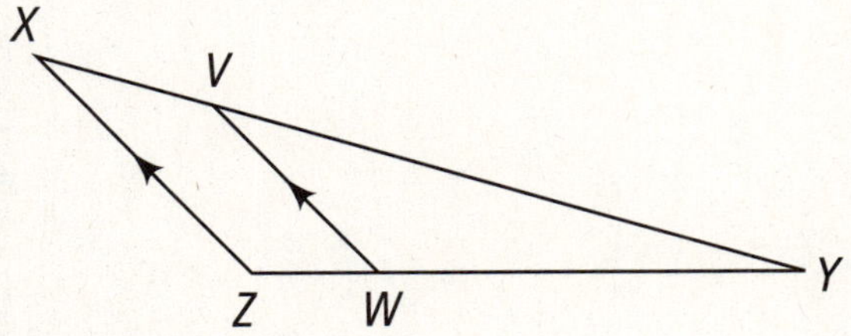

$\triangle VYW \sim \triangle ZYX$

$\triangle ZXY \sim \triangle WVY$

$\triangle VWY \sim \triangle XZY$

Do you UNDERSTAND?

3. Reasoning Given that $BD \parallel AC$, is it possible to conclude that $\triangle ABC \sim \triangle DCB$? Explain.

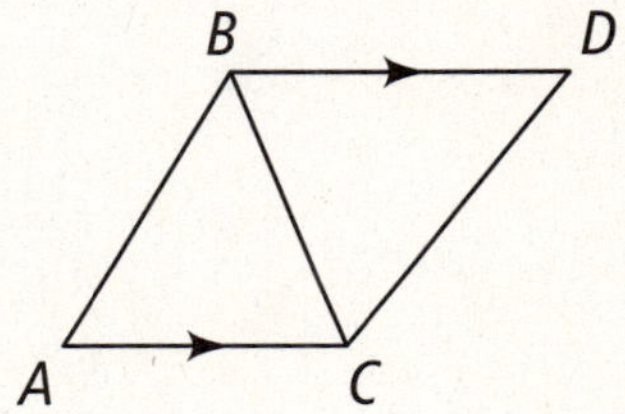

4. Error Analysis Your friend says that if two angles of one triangle are congruent to two angles of another triangle, then the triangles are congruent. Do you agree? Explain.

25-6 Problem Solving

Common Core State Standards: 8.G.5: Use informal arguments to establish facts about the angle sum and exterior angle of triangles, about the angles created when parallel lines are cut by a transversal, and the angle-angle criterion for similarity of triangles … .

Launch

Lines 1 and 2 are parallel horizontal lines. Draw a transversal *p* that passes through point *A* and makes the greatest number of angles with equal angle measure. Justify your reasoning.

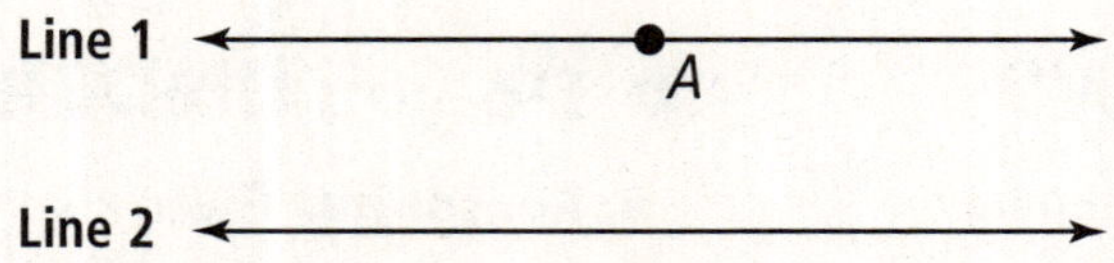

Reflect

How many correct answers does this problem have? Why?

Close and Check

Focus Question

You can use relationships between angles to solve complex problems. How do you decide which relationships to use?

Do you know HOW?

Use the diagram to answer Exercises 1 and 2.

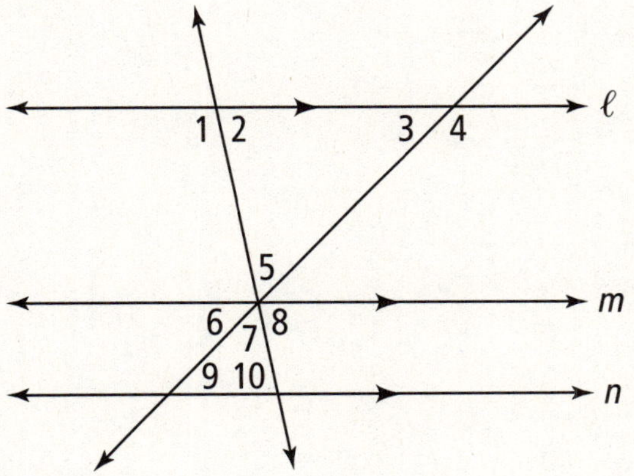

1. Given $\ell \parallel m \parallel n$, and $m\angle 3 = x$, $m\angle 5 = x + 12$, and $m\angle 8 = 2x - 12$, find the angle measures.

$m\angle 2 =$

$m\angle 1 =$

$m\angle 7 =$

$m\angle 4 =$

2. Are the triangles formed by the transversals and parallel lines similar?

Do you UNDERSTAND?

3. Reasoning Is it possible to determine the measures of the remaining unlabeled angles in the diagram? Explain your strategy.

4. Error Analysis A classmate says $\angle 6 \cong \angle 8$. Do you agree? Explain.

26-1 Surface Areas of Cylinders

Common Core State Standards: 8.G.9: Know the formulas for the volumes of cones, cylinders, and spheres and use them to solve real-world and mathematical problems.

Launch

Your friend invents a new pop-up snake can. She says the height is 5 in. and traces the top of the can on an inch grid.

Draw a label that will cover the whole can except for the top and bottom. Estimate its approximate area. Explain your reasoning.

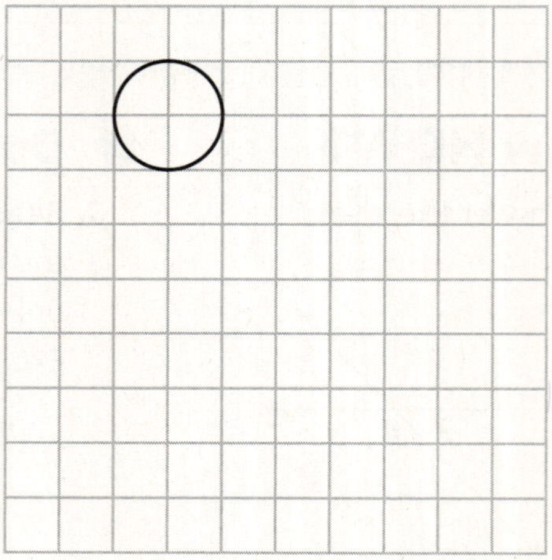

Reflect

What previous mathematical knowledge did you need to solve the problem? Explain.

Close and Check

Focus Question

What types of things can you model with a cylinder? Why might you want to find the surface area of a cylinder?

Do you know HOW?

1. Use the net to find the surface area of the cylindrical can to the nearest tenth. Use 3.14 for π.

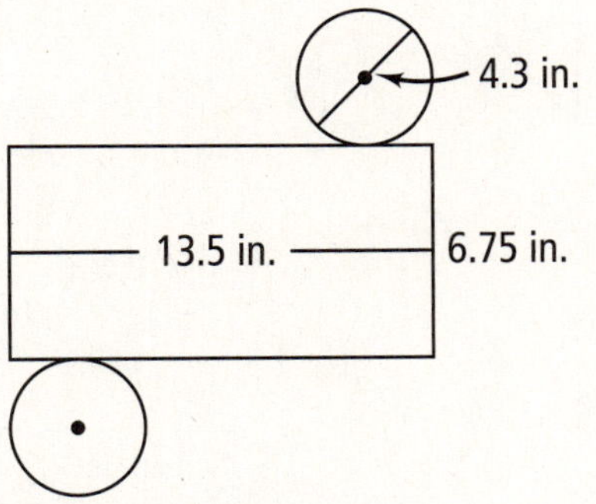

2. Find the surface area of the cylinder to the nearest tenth. Use 3.14 for π.

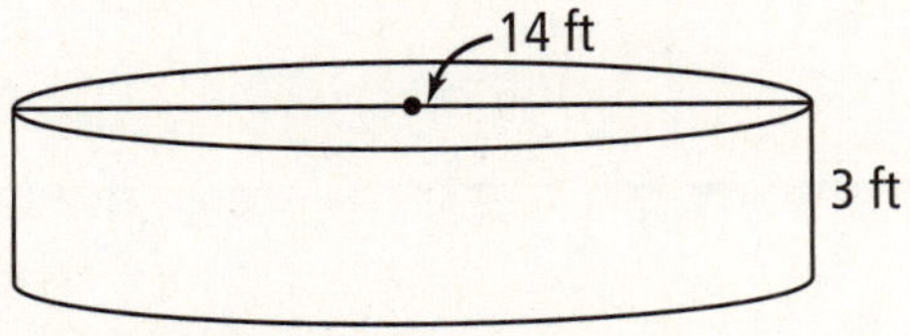

Do you UNDERSTAND?

3. **Writing** Explain how using the calculator key for π rather than 3.14 affects the solution to a surface area problem.

4. **Error Analysis** Your friend decides that the 2 cylinders have the same surface area. Do you agree? Explain.

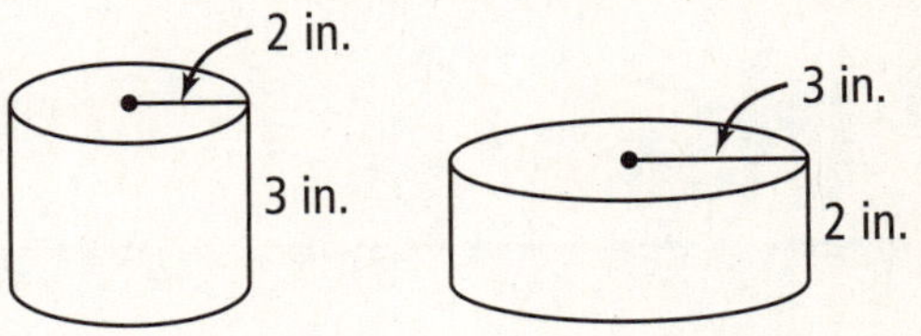

26-2 Volumes of Cylinders

Common Core State Standards: 8.G.9: Know the formulas for the volumes of cones, cylinders, and spheres and use them to solve real-world and mathematical problems.

Launch

Your friend claims that 20 $in.^3$ of stuffed snake will fit in her new can. Her assistant says, "She better use the box."

Will the can work? Why did the assistant say she should use the box? Explain.

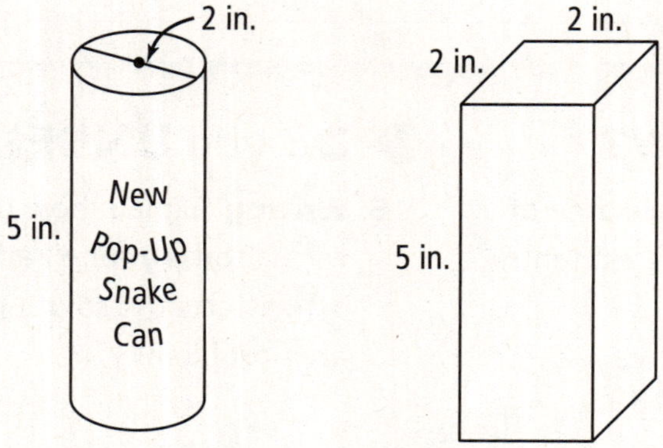

Reflect

How much snake do you think the can would hold? Explain your reasoning.

Close and Check

Focus Question

Why might you want to find the volume of a cylinder?

Do you know HOW?

1. Find the volume. Leave the answer in terms of π.

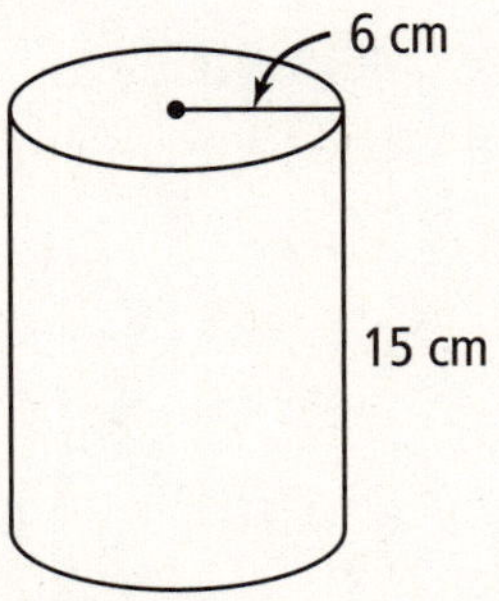

2. The volume of a can of tuna is 562.76 cm^3. Find the radius of the can to the nearest tenth. Use 3.14 for π.

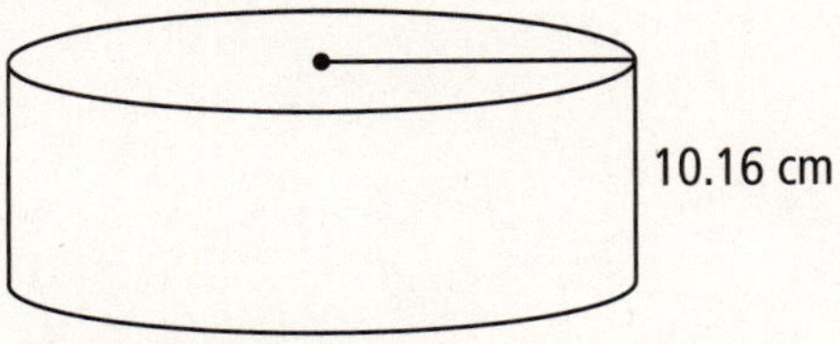

Do you UNDERSTAND?

3. Reasoning A pitcher holds 1,614.7 $in.^3$ of liquid. Each can of punch is 15 in. tall with a diameter of 8 in. How many full cans will the pitcher hold? Explain.

4. Error Analysis A large can of beans has twice the radius and height of a small can of beans. Your friend says that the large can has twice the volume of the small can. Is he correct? Explain.

26-3 Surface Areas of Cones

Common Core State Standards: 8.G.9. Know the formulas for the volumes of cones, cylinders, and spheres and use them to solve real-world and mathematical problems.

Launch

Your friend follows with a plan for a cone-shaped party hat. She says it is 5 in. tall and traces the bottom on the inch grid.

Draw the hat and estimate its surface area. Explain your reasoning.

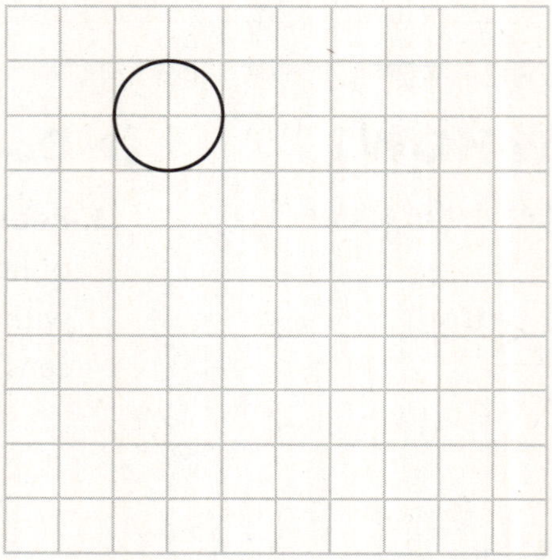

Reflect

Do you think drawing a net of a cone will give you a precise area? Explain.

Close and Check

Focus Question

What types of things can you model with a cone? Why might you want to find the surface area of a cone?

Do you know HOW?

1. Use the net to find the surface area of the cone to the nearest square meter. Use 3.14 for π.

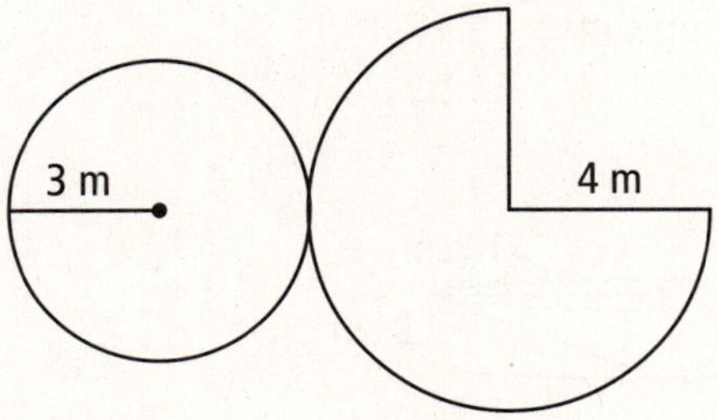

2. Spiced pecans are sold in cone-shaped containers that include a circular lid. Find the surface area of the container to the nearest square inch. Use 3.14 for π.

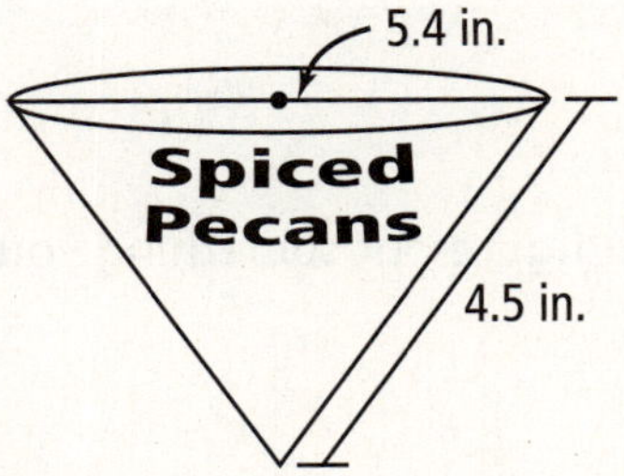

Do you UNDERSTAND?

3. Compare and Contrast Explain the difference between the height of a cone and the slant height of a cone. How do the measures compare?

4. Reasoning Explain the differences between the surface areas of a cylinder and a cone with the same diameter.

26-4 Volumes of Cones

Common Core State Standards: 8.G.9. Know the formulas for the volumes of cones, cylinders, and spheres and use them to solve real-world and mathematical problems.

Launch

Look for a pattern in the volumes of the cylinder and cone pairs in terms of π. Then find the volume of the fourth cone in terms of π. Explain your reasoning.

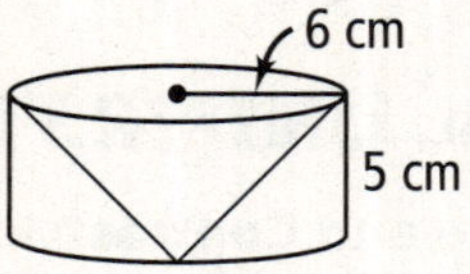

Cone volume: $60\pi cm^3$

Cylinder volume:

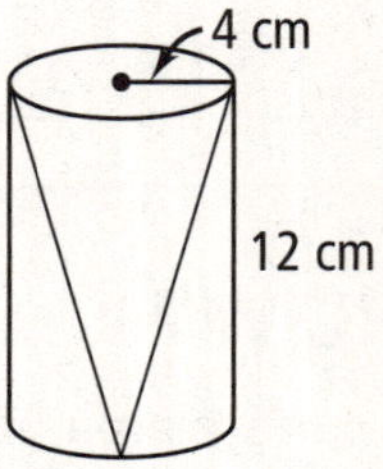

Cone volume: $64\pi cm^3$

Cylinder volume:

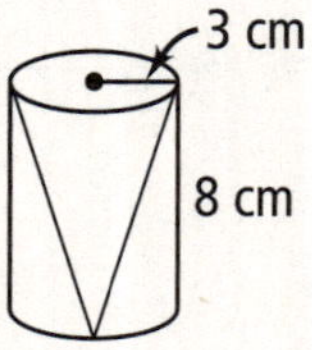

Cone volume: $24\pi cm^3$

Cylinder volume:

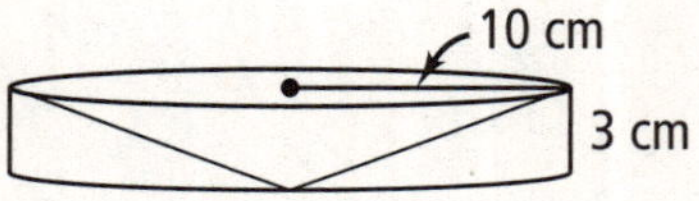

Cone volume:

Cylinder volume:

Reflect

Describe another situation where you can use a pattern to figure out something you don't know.

Close and Check

Focus Question

Why might you want to find the volume of a cone?

Do you know HOW?

1. Number the cones from 1 to 3 in order from least to greatest volume.

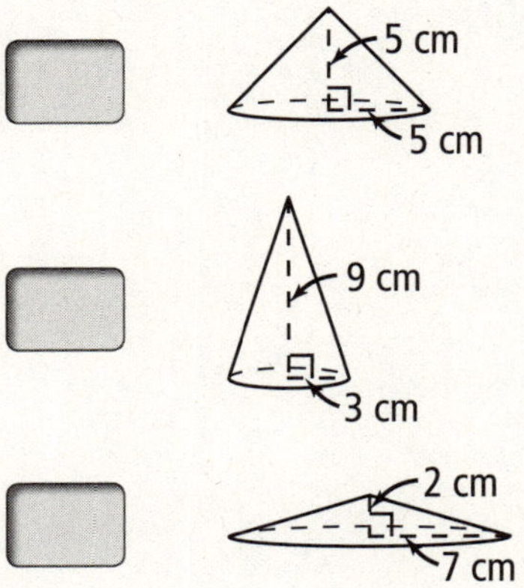

2. Find the volume of the funnel to the nearest cubic centimeter. Use 3.14 for π.

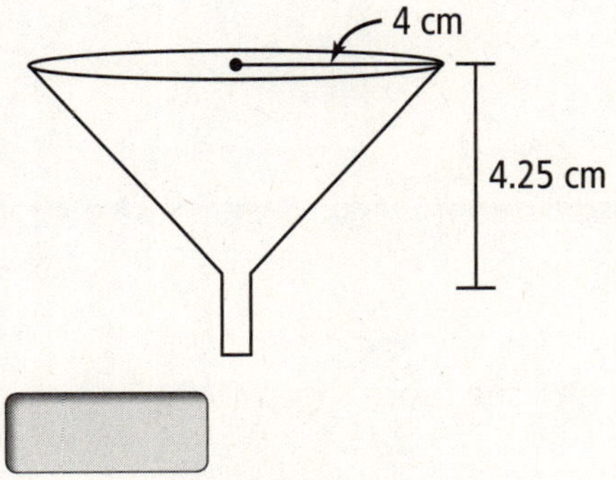

Do you UNDERSTAND?

3. Reasoning A juice company repackages individual juice cans in cone-shaped containers with the same volume. The can is 3 in. tall with a diameter of 2 in. What could be the dimensions of the cone container? Explain.

4. Writing A baker pours sugar into a cylindrical jar using the funnel from Exercise 2. If the jar holds 850 cm^3, about how many times will he have to fill the funnel before the jar is full? Explain.

26-5

Surface Areas of Spheres

Common Core State Standards: 8.G.9. Know the formulas for the volumes of cones, cylinders, and spheres and use them to solve real-world and mathematical problems.

Launch

Which two-dimensional world map, Map #1 or Map #2, would you use to more accurately calculate the surface area of Earth? Explain your reasoning.

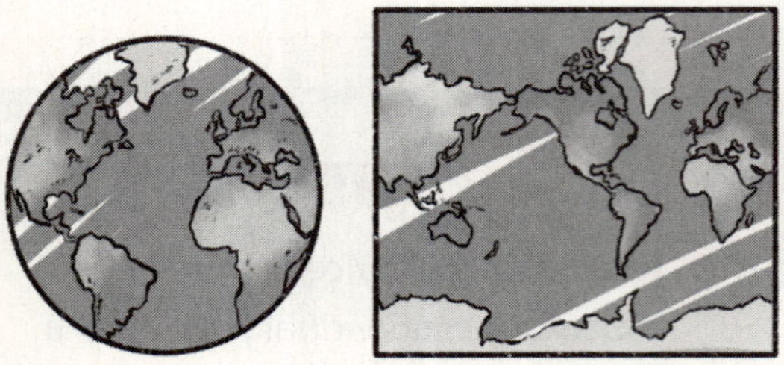

Map #1

Map #2

Reflect

Which type of two-dimensional world map do you use and see more often? Why?

Close and Check

Focus Question

What types of things can you model with a sphere? Why might you want to find the surface area of a sphere?

Do you know HOW?

1. Find the surface area of the sphere to the nearest tenth of a square centimeter. Use 3.14 for π.

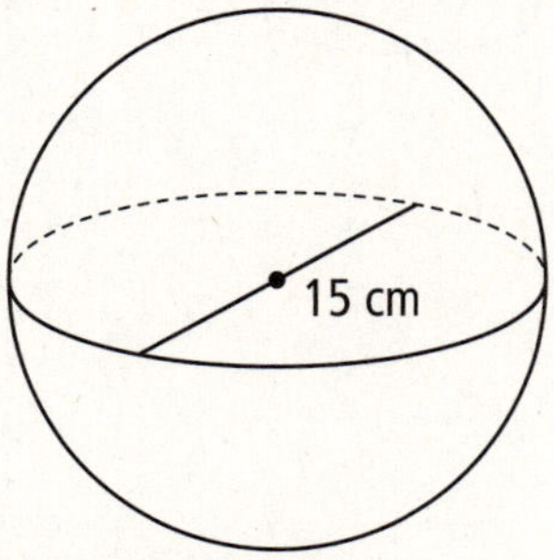

2. The circumference of a giant beach ball is 383.08 cm. Find the surface area of the beach ball to the nearest tenth of a centimeter. Use 3.14 for π.

3. The surface area of a sphere is 651 ft^2. Find the radius of the sphere to the nearest tenth of a square foot. Use 3.14 for π.

Do you UNDERSTAND?

4. Writing Explain how to use the circumference to find the surface area of a sphere.

5. Error Analysis A classmate says it is impossible to find an exact solution for the surface area of a sphere because π is an irrational number. Do you agree? Explain.

26-6 Volumes of Spheres

Common Core State Standards: 8.G.9. Know the formulas for the volumes of cones, cylinders, and spheres and use them to solve real-world and mathematical problems.

Launch

Your friend claims that 40 in.^{3} of party confetti will fit in her new party globe. Her assistant says, "She better use the cylinder."

Will the party globe work? Why did the assistant say she should use the cylinder? Explain.

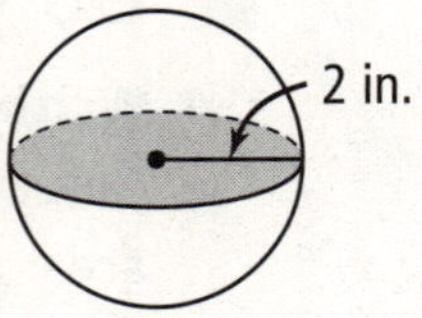

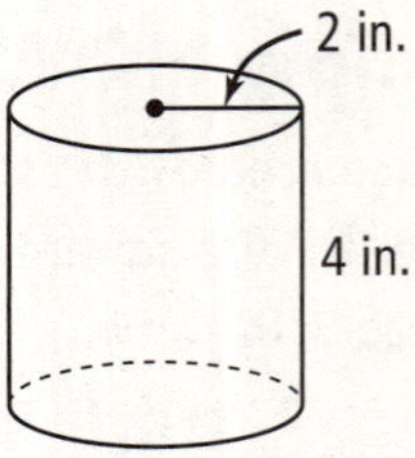

Reflect

If you had to identify the height and width of a sphere with a radius of 2 inches what would it be?

Close and Check

Focus Question

Why might you want to find the volume of a sphere?

Do you know HOW?

1. To the nearest cubic inch, how much space is there inside the ball for the hamster? Use 3.14 for π.

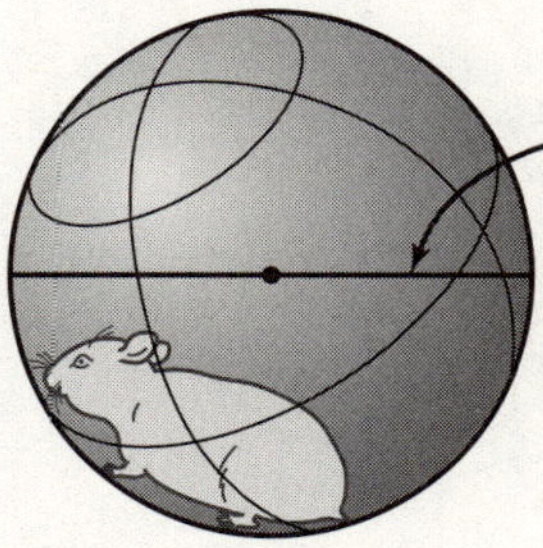

2. A gazing ball in the center of a garden has a volume of 904.3 cm^3. To the nearest centimeter, find the diameter of the gazing ball.

3. To the nearest tenth of a cubic foot, find the volume of a 9 ft diameter inflatable ball.

Do you UNDERSTAND?

4. **Writing** The height and diameter of a cylinder is equal to the diameter of a sphere. Explain the relationship between the volume of the sphere and the volume of the cylinder.

5. **Reasoning** A ball of twine has a diameter of 3.4 m. More twine is added until the diameter is 12 m. A classmate subtracts the diameters and uses the result to find the change in volume of the sphere. Is he correct? Explain.

26-7 Problem Solving

Common Core State Standards: 8.G.9. Know the formulas for the volumes of cones, cylinders, and spheres and use them to solve real-world and mathematical problems.

Launch

The cylinder, cone, and sphere all have the same radius and height (or diameter). Describe how the volumes compare given these dimensions. State the volumes in terms of π.

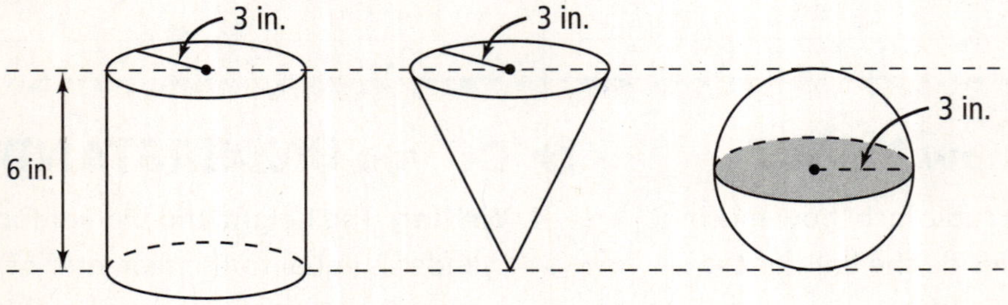

Reflect

How could you use what you know about the relationships between the volumes of the shapes to make solving problems easier? Explain.

Close and Check

Focus Question

How can you apply what you know about surface areas and volumes of cylinders, cones, and spheres to solve problems?

Do you know HOW?

1. A greenhouse is built in the shape of half of a sphere. To the nearest tenth of a cubic foot, find the volume of the greenhouse. Use 3.14 for π.

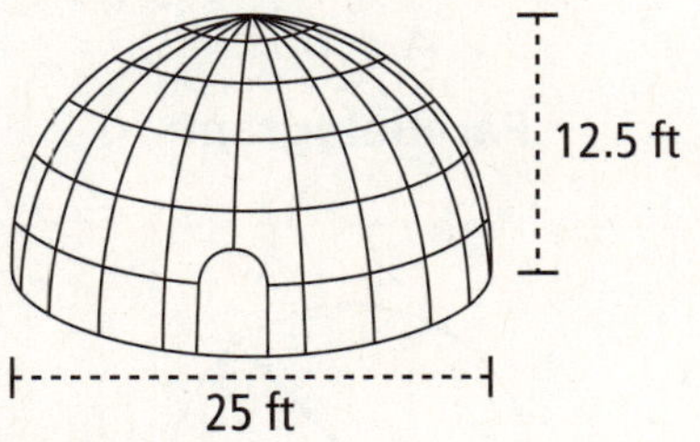

2. Find the surface area of the serving dish to the nearest tenth of a square inch. Use 3.14 for π.

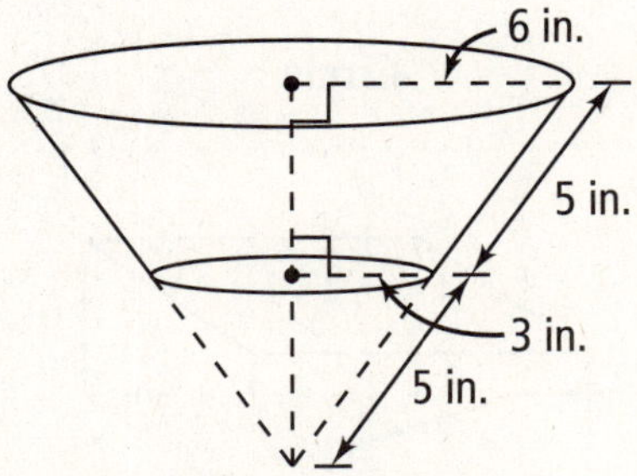

Do you UNDERSTAND?

3. Writing Explain how to find the total volume of the silo.

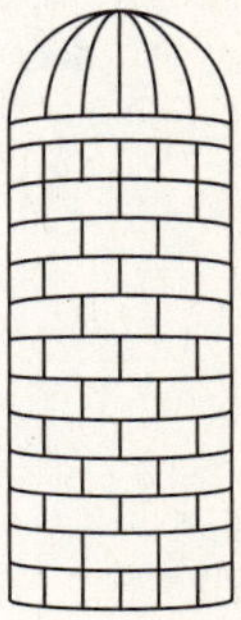

4. Reasoning You want the container with the largest volume. If the height and diameter of each container are equal, should you choose a sphere, cylinder, or cone? Explain.

Formulas

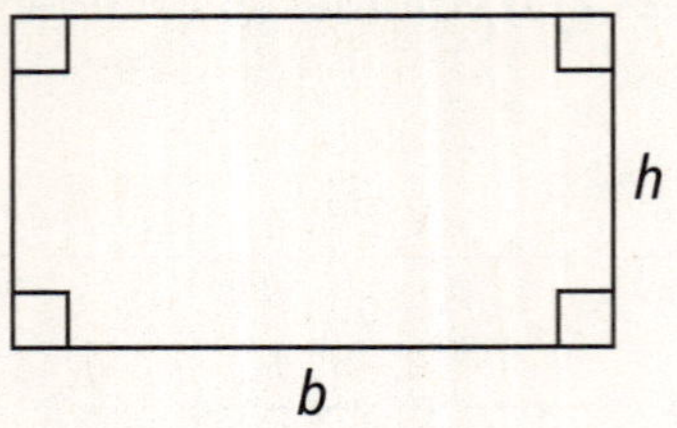

$P = 2b + 2h$

$A = bh$

Rectangle

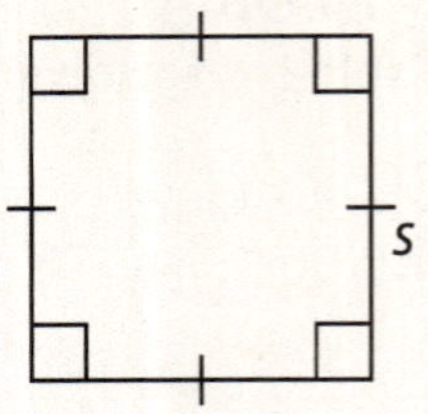

$P = 4s$

$A = s^2$

Square

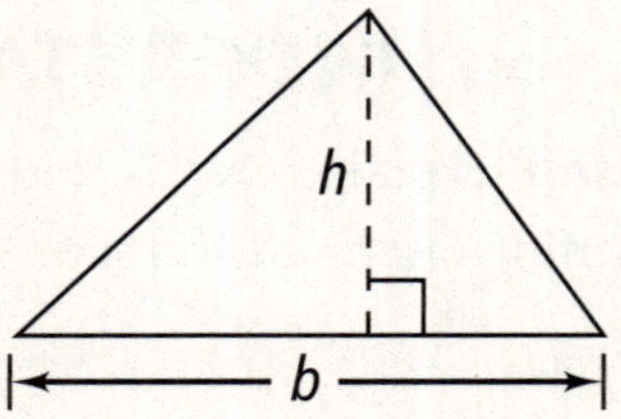

$A = \frac{1}{2}bh$

Triangle

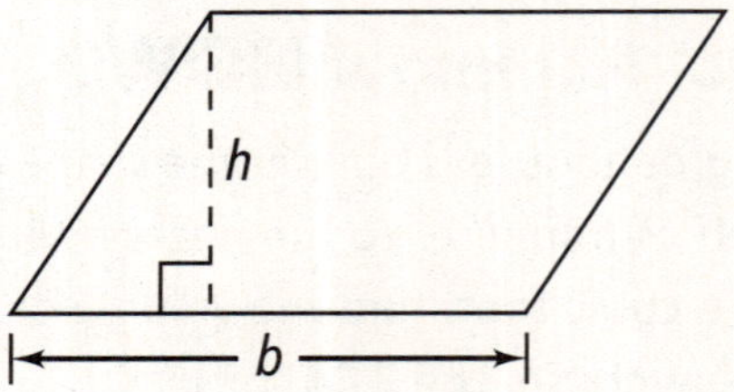

$A = bh$

Parallelogram

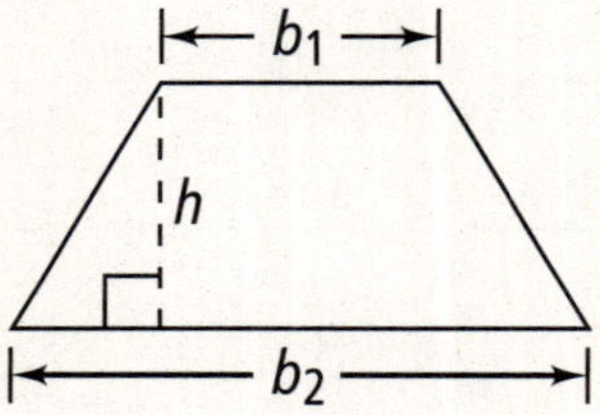

$A = \frac{1}{2}h(b_1 + b_2)$

Trapezoid

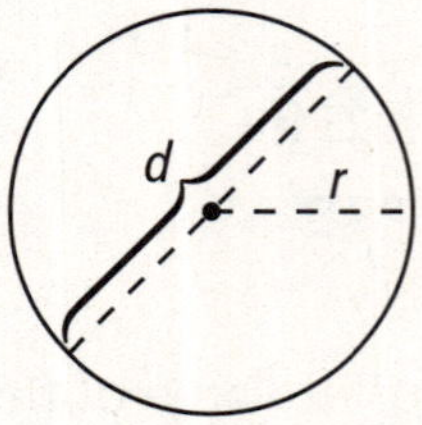

$C = 2\pi r$ or $C = \pi d$

$A = \pi r^2$

Circle

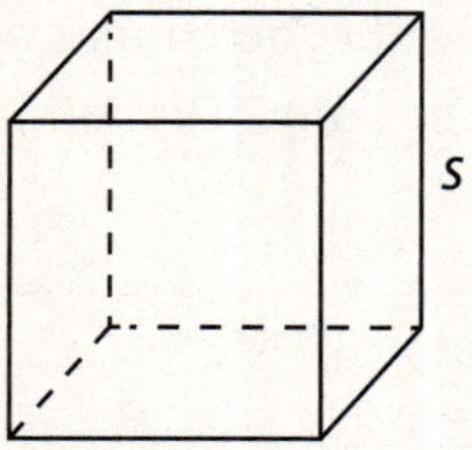

S.A. $= 6s^2$

$V = s^3$

Cube

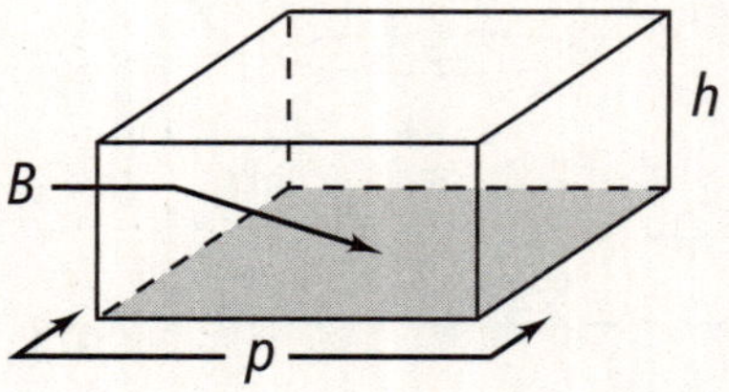

$V = Bh$

L.A. $= ph$

S.A. $=$ L.A. $+ 2B$

Rectangular Prism

Formulas

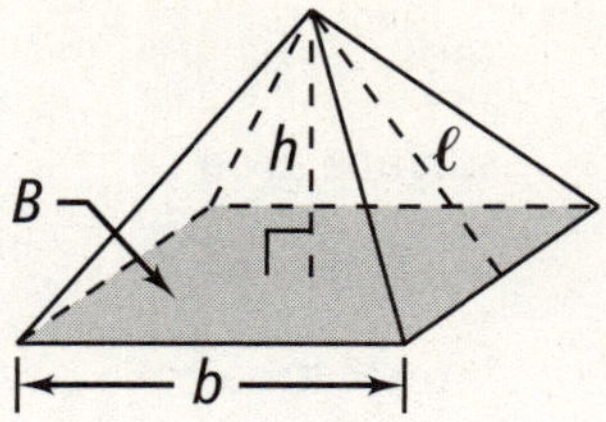

$V = \frac{1}{3}Bh$

L.A. $= 2b\ell$

S.A. $=$ L.A. $+ B$

Square Pyramid

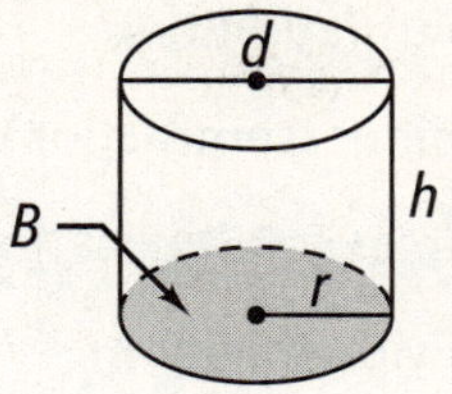

$V = Bh$

L.A. $= 2\pi rh$

S.A. $=$ L.A. $+ 2B$

Cylinder

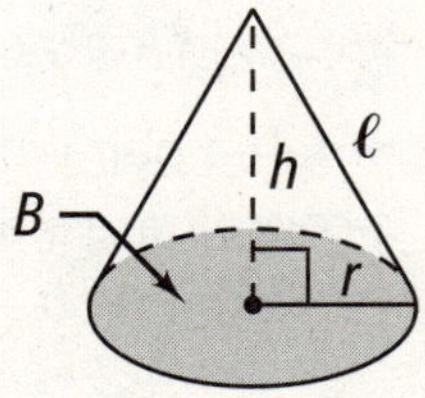

$V = \frac{1}{3}Bh$

L.A. $= \pi r\ell$

S.A. $=$ L.A. $+ B$

Cone

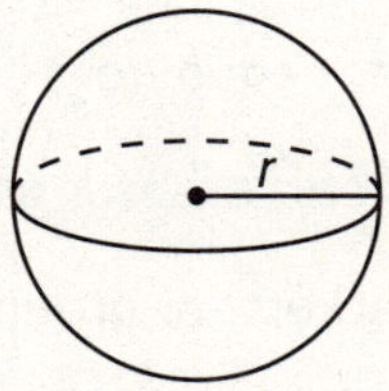

$V = \frac{4}{3}\pi r^3$

S.A. $= 4\pi r^2$

Sphere

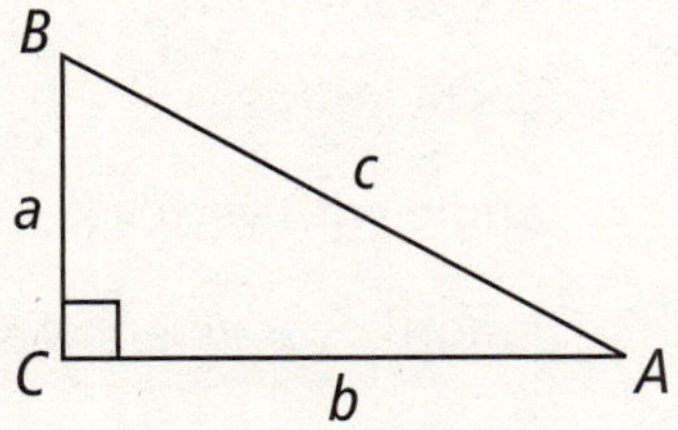

$a^2 + b^2 = c^2$

Pythagorean Theorem

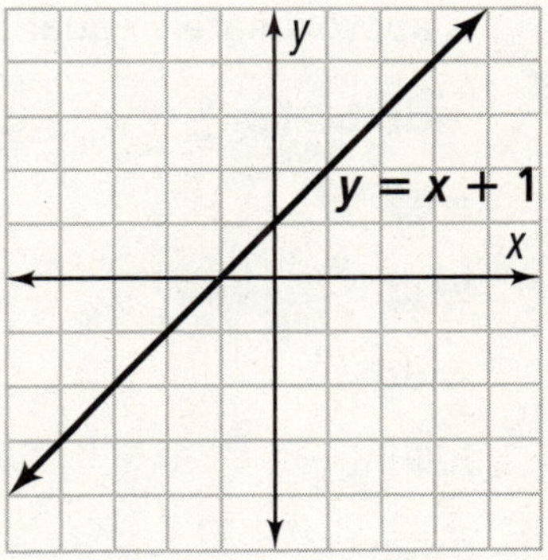

$y = mx + b$, where
$m =$ slope and
$b = y$-intercept

Equation of Line

Math Symbols

$+$	plus (addition)
$-$	minus (subtraction)
$\times$, $\cdot$	times (multiplication)
$\div$, $\overline{)\ }$, $\frac{a}{b}$	divide (division)
$=$	is equal to
$<$	is less than
$>$	is greater than
$\leq$	is less than or equal to
$\geq$	is greater than or equal to
$\neq$	is not equal to
( )	parentheses for grouping
[ ]	brackets for grouping
$-a$	opposite of a
. . .	and so on
$^\circ$	degrees
$\lvert a \rvert$	absolute value of a
$\stackrel{?}{=}$, $\stackrel{?}{<}$, $\stackrel{?}{>}$	Is the statement true?
$\approx$	is approximately equal to
$\frac{b}{a}$	reciprocal of $\frac{a}{b}$
A	area
ℓ	length
w	width
h	height
d	distance
r	rate
t	time
P	perimeter
b	base length
C	circumference
d	diameter
r	radius
S.A.	surface area
B	area of base
L.A.	lateral area
ℓ	slant height
V	volume
a^n	nth power of a
$\sqrt{x}$	nonnegative square root of x
π	pi, an irrational number approximately equal to 3.14
(a, b)	ordered pair with x-coordinate a and y-coordinate b
$\overline{AB}$	segment AB
A'	image of A, A prime
$\triangle ABC$	triangle with vertices A, B, and C
$\rightarrow$	arrow notation
$a : b$, $\frac{a}{b}$	ratio of a to b
$\cong$	is congruent to
$\sim$	is similar to
$\angle A$	angle with vertex A
AB	length of segment $\overline{AB}$
$\overrightarrow{AB}$	ray AB
$\angle ABC$	angle formed by $\overrightarrow{BA}$ and $\overrightarrow{BC}$
$m\angle ABC$	measure of angle ABC
$\perp$	is perpendicular to
$\overleftrightarrow{AB}$	line AB
$\parallel$	is parallel to
%	percent
P (event)	probability of an event

Measures

Customary	Metric
Length	**Length**
1 foot (ft) = 12 inches (in.) 1 yard (yd) = 36 in. 1 yd = 3 ft 1 mile (mi) = 5,280 ft 1 mi = 1,760 yd	1 centimeter (cm) = 10 millimeters (mm) 1 meter (m) = 100 cm 1 kilometer (km) = 1,000 m 1 mm = 0.001 m
Area	**Area**
1 square foot (ft^2) = 144 square inches ($in.^2$) 1 square yard (yd^2) = 9 ft^2 1 square mile (mi^2) = 640 acres	1 square centimeter (cm^2) = 100 square millimeters (mm^2) 1 square meter (m^2) = 10,000 cm^2
Volume	**Volume**
1 cubic foot (ft^3) = 1,728 cubic inches ($in.^3$) 1 cubic yard (yd^3) = 27 ft^3	1 cubic centimeter (cm^3) = 1,000 cubic millimeters (mm^3) 1 cubic meter (m^3) = 1,000,000 cm^3
Mass	**Mass**
1 pound (lb) = 16 ounces (oz) 1 ton (t) = 2,000 lb	1 gram (g) = 1,000 milligrams (mg) 1 kilogram (kg) = 1,000 g
Capacity	**Capacity**
1 cup (c) = 8 fluid ounces (fl oz) 1 pint (pt) = 2 c 1 quart (qt) = 2 pt 1 gallon (gal) = 4 qt	1 liter (L) = 1,000 milliliters (mL) 1000 liters = 1 kiloliter (kL)

Customary Units and Metric Units	
Length	1 in. = 2.54 cm 1 mi ≈ 1.61 km 1 ft ≈ 0.3 m
Capacity	1 qt ≈ 0.94 L
Weight and Mass	1 oz ≈ 28.3 g 1 lb ≈ 0.45 kg

Properties

Unless otherwise stated, the variables a, b, c, m, and n used in these properties can be replaced with any number represented on a number line.

Identity Properties

Addition $n + 0 = n$ and $0 + n = n$

Multiplication $n \cdot 1 = n$ and $1 \cdot n = n$

Commutative Properties

Addition $a + b = b + a$

Multiplication $a \cdot b = b \cdot a$

Associative Properties

Addition $(a + b) + c = a + (b + c)$

Multiplication $(a \cdot b) \cdot c = a \cdot (b \cdot c)$

Inverse Properties

Addition

$a + (-a) = 0$ and $-a + a = 0$

Multiplication

$a \cdot \frac{1}{a} = 1$ and $\frac{1}{a} \cdot a = 1$, $(a \neq 0)$

Distributive Properties

$a(b + c) = ab + ac$ $(b + c)a = ba + ca$

$a(b - c) = ab - ac$ $(b - c)a = ba - ca$

Properties of Equality

Addition If $a = b$, then $a + c = b + c$.

Subtraction If $a = b$, then $a - c = b - c$.

Multiplication If $a = b$, then $a \cdot c = b \cdot c$.

Division If $a = b$, and $c \neq 0$, then $\frac{a}{c} = \frac{b}{c}$.

Substitution If $a = b$, then b can replace a in any expression.

Zero Property

$a \cdot 0 = 0$ and $0 \cdot a = 0$.

Properties of Inequality

Addition If $a > b$, then $a + c > b + c$. If $a < b$, then $a + c < b + c$.

Subtraction If $a > b$, then $a - c > b - c$. If $a < b$, then $a - c < b - c$.

Multiplication

If $a > b$ and $c > 0$, then $ac > bc$.

If $a < b$ and $c > 0$, then $ac < bc$.

If $a > b$ and $c < 0$, then $ac < bc$.

If $a < b$ and $c < 0$, then $ac > bc$.

Division

If $a > b$ and $c > 0$, then $\frac{a}{c} > \frac{b}{c}$.

If $a < b$ and $c > 0$, then $\frac{a}{c} < \frac{b}{c}$.

If $a > b$ and $c < 0$, then $\frac{a}{c} < \frac{b}{c}$.

If $a < b$ and $c < 0$, then $\frac{a}{c} > \frac{b}{c}$.

Properties of Exponents

For any nonzero number n and any integers m and n:

Zero Exponent $a^0 = 1$

Negative Exponent $a^{-n} = \frac{1}{a^n}$

Product of Powers $a^m \cdot a^n = a^{m+n}$

Power of a Product $(ab)^n = a^n b^n$

Quotient of Powers $\frac{a^m}{a^n} = a^{m-n}$

Power of a Quotient $\left(\frac{a}{b}\right)^n = \frac{a^n}{b^n}$

Power of a Power $(a^m)^n = a^{mn}$